HENRY WADSWORTH LONGFELLOW
1855

By an unknown photographer. Original in
the Craigie-Longfellow House,
Cambridge, Massachusetts

LONGFELLOW
His Life and Work

Books by NEWTON ARVIN

HAWTHORNE

WHITMAN

HERMAN MELVILLE

THE HEART OF HAWTHORNE'S JOURNALS
(*Editor*)

THE SELECTED LETTERS OF HENRY ADAMS
(*Editor*)

LONGFELLOW: HIS LIFE AND WORK

LONGFELLOW
His Life and Work

Newton Arvin

An Atlantic Monthly Press Book

LITTLE, BROWN AND COMPANY · BOSTON · TORONTO

LIBRARY OF CONGRESS CATALOG CARD NO. 63–8312

FIFTH PRINTING

The lines from Laurence Binyon's translation of *The Divine Comedy
of Dante Alighieri* are quoted by kind permission of The Society of
Authors and Mrs. Cicely Binyon.

ATLANTIC–LITTLE, BROWN BOOKS
ARE PUBLISHED BY
LITTLE, BROWN AND COMPANY
IN ASSOCIATION WITH
THE ATLANTIC MONTHLY PRESS

*Published simultaneously in Canada
by Little, Brown & Company (Canada) Limited*

PRINTED IN THE UNITED STATES OF AMERICA

TO
VAN WYCK BROOKS

. . . il est si haut, le prix d'un naturel
qui ne doit rien à l'automatisme; on ap-
préciera davantage demain l'aisance et la
liberté que donne une certaine ingénuité.

— *Marcel Raymond*

Contents

Note

FOR THE biographical portions of this book I have been indebted to the following sources: *Henry Wadsworth Longfellow: His Life, His Works, His Friendships*, by George L. Austin (1883); *Life of Henry Wadsworth Longfellow*, by Samuel Longfellow (1886); *Final Memorials of Henry Wadsworth Longfellow*, by Samuel Longfellow (1887); *Literary Friends and Acquaintances*, by William Dean Howells (1900); *Henry Wadsworth Longfellow*, by Thomas Wentworth Higginson (1902); *Random Memories*, by Ernest W. Longfellow (1922); *New Light on Longfellow*, by James Taft Hatfield (1933); *Young Longfellow*, by Lawrance Thompson (1938); *Longfellow and Scandinavia*, by Andrew Hilen (1947); *Longfellow: A Full-Length Portrait*, by Edward Wagenknecht (1955); and *Mrs. Longfellow: Selected Letters and Journals of Fanny Appleton Longfellow*, edited by Edward Wagenknecht (1956).

I am also much indebted to my friends Daniel Aaron, Howard Doughty, and Alfred Young Fisher, who have read the manuscript of this book and made many useful suggestions. My thanks are further due to Mr. Thomas H. de Valcourt for kindly furnishing the photograph used as the frontispiece.

LONGFELLOW
His Life and Work

I

The Thoughts of Youth

OR A WRITER who was to be, on the whole, a poet of acceptance, rather than of rebellion and rejection, there was a
peculiar felicity in all the circumstances of Longfellow's
origin and early life; a felicity in the time, the place, the family
entourage, the whole historic setting. A generation earlier would
have been too early; with the same aspirations to poetic fame,
Longfellow, who was born in 1807, would soon have been dis-
heartened and silenced by that chill in the literary climate that
made so early an end of the poetic labors of the Revolutionary
generation — of Trumbull's and Dwight's and Barlow's — and
that cut short so early the career of the even more gifted Brockden Brown. A generation later would have been too late; the crest
of the wave of New England vitality would already have passed,
and Longfellow, at the best, would have had to be content with
the status, unsuitable to him, of a literary epigone. Some poets,
poets both greater and smaller than he, have waged a constant
war with their age, and this has either made them or destroyed
them; such a conflict would certainly have destroyed Longfellow,
who, fortunately for him, was born when Jefferson was President, came of age during the "presidentiad" of John Quincy
Adams, and flourished — the word, for once, is not too strong —
during that long genial summer that elapsed between then and
the Civil War. He was no *poète maudit*, either by nature or by the

pressure of circumstances, and he did not have to resist the current of his time.

A similar thing is true of the *place* of his birth and most of his early life — New England and particularly Portland, in the District of Maine, during the years when New England was passing through its early, expansive, and culturally most vigorous period. Some poets have hated the place of their birth and early environment; not so Longfellow. For him Portland was always "the beautiful town / That is seated by the sea"; and never, early or late, did he resent and reject it as Hawthorne, for example, resented and rejected Salem, or as some Middle Western writers have resented and rejected their milieu. And was it not wholly natural that Longfellow should have felt as he did? For a person of his temper and tendency the Portland of his childhood must have been exactly the right setting; not a great city, not an obscure village, but a small, busy, active, and prosperous seaport, its streets and wharves lively with the coming and going of sea captains and sailors, its beautiful harbor, Casco Bay, dotted with islands ("islands that were the Hesperides / Of all my boyish dreams") and alive with the sails of seagoing vessels.* It was a town that already had its memories: it had been cruelly bombarded by the British during the Revolution and all but wiped out. It had its historic moments, too, in Longfellow's own childhood: the inhabitants of Portland, one September day in 1813, could hear in the distance the guns of the two brigs, British and American, the *Boxer* and the *Enterprise*, in their sea fight just off the coast; and Longfellow was never to forget how the bodies of the two captains, both killed in the fight, had been brought to land the next day and buried with full military honors in the old burial ground on the hill "o'er-looking the tranquil bay." This was during the War of 1812, and Portland, which had suffered commercially under Jef-

---

* Timothy Dwight, early in the century, after praising the pure air of Portland for its healthfulness, went on to say: "No American town is more entirely commercial; and of course none is more sprightly."

ferson's Embargo, was about to enter upon a period of renewed prosperity; this was mostly to be its character during the nineteenth century.

Since it was primarily a seacoast town, Longfellow's sensibility was from the beginning powerfully molded by the near presence of the sea — by its calm or stormy beauty, its mysterious horizons, its endlessly shifting aspects, its covert menace, its ebbing and flooding tides, the sands and rocks of its rugged coastline. In his way, Longfellow was to be as much a poet of the sea, as little a poet of the hills or mountains, as Whitman; the breathing of the sea is audible in his work from almost the beginning to the end. Yet there were other features of the small town that touched his imagination too, and lingered for years in his memory. There were "the shadows of Deering's woods," a beautiful grove of oaks on what were then the outskirts of the town, and near Deering's woods there was a pottery under a hawthorn tree where Longfellow as a boy loved to stand and watch the black-aproned potter at his wheel, drawing up and molding the ductile clay into bowls and pitchers as he "plied his magic art — / For it was magical to me." There was also an old-fashioned mill for the making of ropes, a "ropewalk," a long low building with a row of windows "like the port-holes of a hulk," and an open door at one end through which one could gaze into the interior and watch the human spiders spinning and spinning, and listen to the whirring of a wheel that

> Dull and drowsy, makes me feel
> All its spokes are in my brain.

Both the pottery and the ropewalk fascinated the boy, and years later their unforgotten images furnished him with symbols for two of his finest poems.

If he was fortunate in the time and place of his birth, Longfellow was equally fortunate in the family into which he was born. It is wholly characteristic that there was no more bitterness in

his relations with his family than in his relations with his surroundings generally; and there was no need for it. In this respect
as in others his childhood was a prevailingly happy one. For one
thing, it was a family that, on both sides, had played and was
playing an honorable role in the public life of the country; who
can say how much the awareness of this fact — though it never
appears on the surface of his work — gave Longfellow the deep
natural sense he had of an intimate connection with the historic
life of the Republic? A national piety was for him an all but unconscious possession; anything like estrangement or disaffiliation
would have been quite out of the question.

The Longfellows had been respected citizens of Portland since
the middle of the eighteenth century, when the town was still
known as Falmouth. One of the houses the British burned on that
October day in 1775 had been the house of Henry's great-grand-
father, Stephen Longfellow, a clerk of the judicial court in Falmouth. His grandfather, a second Stephen, represented the district in the Massachusetts legislature for some years (Maine was
still not an independent state) and later became a judge of the
Court of Common Pleas. Well into the nineteenth century this
Stephen Longfellow continued, like Melville's grandfather, to
wear with old-fashioned dignity the costume of the Revolutionary period — "long-skirted waistcoat, small-clothes, and white-
topped boots, his hair tied behind in a club, with a black ribbon."
The third Stephen Longfellow, the poet's father, had been sent
to Harvard at the very end of the eighteenth century, and had
there been a classmate and friend of such youths as William Ellery
Channing and Joseph Story. This Stephen Longfellow, practicing
law in Portland, seems to have been the very pattern of the Federalist gentleman of his day — stately, grave, a little pompous, but
generous, humane, affectionate toward his children, and filled
with a high sense of public responsibility. He too, like his father,
represented the district in the Massachusetts legislature, and was
therefore much away from home when Longfellow was a boy of

seven or eight. It was during his term there that he went as a dele-
gate to the ill-fated Hartford Convention, but he seems not to
have suffered any great obloquy as a result. Less than ten years
later he was elected to Congress; it was during Monroe's second
administration, and the Federalist party had by that time long
passed its meridian. Nevertheless Stephen Longfellow remained
one of the first citizens of Portland, and when, in 1825, Lafayette
visited the town on his great tour, it was he who was delegated
to pronounce the address of welcome.

On Longfellow's mother's side the prowess of the family was
military rather than legal or political. His grandfather had played
a conspicuous role in the events of the Revolution. General Peleg
Wadsworth, who had raised a company of minutemen at the out-
break of hostilities, and had soon become adjutant general, was
put in command of the whole eastern department of Maine; during his service there he was captured by the British at Thomaston
and imprisoned in Fort George at Castine. From this incarceration
he had made his escape, with another officer, in a quite adventur-
ous manner, as the boy Longfellow was to hear from his own lips.
After the Revolution, General Wadsworth too was elected to the
Massachusetts legislature and later to Congress. In Longfellow's
childhood he was living not in Portland but in a great house he
had built in the country near the village of Hiram, more than
thirty miles from Portland. Here, in an almost primitive setting,
Longfellow as a boy was sometimes taken to spend the months
of the summer vacation; he was to know the old rural life of
Maine as well as he did that of the town. Meanwhile there was not
only military but naval glory on his mother's side of the family.
Longfellow himself was named after his mother's brother, Henry
Wadsworth, a lieutenant in the Navy, who died heroically when
an American fireship on which he served was voluntarily blown
up before the walls of Tripoli to save it from falling into the
hands of the enemy. This was three years before Longfellow was
born. Another uncle, Alexander Scammell Wadsworth, also a

lieutenant in the Navy, took part in the fight between the *Consti-tution* and the *Guerrière* in 1812 when Longfellow was a boy of five. This uncle later became a commodore in the Navy.

There was, in short, a certain glow of eminence, or at least of distinction, in the setting of Longfellow's early life; the obscurity out of which so many writers have emerged was never part of his lot, and in that sense good fortune was with him from the be-ginning. It was with him too in the fact that he grew up in an atmosphere neither of penury nor of great wealth, but of well-to-do comfort and a modest prosperity. His father's law practice was evidently an important one, and the family life in the big handsome Georgian house on Congress Street which General Wadsworth had built — the first brick house in Portland — typi-fied perfectly the way of life of the old Federalist gentry. If that way of life was respectably sober, it was by no means austere; it was the cheerful and even gay social life of the first families of Portland. It included dancing lessons for the children as a matter of course; it included a great deal of music. The Longfellows, we are told, owned the first piano known in Portland; Henry's mother, Zilpah Longfellow, is said to have been passionately in-terested in music, and he, in his boyhood days, was taught to play both the piano and the flute, while he also attended a singing school. No doubt the music he learned and played, along with the others, was of an "unsophisticated" sort, and consisted mainly of popular marches, lyrical airs, and dance tunes — "The Battle of Prague," "Washington's March," "Brignal's Bank," "The Fisher's Hornpipe" — rather than of Haydn or Mozart. But if this was an unsophisticated, it was a genuine, musicality; and Longfellow's natively fine ear was cultivated by it in his boyhood. It was to have a good deal to do with the best of his accomplishment as a poet.

The household was also, as all such households were, a highly literate one. Stephen Longfellow had accumulated a small but carefully selected library, and the boy seems to have had the run

of it. It was possible for him also to borrow books from the old
Portland Library, and to browse among the new books in John-
son's bookstore. His literary passions he could share with his
mother, who, as later letters between them show, had a cultivated
taste for poetry. That taste was naturally of a rather old-fashioned
kind, and the earliest poetry young Longfellow read was bound
to include the eighteenth-century writers — Thomson, Gold-
smith, Cowper — who were still, in his boyhood, current in men's
minds and mouths. The boy's sensibility was formed by these
very quiet writers, but it was formed also by the writings of the
older contemporary poets — the verse romances of Sir Walter
Scott, the lyrics of Campbell and Moore, the descriptive verse of
Samuel Rogers (*Pleasures of Memory*). It was probably this
easily accessible and not very unconventional poetry that was the
staple of his reading in his teens. The names of greater poets, accessible in fact but not yet quite fully "established" — the names
of Coleridge, Wordsworth, Byron — are missing from accounts
of his boyhood reading; these poets certainly swam into his ken
later, but except perhaps for Byron, he was never to owe much
to them directly. He was to owe much more to a young American poet of the time, whose verse was to be found in many a periodical; and later, meeting Bryant in Heidelberg, he told the
older writer how strong his influence had been: "When I look
back upon my earlier years," he said, "I cannot but smile to
see how much in them is really yours." Bryant himself, interestingly enough, had praised some of Longfellow's earliest published poems, without knowing then what the initials H. W. L.
stood for. Some of these poems, indeed, have a distinctly Bryantesque cachet.

Bryant's verse was, among other things, an expression of the
Unitarian mind at its calmest and most reasonable, and this would
have accounted for some of its effect on young Longfellow,
whose early religious influences were of the same sort. After
many decades of mildly Calvinist teaching, the First Parish

Church in Portland had called in as pastor a young Harvard graduate and theological liberal, the Reverend Ichabod Nichols — this was in Longfellow's infancy — and the Portland church became virtually Unitarian. Longfellow's mother had long been a devout church member; it was only later, and then under the influence of his classmate Channing, that Stephen Longfellow became a regular member of the church. "It was in the doctrine and the spirit of the early Unitarianism," says Longfellow's brother and biographer, himself a Unitarian minister, "that Henry Longfellow was nurtured at church and at home." And he adds that there is no reason to suppose that he ever found these insufficient. The truth was probably somewhat less simple than this; Howells tells us that, in his old age, Longfellow's hold on anything like a creed weakened, and that latterly he did not even go to church. His latest writings do not express a perfectly unquestioning acceptance even of Unitarian doctrine, but however this may be, it is true that Longfellow's work is pervaded by the fragrance of nineteenth-century religious liberalism — undogmatic, eclectic, latitudinarian, and rather vague.

On the whole, in short, his childhood and boyhood were spent amid mild and kindly influences, and in a household from which the most demoralizing cares were absent: it was quite evidently an essentially happy inauguration into life. As a boy Henry seems to have been normally cheerful, eager, even high-spirited, and affectionate. Of course the general brightness of the picture ought not to be exaggerated. Longfellow, in his mature years, was far from being wholly free, as we shall see, from emotional and nervous tensions, anxieties, and miseries; and though these may have been due in part to circumstances in the later period, we can assume that some of their roots were in his earliest years. There was a certain precariousness, even at an early date, in his emotional makeup, as indeed we should expect — for was he not, with all his apparent stability, to be a poet? — and when we hear of a childhood dislike of loud noises and "rude excitements," of his having to be taken out of a public school owing to his fear of the "rough boys," of "indefinite longings" and feelings of loneliness, in early boyhood, we realize that there were shadows even in a scene that was prevailingly sunny and cheerful.

Longfellow's formal schooling was, in its old-fashioned way, probably as sound as the best schooling of the time. At the age of five, after the unhappy experiment with a public school, the boy was sent with his brother Stephen to a private school in Portland and a year later to the Portland Academy, another private institution, where he remained a pupil until, at the age of fourteen, he was ready for college. From the outset he appears to have been a studious and conscientious, not a rebellious, small boy. In the spring of 1814 he is reported to have gone through half his Latin grammar; he stood, said the report, "above several boys twice as old as he." The substance of his schooling was of course primarily literary and classical; in order to be admitted to college, as he was, it was necessary for him to write Latin grammatically and to be familiar with such classical writings as Cicero's orations, Vergil's *Eclogues, Georgics*, and *Aeneid*, the Greek Testament, and the Greek writers represented in the old standard school-anthology, the *Collectanea Graeca Minora*. At the age of fourteen Longfellow must already have been a fair classicist.

Though his father was a Harvard man, it was not to Harvard that he was sent but to Bowdoin, the young college at Brunswick, Maine, of which his grandfather had been one of the founders and of which his father was now a trustee. He was admitted to Bowdoin in 1821 with the class of 1825 — the class to which Hawthorne also belonged — but as he was not yet fifteen, the family seems to have felt that he was a little too young to be plunged into even a decorous college life, and during his freshman year Henry remained at home in Portland, going on with his studies at the Portland Academy.

In the fall of 1822 he and his brother Stephen at last went to Brunswick as sophomores in residence. He was to be, on the whole, an unproblematic undergraduate as he had been an un-problematic schoolboy. Except for some dissatisfaction with the rigid theological orthodoxy that prevailed officially, there was nothing of the rebel in Longfellow as a college student. On the contrary, in his quiet and undemonstrative way, he evidently set himself to make the most of what Bowdoin could furnish him; in imagination, one can see him growing intellectually, almost visibly, day by day. And what Bowdoin could furnish him was not to be disdained. Longfellow's Bowdoin may have been young and raw and in a sense provincial, but it was a college of very nearly the first order, and would not have suffered much from the comparison with Harvard. There were on the small faculty some men of genuine learning and power. There was Parker Cleaveland, Professor of Natural Philosophy, author of a widely used treatise on mineralogy, a man of real force, to whose mem-ory, many years later, Longfellow dedicated a sonnet ("Among the many lives that I have known"). There was Samuel P. New-man, Professor of Rhetoric and Oratory, author also of a textbook on his subject, who had the insight to discern the promise of Longfellow's classmate Hawthorne, and whose teaching proved a great stimulus to young Longfellow. In Longfellow's senior year there appeared as Professor of Mental and Moral Philosophy a young Dartmouth graduate, Thomas Cogswell Upham, who was later to be the author of a *Treatise on the Will*, but who had already published a volume of verse, *American Sketches*, that dealt, suggestively if not brilliantly, with New England legendry and with Indian lore. Longfellow had already known these poems for some time; he took to Upham at once as a man——he seems to have treated undergraduates with a somewhat unconventional informality and friendliness — and almost certainly the association was an important one for the boy.

For, decorous as he was outwardly, Longfellow in his teens had his own inner intensities, and the longing for literary fame had become, by this time, an obsession with him. "The fact is," he wrote to his father in the winter of his senior year, "— and I will not disguise it in the least, for I think I ought not, — the fact is, I most eagerly aspire after future eminence in literature, my whole soul burns most ardently after it, and every earthly thought centres in it. . . . Whether Nature has given me any capacity for knowledge or not, she has at any rate given me a very strong predilection for literary pursuits, and I am almost confident in believing, that if I can ever rise in the world it must be by the exercise of my talents in the wide field of literature." "Nothing could induce me," he wrote a little later, "to relinquish the pleasures of literature — little as I have yet tasted them."

With these literary aspirations in themselves Stephen Longfellow was intelligently sympathetic ("I am happy to observe that you are ambitious of literary distinction," he wrote), but his duty as a father forced him to point out how little room there was in American society for the literary career in any practical sense, and how necessary it was, even for an ambitious poet, to have another profession by which he could support himself. The position of the man of letters, indeed, in American life was a subject to which Henry Longfellow — no doubt like other young Americans — had given a good deal of thought. He had given it enough thought to devote his commencement oration to the subject. This oration is entitled "Our Native Writers," and although it is in a vein of nationalist literary ardor that was even then not unfamiliar, the little speech has an individual accent of youthful enthusiasm that is anything but perfunctory. It is true, says the young orator, that the mind of America is almost exclusively occupied with the practical and the "operative," but the land itself is rich in the materials of poetry, and the time is coming when it is to be "indeed the land of song." There must be patronage for writers, but there must also be a high dedication on the part of poets themselves: "with them there must be a deep and thorough conviction of the glory of their calling, — an utter abandonment of everything else, — and a noble self-devotion to the cause of literature."

Meanwhile, these aspirations had not been merely insubstantial dreams; they had had a substance that, for a boy of Longfellow's age, had not been unimpressive. Beginning apparently in his junior year — though he had written and even printed one or two precocious poems earlier — and continuing until after his graduation, at a time when Longfellow was but seventeen or eighteen, he had passed through a period of what can only be called youthful efflorescence as a productive poet, and as a published and recognized one. The results had no permanent value, it is true, but the productivity itself is eloquent not only of an intense literary ambition but of an undeniable literary force. Between January, 1824, and some time late in 1825, young Longfellow had written and published nearly forty poems in various newspapers and magazines. Years later, when he published his first collection of poems, *Voices of the Night,* Longfellow reprinted seven of these — seven that deserved to be revived if any did; the others waited for editors to ferret them out and reprint them. These youthful pieces had been published in a Portland newspaper, or a giftbook put out in Philadelphia, or — and these were the larger number — in a short-lived Boston magazine called the *United States Literary Gazette,* which was publishing much of Bryant at the same time, and whose editor, Theophilus Parsons, was particularly hospitable and encouraging to Longfellow.

As one would expect, these boyish pieces have no very obvious idiosyncrasy, no very striking character of their own; they seem to belong to the common run of competent magazine verse of the decade, hardly distinguishable from the poems of the Pierponts, the Percivals, the Spragues, which adorned the pages of the same periodicals; the echoes of Bryant, in particular, are almost those of a deliberate mimic:

> . . . and all the fair
> And beautiful forms of nature, had a voice
> Of eloquent worship.

Yet, faint as it is, there *is* a personal note in these poems, just barely perceptible, in which one can detect some premonition of the mature poet that was to come. The strain of mild and pensive melancholy might be disposed of as the normal moodiness of adolescence if there were not discernible in it something of the characteristic sadness of the later Longfellow:

> I stand deep musing here,
> Beneath the dark and motionless beech,
> Whilst wandering winds of nightfall reach
> My melancholy ear.

The boy represents himself, in another poem, "Musings," as seated beside his window at night, watching the stars as they come out one by one, and reflecting on the mournful transitoriness of all human joys. The language is commonplace and the verse halting, but the nocturnal setting and the minor mood have a recognizable Longfellow stamp.

The best of these little poems, predictably, have to do with nature; one of them, indeed, "The Spirit of Poetry," in Bryantesque blank verse, expresses the already familiar conception of poetry as "a bright image of the light and beauty / That dwells in nature." And no doubt an earlier influence than that of Bryant helps to account for the young poet's preoccupation with "the seasons": spring ("An April Day"), autumn ("Autumn" and "Autumn Nightfall"), winter ("Woods in Winter") — these are favorite themes, and an occasional fine line or two testifies to their spontaneity:

> Morn on the mountain, like a summer bird,
> Lifts up her purple wing.

> Shrilly the skater's iron rings.

> . . . her silver voice
> Is the rich music of a summer bird,
> Heard in the still night, with its passionate cadence.

Good as these lines are, they are good in a way that suggests some earlier English poet, Elizabethan or Augustan, not Longfellow himself as he was to become; what is his own — what he has already made his own — is the sense of a genuine emotional relation to the seasons, to the "sober gladness" of autumn or the frozen landscape of winter.

Premonitory, too, are four early poems on the Indians, poems such as Freneau and his imitators had already made familiar — elegiac, pathetic, funereal. They deal with such subjects as the suicide of a deserted maiden ("Lover's Rock") or of a forlorn hunter ("The Indian Hunter"), the burial rites of a warrior fallen from a cliff ("Jeckoyva") or of a young brave ("The Burial of of the Minnisink").* At this stage Longfellow could associate Indians only with the idea of death, and only the last of the poems mentioned rises above sentimental woodenness; this, partly because the natural setting of the Minnisink's burial, an autumnal forest at twilight, is rather finely sketched, and partly because the liberation, as a ritual gesture, of the dead man's horse — "uncurbed, unreined, and riderless" — brings the poem to a pictorially effective close.

Quite unlike any of these other poems, but curiously characteristic in its literary and patriotic derivation, is the "Hymn of the Moravian Nuns of Bethlehem," which Bryant praised before he knew more than the initials of the young poet. It was suggested to the boy by an account in a magazine article of the flag that

---

* Longfellow found the word "Minnisink" in Heckewelder's book on the Indian "nations" of Pennsylvania, where, however, "Minnisink" is said to have been a place, not a tribe — a place on the Hudson where the Minsi Indians had formerly had their council seat and fire. The undergraduate poet may have read Heckewelder carelessly or he may well have thought "Minnisink" a more poetic word than "Minsi."

Pulaski, the Polish hero of the Revolution, had ordered from the Moravian sisters (not nuns) at Bethlehem, Pennsylvania; it has, with no distinction of language, and thanks no doubt to the imitation of Scott, a certain vigor of rhythm and rhetoric:

> "Take thy banner! and if e'er
> Thou shouldst press the soldier's bier,
> And the muffled drum should beat
> To the tread of mournful feet,
> Then this crimson flag shall be
> Martial cloak and shroud for thee."
>
> The warrior took that banner proud,
> And it was his martial cloak and shroud!

The undergraduate poet had not yet found an unmistakable voice of his own, but we can hardly reproach Bryant, Parsons, and others for seeing signs of promise in these youthful "effusions." Nor was it only in verse that the boy's literary energy manifested itself during these last months of college: at this stage, as well as later, he aspired to become a prose writer too; he would try his hand at the essay as well as at poetry. Between March and October, 1825, there appeared, also in the *United States Literary Gazette*, five short essays under the general title "The Lay Monastery," signed by "The Lay Monk." They give one, if anything, a stronger impression of Longfellow's innate gifts than the poems. It is true that they are unmistakably imitative — imitative particularly of Washington Irving. As a schoolboy Longfellow had fallen in love with *The Sketch Book*, which had appeared before he went to college; Irving's particular quality of gentle, daydreaming, recreative romanticism, without vehemence and without deep inquietude, was bound to be congenial to him. Years later, in some remarks at the time of Irving's death, he acknowledged this early passion: "Every reader has his first book; I mean to say, one book among all others which in early youth first fascinates his imagination, and at once excites and satisfies the desires of his mind. To me, this first book was *The Sketch Book* of Washington Irving."

Given this enthusiasm, and Longfellow's youthful plasticity, one is not surprised to come upon almost literal echoes of Irving in "The Lay Monastery." "I still love to indulge," he says in the essay on "Valentine Writing," "in conjectures upon the superstitious beliefs and observances of mankind. . . . Having thus been from my youth up a kind of arrant poacher in the rich fields of legend and romance, it is not strange that I should find it a pleasure even now . . . to look into those ancient things, which I should be looking and searching into, were I young again." The Irving of "The Author's Account of Himself" could hardly be more audible than he is in such ventriloquistic phrases. Yet these little essays are not merely exercises in imitation: they have a touch of individual character, however faint and faded. In an introductory essay, "The Author," the youthful experimenter creates a poetic persona for himself that is not simply that of his master — the persona of a "lay monk" whose chief joy is in "seclusion and solitary musing," but who in his mildly melancholy retirement looks out upon suffering mankind and finds his self-enjoyment "spiritualized . . . to a glowing philanthropy." This is the benevolent Longfellow, not the indifferent Irving, and the writing in another essay, "Winter Months," has a maturity — and a sharpness of perception — that none of the verse has:

> The forest and the valley and the upland are silent around me, save when the icicle drops from the withered branch and slides away on the crusted snow. . . . The giant oak heaves out its arms to the wind, — the withered vine hangs, covered with hoarfrost, from the brown elm, and the dark moss is frozen upon its trunk.

The April essay, "The Literary Spirit of Our Country," anticipates much that Longfellow was to say in his commencement oration the following summer, but it includes one observation that he did not repeat; namely, that America is by no means wanting in those "rich associations" that so many commentators have denied it; in time, at least, he argues, the melancholy romance of Indian life will make so deep an impression on men's imaginations that "our land will become, indeed, a classic ground." The Indians had already begun to glide through Longfellow's work.

The last of the essays in "The Lay Monastery" appeared in October, 1825. By that time Longfellow had put Bowdoin behind him, and was on the eve of a wholly unexpected and unpredictable change of scene that was to give much of its direction to his future life and work.

II

A Pilgrimage Beyond the Sea

THE EVENTS that followed Longfellow's graduation from college have in retrospect, and must have had even at the time, a quality of happy improbability. During his senior year, naturally enough, Henry had been anxiously concerned about his future. His deepest wish was to throw himself into a purely intellectual, a purely literary career, and to make an illustrious name for himself as a writer. Yet he had to recognize the cogency of his father's demurrers; he had to recognize that, in the America of his time, a purely literary career was a practical impossibility, that the most dedicated of creative spirits must have some other profession or occupation "which," as his father said, "will afford [him] a subsistence as well as a reputation." Bryant and Irving had already proved the truth of this discouraging generalization in their careers, as Hawthorne and Emerson and Poe were very soon to do, and Longfellow was now trying to resign himself to the necessity, in the family tradition, of becoming a lawyer: "I can be a lawyer," he wrote to his father, "for some lawyers are mere simpletons. This will support my *real* existence, literature an *ideal* one."

The prospect, however, was disheartening: the idea of becoming a practicing member of the bar was utterly alien to the bookish and ardent young Longfellow, and he had formed the wish to be allowed to spend a year at Harvard — what we should call a year of graduate work — studying "general literature," and particularly gaining a knowledge of the French and Italian languages. In his generous way, Stephen Longfellow had acceded to this wish, and during the second term of his senior year the anticipation of a year in Cambridge devoted to literary studies must have done something to compensate Henry for the more remote dread of the law office.

What happened in fact could surely not have been foreseen by anyone, and it transformed the whole future course of Longfellow's life. The trustees of Bowdoin had come to the decision to establish a chair of modern languages — in the 1820's a remarkably enlightened step to take — and at the suggestion of one of their number, who had been much impressed by the boy's translation of an ode of Horace for the senior examination, it was decided to offer the professorship to the eighteen-year-old Longfellow. As it happened, the trustees of Bowdoin could not possibly have made a better choice, but this does not keep one from marveling, even now, at its boldness. Not only was the appointee outrageously young, but, at the time, his knowledge of foreign languages was confined to a smattering of French he had picked up from studying with a church organist in Portland, Charles Nolcini, during the winter vacation of his sophomore year — a study supplemented by some independent reading in French during the years that followed. Nevertheless, unequipped as he was, the appointment was made; it was of course accepted with relief and eagerness; and since the trustees recommended that the new professor should prepare himself for his role by traveling and studying in Europe, Longfellow was suddenly presented with the heady prospect of two or three years abroad. It must have seemed like the wholly improbable realization of a mere dream.

Because of the risks and discomforts of ocean travel late in the year, however, it was decided that Henry should postpone his departure to the following spring, and meanwhile, after all, spend the autumn and winter months reading law in his father's office: to what end, who can say? In any case those months were spent in Portland, probably not very diligently so far as the law was concerned; Longfellow doubtless gave much more time and thought to the essays he wrote in collaboration with his friends and fellow law students in imitation of Irving's and Paulding's *Salmagundi* papers — essays they contributed pseudonymously to the Portland *Advertiser*. It was not until April, 1826, that the young scholar left home at last, and not until the middle of May that he embarked for Europe on the packet ship *Cadmus*.

As it turned out, Longfellow was to spend a little more than three years abroad — three years during which he was at the most sensitive, impressionable, and assimilative period of a man's life. Of course it was decisive for him as a writer. No other American writer, not even Irving, had hitherto had just that experience and few were to have it later; it meant that Europe — France, Spain, Italy, Germany — was to enter into the tissue of Longfellow's sensibility as it has entered into that of few Americans, and that his work was to be a subtle and very special, but wholly spontaneous, fusion of the native and the foreign. The experience was entirely untouched by the harsh traits of rejection, of repudiation, of impatient "escape": Longfellow immersed himself in European life and culture as naturally and as easily as he later immersed himself in Cambridge. It is unimaginable that the thought of becoming an "expatriate" should for a moment have occurred to him: he was never more toughly, one might say amusingly, American than when he was soaking himself most thoroughly in the stream of European life. The results were unique and they have never quite been repeated. No one has described them better than Henry James, in his life of that real expatriate, William Wetmore Story. Longfellow, as James says, was simply not a case of "fellowship in nostalgia for Europe with our friend":

> For, complete and established, attuned and settled, Mr. Longfellow, precisely, was perhaps interesting for nothing so much as for the secret of his harmony . . . and for the way in which

his "European" culture and his native kept house together. Did he owe the large, quiet, pleasant, easy solution at which he had arrived . . . to his having worked up his American consciousness to that mystic point — one of those of which poets alone have the secret — at which it could feel nothing but continuity and congruity with his European?

James professes not to be able to answer the question, but he goes on to record his impression of something in Longfellow's liberal existence that was like "a fine ambiguity":

> If it seemed a piece of the old world smoothly fitted into the new, so it might quite as well have been a piece of the new fitted, just as intimately, into the old.

It was both, of course, and the clue to the adjustment perished with Longfellow.*

Meanwhile, by instinct, by unconscious rather than deliberate tendency, Longfellow was putting his first long stay in Europe to the best possible use. He was not preparing himself to teach modern languages as any young scholar would do today; from a certain professional point of view it must be admitted that there was something decidedly easygoing, amateurish, and reprehensible in Longfellow's apprenticeship to "the tongues." So far as can be made out from his letters, he never enrolled formally in any university, except perhaps Göttingen. For the sake of the languages, he attended university lectures in Paris and in Göttingen, but he never took a course for its own sake. Except in Germany he seems to have done little or no systematic reading in libraries. In Madrid he employed someone as an instructor in Spanish, and in Göttingen studied German under the guidance of Professor Georg Benecke, who had taught Bancroft, Ticknor, and all the Americans. This seems to be as near as he came to formal study. He wished, he needed, to learn three or four lan-

---

* In his old age he wrote to Louise Chandler Moulton, who was about to sail for Europe: "Please don't get expatriated. Ah, no, life is not all cathedrals and ruined castles, and other theatrical properties of the Old World."

guages as thoroughly as possible; his way of learning them was to hear them spoken, and to speak them himself, as constantly as might be, and meanwhile to read and even write them too. But he knew intuitively that a language is not a mere mode of communication but a complex expression of the whole life — the "soul" — of a people, and that to learn it well is to saturate oneself as best one can in that life itself, even in its apparently more trifling aspects.

It might not have worked for another kind of student, but it worked for Longfellow. If he became, as he did, a great teacher of modern languages and literatures, it was partly for formal professional reasons, but it was also because he had stored up, like the poet he was, an inexhaustible fund of sensuous and social impressions — impressions of French types and French manners, of the Spanish landscape, of the Carnival in Rome and a conversazione in Venice, of coffee-houses in Dresden and of mediaeval castles on the Rhine. In Paris he went to the theater and the opera, but he also, during his one autumn in France, went on a walking trip alone in the Loire valley, equipped with knapsack and flute, and not only visited the châteaux but mingled easily and spontaneously with the peasants and the vintagers. In Madrid — thanks to Washington Irving, who was working there on his life of Columbus and whom Longfellow, to his delight, came to know — he went several times to the evening "jams" of the Marchioness of Casa-Yrugo and thus had a peep into "good Spanish society"; but he also spent a week or two in the little village of Pardillo and joined in with the villagers as they danced the vigorous dance of the Manchegas. At the village of Ariccia, near Rome, where he spent some summer weeks, he sought out and talked with the monks of the Capuchin convent there. He could not seem to weary of these human encounters, admirably miscellaneous as they were.

He was becoming all the while a remarkable linguist, and this was to color his work in a hundred intangible but definitive ways.

For the time being his plans for a literary career were giving place to his passion for learning languages. To his mother, from Rome, he wrote that he was "passionately fond" of this study and indeed "completely enchanted" with it. Some months later he wrote, with characteristic ardor, to one of his sisters: "I assure you that, by every language you learn, a new world is opened before you. It is like being born again." So far as this from dutiful and perfunctory was the preparation of the future professor at Bowdoin and Harvard. Few poets have found more joy than Longfellow did in the discovery of new worlds through new languages: it is what helps to give his own work the special cosmopolitanism it has. There may have been a loss involved, but that was in the nature of the case.

With the quick imitativeness that was part of his talent, he came to speak several languages with ease and even to write them, if not with perfect correctness, at least with a certain dash. From Venice, on his way to Dresden, he wrote to his father: "With the French and Spanish Languages I am familiarly conversant — so as to speak them correctly — and write them with as much ease and fluency as I do the English. The Portuguese I read without difficulty: — and with regard to my proficiency in the Italian, I have only to say, that when I came to this city, all at the Hotel where I lodge took me for an Italian, until I gave them my passport, and told them I was an American." This, to be sure, was Longfellow's own claim to mastery, but there is some confirmation of it from other sources. "He writes and speaks Spanish," said George Ticknor, "with a degree of fluency and exactness which I have known in no American born of parents speaking English as their vernacular." In Spain and later he kept a journal in Spanish; we are told that, though it is not free from grammatical errors, it shows a thorough grasp of the spirit of the language. And his friend Julie Hepp in Heidelberg, years later, said, "Sie schreiben Deutsch beinahe wie ein Deutscher." As to the perfect correctness of his Italian sonnet ("Il Ponte Vecchio di Firenze"), of his French

Christmas poem for Agassiz ("Quand les astres de Noël"), or of his attempts at German verse ("Verlangst du, Erdgeboren!" and others), reservations have been made by those in a good position to pass judgment. But the linguistic zest that dictated them is the important thing, and their spiritedness is unmistakable.

Longfellow had spent more than eight months of his first year abroad in France. He had then moved on, early in 1827, to Spain, and remained there for an equal length of time. His stay in Italy, from December, 1827, when he reached Genoa, to December, 1828, when he left Venice to journey to Dresden, was the longest of his sojourns in any one country. He was in Germany for six months, mostly in Göttingen, and his father, pleased by the progress Henry had obviously been making, would have been willing for him to remain in Göttingen to the end of the summer — the summer of 1829. But the homesickness that had been recurrent all along, perhaps from the day he set foot on French soil, was at last overpowering, and Longfellow left Göttingen incontinently early in June, made his way to Paris and then London, and finally sailed on the ship *Manchester* from Liverpool to New York, where he arrived in the middle of August. In September he was to take up his duties at Bowdoin.

During his first months back in Brunswick there must have been much that was exhilarating to Longfellow in the role he had assumed. Certainly it was one that he was forced to create almost from scratch. He had never had any formal language teaching himself in college, and since there were at the time only three other colleges in the country — William and Mary, Harvard, and the University of Virginia — where modern languages were taught, there were no well-tried models for him to follow. There were not even any satisfactory textbooks, and this gap, as we shall see, he himself was forced, or felt himself forced, to fill. His "methods" he must have worked out almost entirely on his own. Much of his teaching necessarily consisted at first of elementary language instruction — instruction, for the time being, only in French and Spanish — but even during his first year at Bowdoin we hear of Longfellow's writing a course of lectures on French, Spanish, and Italian literature; and he was soon contributing articles on these languages and literatures to the *North American Review*. The life of a scholar and teacher, at least in some of its aspects, was temperamentally congenial to him, and we find him writing to a friend: "I am delighted more and more with the profession I have embraced." Of that profession he entertained the most serious and ideal conception: it was far from being a mere "career" for him, as he indicated, with old-fashioned stateliness, in his inaugural address at Bowdoin as Professor of Modern Languages:

> I regard the profession of teacher in a far more noble and elevated point of view than many do. I cannot help believing that he who bends in a right direction the pliant disposition of the young, and trains up the ductile mind to a vigorous and healthy growth, does something for the welfare of his country and something for the great interests of humanity.

Specifically the teaching of languages he defended as having a far greater importance than mere linguistic training; it was a means, as he said, to something much more valuable, an understanding of "the progress of the human mind," an enrichment of the understanding "by opening up to it new sources of knowledge," the becoming "a citizen of the world."

Given this high view of his profession, and given the warmth and exuberance of his nature, Longfellow could not fail to become one teacher in a thousand, and from the beginning he seems to have inspired not only respect but affection in his students. One of them remembered that "his manner was invariably full of that charming courtesy which it never lacked throughout his whole life. . . . We were fond of him from the start; his speech charmed us; his earnest and dignified demeanor inspired us. A better teacher, a more sympathetic friend, never addressed a class of young men."

This was one side of the pedagogic coin; the other was less shining. For one thing, it proved harder than Longfellow had foreseen to return to a small Maine town — slow, provincial, socially narrow, and just physically rather raw and bleak — after three rich years in the capitals and university cities of Europe. Almost from the beginning he chafed against the bareness, as it was for him, of Brunswick. In the spring of his first year there, he was writing to a friend that he took his exercise on horseback alone, "for I lead the life of an anchorite; to be sure I have many *acquaintances,* — mais elles ne sont pas du bois dont on fait les amis." He lamented the want of any opportunity to make use of his languages except in the classroom, "for nobody in this part of the world pretends to speak anything but English — and some might dispute them even that prerogative." In January, 1831, he was describing Brunswick as "this land of Barbarians — this miserable Down East. I feel," he added in the tone of Ovid at Tomis, "as if I were living in exile here."

In the fall of that year he was married to Mary Storer Potter, a charming and cultivated Portland girl, and after the two began housekeeping in Brunswick, life was certainly less dreary for Longfellow than it had been during his first two years. But neither he nor his wife was genuinely happy there, and moreover, along with his enthusiasm for the higher tasks of a teacher, there went inevitably, for Longfellow, a rebellious impatience with its inescapable humdrum, especially on the elementary level. "You call it a dog's life," he wrote to his sister before his marriage: "it is indeed — my dear Anne: I do not believe that I was born for such a lot." "This teaching boys their a,b,c," he wrote later to a friend, "is growing somewhat irksome. Morning, noon, night — *toujours perdrix!*" True, these outbursts of weariness and vexation contravened the high sentiments of the inaugural address, but Longfellow was paying the price for having the nature of an artist as well as the inclinations of a scholar.

As time wore on, he began to think more and more seriously of getting away from Brunswick, if not from teaching itself, and to cast about for avenues of escape. At one time he had high hopes of an appointment at New York University, which would at least have given him "a stage on which I can take longer strides and spout to a larger audience" — but nothing came of these hopes. Later he was similarly frustrated in a hope that he might be called to the University of Virginia. In the summer of 1833 he heard that the Secretary of the Legation at Madrid had just died; at once the wish flared up in his mind that he might succeed to this attractive post, and thus not only escape from teaching but return to live, for a time at least, in his beloved Spain. These hopes also were destined to be dashed, and the following winter, as if reluctantly reconciled to a pedagogic life, and having heard that George Bancroft and Joseph Cogswell were planning to dispose of their Round Hill School at Northampton, he journeyed to the Massachusetts town in the depths of winter to discuss the possibility of taking the school over from them. Friends in Boston, however, advised him strongly against the folly of taking over a *"run down"* institution, and Longfellow quickly abandoned this not very promising project.*

Disheartening as all this was, the fates that were essentially benevolent to Longfellow were for some months at work on his

* "I reached Northampton safe and sound," he wrote to his friend Greene, "and remained there two days. . . . The spot is lovely indeed — lovely even beneath its mantle of snow. I have seen it in summer — and I believe it one of the most beautiful places in New England." In fact it was not exactly in summer that Longfellow had once before visited Northampton, but in the spring of 1826, on the eve of his departure for Europe; he had gone there to ask Bancroft and Cogswell for advice about his studies in Europe and for letters of introduction. Longfellow's impressions of the town did not coincide with Henry James's a generation later, but it must be remembered that James's health at the time was none of the best.

behalf. George Ticknor, the first professor of modern languages at Harvard, was eager to give up teaching and devote himself entirely to his own studies. He had, as we have seen, a high opinion of Longfellow as a linguist; other friends, too, were busy pulling wires in his interest; and in December, 1834, Longfellow received a letter from President Quincy offering him the Smith Professorship of modern languages at Harvard. Curiously enough, Longfellow seems to have hesitated for some weeks to accept the offer, but early in 1835 he decided that he *would* accept it, and wrote to President Quincy to that effect. The offer of the professorship had carried with it the suggestion that he might wish to spend a year or eighteen months in Europe "for a more perfect attainment of the German." Despite his father's advice and Mary Longfellow's reluctance to make the trip, Longfellow was determined to spend a second sojourn in Europe; and in April, accompanied by his wife and two young women friends of hers, Longfellow sailed out of New York harbor, this time for England. His second stay abroad was to be much shorter than his first: he was in Europe only a year and a half, and returned to America in the fall of 1836.

His first visit had been largely spent in France and southern Europe, and had been devoted to the acquisition of the Romance languages, for even in Göttingen he had worked at Spanish literature rather than German. This second stay was to be spent in northern Europe and Germany, and was to open up for him the riches of German and Scandinavian literature, which he had longed to command. In London, where he and his party spent a month, Longfellow, armed with a letter from Emerson, went to call on Carlyle at Cheyne Row; for the first time, perhaps, he heard Goethe spoken of with reverence by a man whose critical powers he had to respect. At his hotel the next day he tore through Carlyle's life of Schiller with mounting excitement. Only now was the power and depth of modern German literature revealing itself to him.

He had no intention, however, despite President Quincy's letter, of moving on at once to Germany. Certainly he wished to perfect his German, but meanwhile he wished also to acquire Swedish and Danish, and the party traveled, by way of Hamburg and Copenhagen, to Stockholm, where they were to spend the summer. It was a disappointing period in some respects: the weather was cold and wet, and Longfellow was frustrated to find that his friend, the Swedish poet Karl August Nicander, whom he had known in Rome, was out of town for the summer vacation. Stockholm itself was not attractive to him — but, despite these setbacks, Longfellow managed to make pleasant and useful acquaintances, partly through the kindness of Berzelius, the great chemist, to whom Professor Cleaveland had given him a letter. In this way he got in touch with Karl Fredrik Lignell, professor of modern languages at Upsala — a very old man, as Longfellow described him, who dressed like a young beau — and began to study Swedish under this eccentric but kindly teacher. Before the summer was over Longfellow had acquired an adequate knowledge of the language — which struck him as "soft and musical, with an accent like the lowland Scotch" — and the beginnings of a knowledge of Swedish literature. Meanwhile he saw something of the literary society of Stockholm, and was taken by the popular novelist Gustaf Henrik Mellin, a clergyman and an imitator of Scott, to a gathering at the Café Allemand, where he met several of the young literati, and was a little surprised by the mild dissipation in which Mellin and another literary clergyman participated. With Mellin, however, who was a Finn, he even took some lessons in Finnish.

A fortnight in September he spent in Copenhagen, a city which, with its spacious streets and handsome houses, Longfellow found much more charming than Stockholm. Here, naturally, he set himself to the task of learning Danish in short order. His tutor was a scholar on the staff of the Royal Library, and even in those few days he seems to have acquired a reading knowledge of

Danish; not content with which he also exchanged, with the antiquary Carl Rafn, lessons in Icelandic for information about the American Indians. Meanwhile he had attended the theater to see a tragedy by the great Danish poet Adam Oehlenschläger, and had been impressed by the silence and attentiveness of the audience. Oehlenschläger himself he once saw in the public walk — a large, dark man who reminded him of Daniel Webster — and came to regret that he had never made his acquaintance.

The stay in Copenhagen would have been perfectly happy if it had not been for an illness of Mary Longfellow's, who was pregnant. In the midst of his exhilarating travels and studies, a great sorrow was in store for Longfellow. He and the three young women had proceeded from Copenhagen to Amsterdam, where Mary was forced to take to her bed and where she had a miscarriage. Overshadowed as his days were by this anxiety, Longfellow had plunged characteristically into the study of Dutch, and before he left Holland was, it is said, "conversing quite freely" in that language. After three weeks in Amsterdam Mary Longfellow had recovered sufficiently so that the party could move on to Rotterdam, but there her condition grew rapidly worse, and on November 29 she died. It was not the first bereavement Longfellow had suffered but, at this time, it was the greatest. During the rest of his stay in Europe, though he distracted himself by study, by social activities, and by travel, the undertone of his thoughts and feelings was one of intense grief. "I cannot study," he writes in his Heidelberg diary two months later. "One thought occupies me night and day. She is dead — she is dead! — All day I am weary and sad — and at night I cry myself to sleep like a child. Not a page can I read without my thoughts wandering from it." And even the following summer, as he walked alone beside the Swiss lakes, he could write: "Good God! what a solitary, lonely being I am! Why do I travel? Every hour my heart aches with sadness."

In spite of his misery, however, Longfellow had not allowed

himself to forget or neglect his intellectual purpose in coming to Europe, and when he could leave Rotterdam, he set out for Heidelberg, where the Younger Romantics — Brentano, Arnim, Eichendorff — had lived and worked a generation earlier, and where he had decided to spend most of his stay in Germany. On his way thither, passing through Bonn, he went to call on August Wilhelm Schlegel, an elderly man now, with a broad high forehead, large eyes, and a pleasant intellectual expression of countenance, who lectured to him rather than conversed, but whom — chiefly, it seems, as the translator of Shakespeare — he was gratified to see. In the middle of December he reached Heidelberg, where he was to remain for the next six months.

These months were spent largely in immersing himself at last in the current of modern German literature. He was to find himself excited, even intoxicated, by it as by the literature of no other language. On another level, it is true, no experience abroad was ever to be so profoundly romantic for him as his months in Spain had been; he was always to be torn, later, by the longing to return to Spain and the fear of returning, with the danger of dissipating this youthful glow; in fact, he never did go back. But there is no substitute, for a young writer, for the literature of his contemporaries, and Spanish literature in Longfellow's generation seems to have been less impressive than ever before or since. For half a century and more, on the other hand, the literature of Germany had been among the richest, perhaps the richest, in Europe; and Longfellow, like no American writer before him, steeped himself in it until the German strains in his own work became so intimately organic to it that they cannot be disengaged.

Not that Longfellow's Germany was Coleridge's or Carlyle's or Emerson's — the severely philosophical Germany of Kant or Schelling. Metaphysical Germany was of little or no significance to a poet so unpretentious intellectually as Longfellow, and it is only the agreeable fragrance of German transcendentalism that, at one or two removes, pervades his work like a gentle presence. It was, for the most part, the easier, the milder, the more accessible aspects of German romanticism that enchanted him — its innocent ideality and rejection of the mundane, its spiritualizing of the material, its ethical purity and aspiration, its frank indulgence of sentiment and all tender feelings, and of course its cultivation of the Middle Ages, of the romantic past, of the poetry of the folk, balladry, and popular tradition. It would not be fair to say that German literature meant only the secondary writers to Longfellow: he came to have a serious understanding and appreciation of Goethe. But certainly the writers who spoke most directly and naturally to him were the poets of sentiment and story (Bürger, Müller, Uhland), the collectors of ballads and *märchen* (Musaeus, Arnim and Brentano, the Grimms), and the writers of romantic fiction (Jean Paul Richter, Tieck, Chamisso, Hoffmann). These were the writers whom he mainly read during the months in Heidelberg, and they must have done as much as poetry could do to assuage his grief.

His time, naturally, was not spent only in reading. He attended lectures at the university, though he had no very high opinion of the literary faculty. Many evenings he spent with the hospitable family of the Hepps, where his one remaining companion, Clara Crowninshield — for the other member of the party had returned to America — was a boarder. He went on long walks in the neighboring woods and hills with his fellow boarder, the young and attractive Estonian landlord Baron Jacques von Ramm, who appears as the Baron of Hohenfels in *Hyperion*. In the summer, weary for the moment of his studies, he set out on a leisurely trip through southern Germany, the Tyrol, and Switzerland. In the coach that took him from Munich to Salzburg he had as a fellow passenger the eminent Austrian dramatist Franz Grillparzer, whose name, oddly enough, seems not yet to have been known to Longfellow, for he misspells it in his diary and calls the great Grillparzer simply "a poet from Vienna." He remarks that this poet, though insignificant in appearance, was a pleasant person in reality. Much of the time on these travels Longfellow was alone and, as we have seen, lonely and dejected. But at Thun, in July, he fell in with a pleasant Boston family, the Appletons, with whom he struck up an acquaintance, and meeting them a few days later at Interlaken, he joined forces with them, and traveled more cheerfully in their company to Lucerne, Zürich, and Schaffhausen. It was one of the Appleton daughters, Frances, with whom he formed the closest friendship; indeed, he fell deeply in love with her, and seven years later she became his second wife. In mid-August, however, it was necessary to part with the Appletons and return to Heidelberg and the somewhat neglected Clara Crowninshield. Later that month the two of them left Germany, and traveling by way of Strasbourg and Paris, reached Le Havre early in October and sailed thence for America. It was not long before Longfellow had established himself in Cambridge — as it proved, for the rest of his life.

It has been remarked more than once, as an oddity, that during the whole of his twenties, when most poets have done so much of their work, Longfellow almost ceased to be a poet. Bryant, at Heidelberg, in the winter of 1836, might have been excused for wondering whether his young friend would ever again, except as a translator, write a line of verse. And Longfellow himself was at times besieged by doubts. "My poetic career is finished," he had written to his sister from Göttingen in 1829, and it is true that, during this whole period, he cannot have written — and that mostly in his journal — more than half a dozen original poems, none of which he preserved. Traveling, studying languages, teaching — activities such as these proved simply too engrossing, for the young Longfellow, for him to have any energy left over for poems of his own; and indeed there is something not quite explicable in his coming back to poetry when he did. It is eloquent of the genuineness of his gift that he ever did so.

During his second year at Bowdoin, to be sure, he had been asked to deliver the annual Phi Beta Kappa poem, as he did in the fall of 1832. A year later he was invited to repeat the performance at Harvard. Only a few stanzas of this poem have ever been published, but "The Past and the Present" was clearly an uncharacteristic effort, and it led nowhere. No doubt it was from this experience that Longfellow learned how unnatural for him was the writing of poems to order for special occasions, and with one exception he never again allowed himself to be led astray in this direction. "The Past and the Present" was a long didactic poem, in six-line stanzas, on the subject of education, in which Longfellow seems to have drawn a contrast, partly satirical, partly serious, between the bigotry of the Dark Ages and the enlightenment of his own. How unpromising such a subject was for a poet like Longfellow may be seen from one stanza:

> Oh holy and eternal Truth! Thou art
>   An emanation of the Eternal Mind!
> A glorious attribute — a noble part
>   Of uncreated being! Who can find,
> By diligent searching — who can find out thee,
> The Incomprehensible — the Deity! *

Yet if Longfellow wrote almost no original poetry during his years at Bowdoin, he was by no means idle in a literary sense. His first publications now sprang directly from his labors as a linguist and teacher; they were textbooks, indeed, and though they have no place in the history of literature, they are small items in the history of Longfellow's mind. During his first year at Bowdoin he translated and adapted for American students a French grammar (C. F. Lhomond's *Éléments de la grammaire française*); he made selections from a French textbook consisting of little

---

* Longfellow published extracts from this Phi Beta Kappa poem in the periodicals during the thirties, and a few lines were incorporated in "The Warning," one of the *Poems on Slavery*, in 1842; but with that exception he wisely refrained from reprinting any of the poem in collections of verse.

dramatic sketches (*Manuel de Proverbes Dramatiques*); and he edited two Spanish tales that had been written in the style of Washington Irving (*Novelas Españolas*). All these were published in Portland in 1830, and they indicate how much absorbed young Longfellow was, during this first year, in the teaching of even elementary languages.

A couple of years later he published two other textbooks, this time for students of Italian. But this was fortunately the end of such hack-work for him. A far more creative offshoot of his teaching was the translating of European poetry that he began in these years. Longfellow, as it turned out, was a born translator; he was to be a remarkable one; and it was during this Bowdoin period that his long career as a translator began. It is true that he had, as we have seen, made an impression as an undergraduate with at least one translation; but it was only now that, as a mature man, he came back to the art. The whole subject of Longfellow's achievement as a translator must be postponed to a later page, but these early years cannot be rightly spoken of without a glance at the subject. No doubt he began by translating poems for his college classes, but if so, he must soon have felt that these experiments were successful enough to justify publication, and in 1833 he published — it was his first real book — his accomplished rendering of the "Coplas" of Jorge Manrique, the fifteenth-century Spanish poet. The volume was prefaced by an essay, already published in the *North American Review*, on Spanish moral and devotional poetry, and it included also some translations of shorter poems by Lope de Vega and other Spanish poets. Longfellow's name appeared on the title page, and the beauty of these versions must have had something to do with his appointment at Harvard. Still more important, it was the, in a sense, creative act of rendering other men's poems in English that, as time went on, helped to liberate Longfellow's mind for his own work.

Meanwhile, during these years at Bowdoin, if he wrote little original verse, Longfellow had again been busy with prose in various forms. Alexander Everett, whom he had known in Madrid as Minister to Spain, had now become editor of the *North American Review*, and in this role appealed to the young scholar for contributions. Longfellow responded with a series of review-articles on linguistic and literary subjects — "Origin and Progress of the French Language," "History of the Italian Language and Dialects," "Spanish Language and Literature" — which strike us now as curiously unsuitable for a periodical with even a small nonacademic circulation. They were in the mode of the time, however, and they gave Longfellow a welcome opportunity to exploit his new philological and literary learning. He used portions of these articles in *Outre-Mer* and, several years later, in his anthology *The Poets and Poetry of Europe;* but they are written, for the most part, in the rather ponderous review style of the period, and they have quite lost their interest now.

With perhaps one exception. In the winter of 1832 Longfellow published in the *North American* a "Defence of Poetry" — ostensibly a review of a new edition of Sidney's "Apology for Poetry" — which is still worth reading, if only for what it tells us of the literary mind of that decade. Seven years earlier, in his commencement oration, Longfellow had defended poetry against the American obsession with the practical; and now, in the early thirties, he is still defending it against the all-pervasive spirit of Utility. In doing so, he is, in his less eloquent way, aligning himself with Shelley in his counterattack on the English empiricists and utilitarians,* and like Sidney, too, he defends poetry as being, in fact, "useful," but in a far higher and more ideal sense than the usual one. What is still more interesting in the essay, however, is that Longfellow, perhaps for the first time in this country, strikes the note of romantic literary nationalism — gives voice to the conviction that "poetry is but the warm expression of the thoughts and feelings of a people, and we speak of it as being

* Yet Longfellow could not at this time have known Shelley's "Defence," which was not published until 1840.

national, when the character of a nation shines visibly and distinctly through it." Appeals enough had been made before this for a genuinely American literature, but just this philosophical view was still an unfamiliar one, and it indicates to what good effect Longfellow had been dipping into Herder or Friedrich Schlegel or both.

There was a great deal of diffuse literary energy in Longfellow's mind during these years, and he tried his hand not only at scholarly criticism but, for the first time, at prose fiction. It was the period of the strongly localized prose tale — "The Legend of Sleepy Hollow," "Peter Rugg, the Missing Man," and others — and even during his first European years, Longfellow's thoughts had turned to the possibility of a "Sketch Book of New England" that might do for his own region what Irving's tales had done for the Hudson Valley. From Dresden he had written to a Philadelphia publisher suggesting such a volume, and listing some of the sketches he would like to include in it. Nothing came of this plan for a book, but he did later write and publish two of the tales he had mentioned by title in his letter. One of them, "The Indian Summer," is a piece of appallingly lachrymose deathbed fiction, but the other, "The Bald Eagle," which appeared anonymously in *The Token* for 1833, abounds in local flavor and is written with admirable spirit and humor. It was formerly thought to be Hawthorne's; it was even included in his collected works, and indeed it has some of Hawthorne's droll localism — one thinks of "Mr. Higginbotham's Catastrophe" or parts of "Ethan Brand" — but it has a stamp of its own, this little tale of the excitement aroused in a sleepy New England village by the news that Lafayette, on his way north, is to pass through the place; of the feverish preparations that are made for his reception, and the bitter disappointment when, late in the day, it is learned that the General has taken a different route.

Another tale that might have been included in the New England Sketch Book, though it is not mentioned in Longfellow's letter to Carey & Lea, is "The Wondrous Tale of a Little Man in Gosling Green," a story with which, in 1834, he won half the prize offered for the best prose tale in a contest conducted by Horace Greeley's weekly, the *New-Yorker*. "The Wondrous Tale" has a kind of poignancy that "The Bald Eagle" does not have, and the New England village which is its setting — Bungonuck, which may be intended for Brunswick — is depicted with a touch of mild satire that one does not find in the other story. It would be the best of Longfellow's tales if it were not so imperfectly unified; two tales, not one, should have been made of it. The mysterious stranger in gosling green who arrives in Bungonuck one day by stage explains to the inquisitive inhabitants that he is on his way eastward to discover where Down East is. He returns some months later to confess that he has not been able to discover it. "The farther he went, the farther it went; it was like trying to tread upon your own shadow." This is the "uncanny" vein of "Peter Rugg"; what follows — the pathetic story of the stranger's lonely life in Bungonuck — is in another style, and pleasant as it is, rather compromises the unity of the tale.

Other anonymous stories Longfellow wrote at the time have been identified, and some of them — particularly a tale with a Spanish setting, "The Convent of the Paular" — have a dark tonality that is too seldom thought of as within Longfellow's range. Meanwhile he had been at work on another project the idea of which, too, had come to him during his first stay in Europe. "I am also writing a book," he wrote to Stephen Longfellow from Göttingen in 1829, "a kind of Sketch-Book of scenes in France, Spain, and Italy." Again Irving is standing behind his shoulder as he writes, but unlike the New England Sketch Book, this European counterpart ultimately came to realization. At first, as with "The Lay Monastery," Longfellow planned this book as allegedly the work of a fictional persona — in this case, a schoolmaster in a New England village ("a son of New-England . . . educated in all her feelings and prejudices"), who has traveled in Europe and is now recalling his experiences as what James would call a "passionate pilgrim." During his second and third years in Brunswick, Longfellow contributed six of his "Schoolmaster" papers to the *New-England Magazine;* but by that time he seems to have thought better of this inhibiting device, and the European sketchbook, when it finally took shape, was alleged, more suitably, to be the work simply of "The Pilgrim of Outre-Mer." *Outre-Mer: A Pilgrimage beyond the Sea* is indeed its final title. In 1833 Longfellow began to publish the work in parts, as Irving had published *The Sketch Book,* but he gave this up with the second number, and in 1835 the whole work was published in New York.

Longfellow himself once said that he felt a kind of reverence for the first books of young authors — so much "audacious hope" and "trembling fear" have gone into them — and in that spirit one should no doubt approach *Outre-Mer* as gently as may be. It is one item in that long series of American books that testify to the intensely American emotion of romantic feeling for Europe, though in Longfellow, as we have seen, it never took the form of unappeasable nostalgia. As an early and ingenuous outpouring of such feeling, *Outre-Mer* will always have a minor interest and charm. "To my youthful imagination," says Longfellow, "the Old World was a kind of Holy Land, lying afar off beyond the blue horizon of the ocean; and when its shores first rose upon my sight, looming through the hazy atmosphere of the sea, my heart swelled with the deep emotions of the pilgrim, when he sees afar the spire which rises above the shrine of his devotion."

One regrets that, with all this ardor behind it, *Outre-Mer* is no more impressive than it is. It suffers of course from being much too consciously and directly the imitation of another book: not to Longfellow was it given, as it might have been, to surpass his model. Irving is a disturbing presence here; and besides, one has to recognize that, as a prose writer, Longfellow did not have

Irving's particular felicity of stroke, his water-colorist's eye for landscape, or that temperamental sense of place, of "atmosphere," that could impart an irresistible magic to evocations of Westminster Abbey, of the Alhambra, or even of a Dutch farmhouse in the Hudson Valley. Unlike verse, prose of this sort was usually an inhibition to Longfellow, and when he forced himself to write about the cathedral at Rouen or the mountains of San Salvador, he succeeded, as a rule, only in being thin and commonplace. There is something curiously unyouthful in many of these notes of travel: Longfellow is sometimes frankly weary of his task, and can be as embarrassingly flat as an inferior guidebook: he speaks of "a steep hill which commands a fine view of the city of Tours and its delightful environs." He is not often so jejune as this, but he is too seldom successful when he attempts to conjure up the beauty or picturesqueness of a building or a scene, and he attempts this frequently.

Yet it would not be fair to say that he always fails. There are characteristic effects of dreamy tranquillity, of late-afternoon or early-evening peacefulness, that he could command even in prose; he does this in his description of the Lago di Albano seen at sunset from the heights of Ariccia:

> The sultry day was closing, and I had reached, in my accustomed evening's walk, the woodland gallery that looks down upon the Alban Lake. The setting sun seemed to melt away in the sky, dissolving into a golden rain, that bathed the whole Campagna with unearthly splendor, while Rome in the distance, half-hidden, half-revealed, lay floating like a mote in the broad and misty sunbeam. The woodland walk before me seemed roofed with gold and emerald, and at intervals across its leafy arches shot the level rays of the sun, kindling, as they passed, like the burning shaft of Acestes. Beneath me the lake slept quietly. A blue, smoky vapor floated around its overhanging cliffs; the tapering cone of Monte Cavo hung reflected in the water; a little boat skimmed along its glassy surface, and I could even hear the sound of the laboring oar, so motionless and silent was the air around me.

It is tempting to say that there is a touch, slight and precarious as it is, of the Vergilian magic in this ("et sol crescentis decedens duplicat umbras"), and the echo of the *Aeneid* — the arrow of Acestes blazing in the air — is a lovely example of Longfellow's more and more characteristic use of literary allusion for purposes of metaphor.

If he usually fails, however, with landscape and architecture, Longfellow is on surer ground when he goes in for sketches of "characters," of "types," for quasi-fictional portraits of encountered individuals. It is what we should expect from his prose tales, and we are not always disappointed in *Outre-Mer*. Unmistakable is the animation in his sketch of the conductor of the Norman *diligence* on the way to Rouen ("a short, pursy man, with a busy, self-satisfied air" who seems almost to have stepped out of Flaubert by anticipation); or of Monsieur d'Argentville, the sexagenarian at Auteuil, with his light nankeen breeches and his russet surtout, who lives in the touching memories of his philandering youth before the Revolution; or perhaps best of all the rascally student of Alcalá whom the author encounters in an innyard at Manzanares and who holds forth shamelessly on his own artful dodges: he seems to owe something to Cervantes and something to real life.

There is no doubt, too, that Longfellow had some of the gifts of a humorous writer, and in *Outre-Mer* there are two interpolated tales — there are indeed three, but only two of them are humorous — which confirm the impression one would have got from "The Bald Eagle." The better of them, which he pretends was related to him by an elderly antiquarian at the Golden Lion Inn in Rouen, is "Martin Franc and the Monk of Saint Anthony." This appears to be simply a retelling of a thirteenth-century Norman *fabliau*, but if so, Longfellow, like other good writers before and since, seems to have improved upon his original, and this tale of a libidinous monk who is accidentally killed by a jealous husband, and whose dead body becomes an embarrassment to a series of perplexed individuals, is told with a comic speed and zest that cannot be too much praised. The humor of the Middle Ages was quite as accessible to Longfellow as their romance.

A reviewer in the *North American Review* of the first two numbers of *Outre-Mer*, which were anonymous, remarked that the work was "obviously the production of a writer of talent and cultivated taste"; but in general the book seems to have made no very great stir either among reviewers or readers. It was not wholly ignored, however, and when Longfellow returned, in prose, to the subject of European travel, as he did three years later in *Hyperion*, he had behind him his very full months in Heidelberg and his roamings through the Tyrol and Switzerland. It remained to be seen whether these would stand him in still better stead.

III

Professor Longfellow

LONGFELLOW had spent six years of his youth as a professor at Bowdoin; he was to spend eighteen years of his early middle life as a professor at Harvard — the years of his renewed productivity as a poet and the genial early summer of his great fame. Was he first of all a scholar? Or was he first of all a poet? There were half a dozen years or so when one can imagine such questions asked by a curious observer, and just as there was, as James said, a fine ambiguity in the relation between Longfellow's native and his European culture, so there was a fine ambiguity here. His work was all but unique in being the product of a complex and fruitful interaction between literary scholarship and literary creation; among poets Longfellow has the air of being quite specially academic; among academicians he has the air of being a poet in the lecture hall. Given the character of his gift, this was an almost wholly fortunate duplicity, and if we end, as of course we do, by calling him primarily a poet, we do not forget that this poet might once have been called a professor on Parnassus.

Officially Longfellow's professorship at Harvard began in the fall of 1836 when he was formally elected Smith Professor by the President and Fellows, and when he himself arrived in Cambridge to live. He did not actually begin lecturing until the following May, but from then on until the spring of 1854 the greater part of his time and energy were devoted to his college duties. During all these years, when college was in session, he lectured, twice a week as a rule, in a pleasant room in University Hall and in his frankly enthusiastic way, on the mediaeval and modern literatures of Europe. It was an honorable and even an important chapter in the history of such instruction in this country. No one before Longfellow, not even Ticknor, had had so great a scope of literary culture, and no one had been so notably a man of letters in the classroom. The age of specialization had not yet begun, and Longfellow could, and indeed was expected to, range majestically over the whole terrain, or most of it, of European literature. In that first spring of 1837 he treated, in his lectures, such subjects as the history of the French language, Anglo-Saxon literature, Swedish literature, the life and writings of Goethe, and the life and writings of Jean Paul Richter. As time went on, his most original contribution was no doubt his teaching of German literature: Longfellow was the first scholar in this country to give a course in *Faust,* and his lectures on Goethe, freely delivered from notes and interspersed with readings from the German and his own translations, made an epoch. But his lectures over many years on Dante were no less significant, and meanwhile he was lecturing, for example, on Molière, on the Spanish drama, and on Italian writers from before Dante to Goldoni, Metastasio, and even "the writers of the present century." It was as if he had taken all literature for his province.

Certainly Longfellow's lecturing was broadly humanistic rather than erudite in any studiously specialized way, and moreover it seems to have been, in style and spirit, vivid and picturesque rather than soberly learned. If we can judge from passages in *Hyperion* which were apparently lifted from his lectures — the pages on Richter, for example — Longfellow's manner was exuberantly "appreciative"; unapologetically imaginative or fanciful; sometimes dramatic, sometimes pictorial; often charmingly allusive or metaphorical.* He aimed much less at the transmission of information than at the contagion of personal enthusiasm. At the end of his last lecture, for the time, on Italian literature, in 1851, he explained to his hearers that in planning the course, he had chosen the method of "history" rather than that of "criticism and analysis" — by which he meant, as he went on to imply, that he had preferred to be sympathetic and descriptive rather than judicial or censorious, and to linger on excellences rather than defects. It was a kind of lecturing that became much more frequent at a later period than it was in Longfellow's day. How much it meant to several generations of Harvard men we can gather, for example, from a letter sent to him at the time of his wife's death, in 1861, by Francis Parkman and four of his classmates in the class of 1844: "the eighteen years that have passed since then, with all the changes they have brought," said these former students, "have served only to make more permanent the recollection of those hours" — the hours spent on Molière — "as among the most agreeable of our college course."

Teaching so fully committed as this must have given not only pleasure to the taught but joy to the teacher; and undoubtedly, most of the time, it gave deep satisfaction to Longfellow. Noting in his journal in 1847 that in that term he had two classes in Molière and one in Dante, he remarked: "No college work could possibly be pleasanter." This satisfaction was certainly real enough, and no doubt persisted to the end; but meanwhile, almost from the beginning, there had been, as at Bowdoin, another face of the coin. Lecturing was only a part of Longfellow's duties as Smith Professor; supervising a department made up of four language instructors, visiting their classes at stated intervals, and sometimes

* See for example the fine extended simile in *Hyperion,* Book I, Chapter V, comparing the reading of Jean Paul with the climbing of a high mountain to see the sun rise: "At times you are enveloped in mist, the morning wind sweeps by you with a shout," etc.

even, when an instructor was lacking, taking over the teaching of elementary sections — these responsibilities were also involved; and the irksomeness of this uncongenial administrative work, as well as the tedium of elementary teaching, worried and wearied him all along. His letters and journals abound in expressions of rebellion — rebellion against the routine of his work itself and against its frustration of his true work, writing.

"Perhaps the worst thing in a college life," he lamented in the fall of 1838, "is this having your mind constantly a playmate for boys, — constantly adapting itself to them, instead of stretching out and grappling with *men's* minds." "Poetic dreams shaded by French irregular verbs!" he wrote a year later. "Hang it! I wish I were a free man!" In that same fall he described himself as "exhausted with labors in college," and began to dally with the idea of giving up teaching entirely and devoting himself wholly to literature. This dream of resigning from his professorship and giving all his energy to writing haunted him during most of his time at Harvard: in 1846 he records in his journal, after Hawthorne had been dining with him: "He thinks I ought by all means to give up college." "And so I think," added Longfellow, "and I mean to do it." Yet from year to year — out of love for the lecturing itself, perhaps, and no doubt out of some temperamental timidity — he postponed so drastic a step, and though he more and more spoke of teaching as a grind and a mill, he came back to it term after term. It was not until he at last felt that he could afford, in the material sense, to surrender his professorship and give himself entirely to writing, that, in the spring of 1854, describing himself to his brother as "pawing to get free," he sent his letter of resignation to President Walker and the Fellows. On April 19 he delivered his last lecture — and began, as he wrote to Sumner, "to rise and right [himself] like a ship that throws out some of its cargo."

He had exulted much of the time in his labors, one can have no doubt, and he had, much of the time, suffered from the genuine misery they had caused him. Both were characteristic of him, the misery as much as the exultation. Simple and translucent as Longfellow's nature has often been described as being — and as, compared with that of many poets, it was — he was by no means wholly free from the painful and problematic complexities that are the familiar penalty of fine gifts. Below the smiling surface of his years at Harvard ran an undertone of physical and emotional distress that, muted and transmuted, is audible in much of his verse, but that breaks out in his journal and even in his letters in its raw and unalleviated form. His physical afflictions span the gamut so familiar in the lives of the poets — dyspepsia, neuralgia, insomnia, eyestrain. In the spring of 1839 he is "Almost crazed with this infernal firebrand burning my life out; namely, dyspepsia." Neuralgic pain was a yearlong trial: "All day and all night," he writes in 1851, "this terrible neuralgia" — but it had begun years before, and never set him free for many months on end. Most serious of all, for a scholar and a writer, was the malady of the eyes that led him to describe himself at one time as half blind. In the summer of 1843, it appears, as he was writing in the twilight, a partial blindness suddenly fell on him, and "For some time I walked in a world of shadows, seeing men as trees." During the next few years the use of his eyes was a constant problem, and it was only because, after that same summer of 1843, his wife could read to him and write for him that Longfellow was enabled to get on with his college work and his writing.

There was certainly a large element of the "psychosomatic" in all this physical misery. Longfellow sometimes called himself a hypochondriac, and clearly a good deal of emotional tension lay below his illnesses. Cheerful and equable as he always seemed outwardly, secretly he struggled with recurrent depressions, anxieties, and fears. "I am neither in good health nor good spirits," he confided to his journal during his second fall in Cambridge; "being foolishly inclined to indigestion and the most unpleasant melancholy." A few days later: "Moped and groped about, un-well. Dejected, — no sunshine in the soul." On the eve of sailing to Europe in 1842 he wrote to Sumner that he had determined to put away all gloomy forebodings, and was sending him back "none of the darkness which . . . at times usurps the empire of my thoughts." Much of this darkness must have been dissipated by the happiness that came to him with his second marriage, but even four years later he confessed, on one occasion, that he had fallen into "a state of dullness and apathy quite woeful! No life — no keen sensations; but a dismal lethargy hanging about me like a darkness." And this heavy apathy sometimes alternated with its opposite, an unreasoning terror. "O heavy heart, be comforted!" he writes. "A kind of panic and wild alarm has seized upon me, which I cannot control! God be merciful to me!"

The seeds of Longfellow's neurosis — the word is not too strong — are buried so deep in the record that one cannot hope to unearth them now. Widowerhood, after the death of Mary Longfellow, and the bachelor existence he led for five or six years in Cambridge, were no doubt, for a man of Longfellow's warm and tender emotionality, a continuous ordeal; the effects of sexual tension cannot be ruled out. In the fall of 1841, in any case, he had become so much disturbed about his health that he applied to the university authorities for a leave of absence, and in the spring of 1842 he departed for Europe again, where he spent most of his stay subjecting himself to a heroic water-cure at Marienberg, just above the town of Boppard on the Rhine. Despite his physical ailments the stay of five or six months had its happy aspects — the hours Longfellow spent in the old cities of Bruges and Nuremberg, the friendship he struck up with the young German poet Ferdinand Freiligrath, and the days he spent as Dickens's guest in London on his way homeward. He had hoped to stay on at Marienberg for a continuation of his cure, but the university could not extend his leave of absence without suspending his salary too, and it was probably with a mixture of regret and homecoming joy that he found himself, early in November, back at the Craigie House and Cambridge.

For it would be a distortion of the truth to represent the years of Longfellow's professorship as merely exacerbated by academic duties or darkened by ill health and melancholia. These latter were always present or latent, but meanwhile there were great and profoundly real satisfactions to compensate. The satisfactions of teaching were among these, as we have seen, and there was the glow and flush of his increasing fame to counterbalance many hours of misery. There was much too in the mere physical setting of his days to give joy to a man so sensitive to his surroundings as Longfellow was.

During his first months in Cambridge he had lived in a professorial boardinghouse on Kirkland Street, but in the late summer of 1837 he had had the good luck to find rooms in the noble old mansion on Brattle Street known as the Craigie House — a stately residence that had been built before the Revolution and had served for months, as Longfellow loved to recall, as Washington's headquarters during the siege of Boston. His rooms themselves were large and elegant, and from the windows of his front chamber he could look out over the slow-winding Charles to the southward and the Brighton meadows beyond. From the beginning he was unconcealedly happy in his living quarters: the great old house, with the elms in front of it and the garden behind, was the perfect haven for Longfellow — as it would not for a moment have been for Thoreau or Whitman — and it was to be his home until the end of his life. After his marriage, his father-in-law, Nathan Appleton, a wealthy Boston industrialist, bought the house for Longfellow and his wife, and permanent possession was assured.

There was little of the stoic, and less of the ascetic, in Longfellow's nature; he was as far as possible, too, from being a sybarite, but undeniably he was dependent on elegance and even a certain luxury in his surroundings, and life at the Craigie

House, with its comfortable furnishings, its well-stocked cellar, and its several servants, was almost as luxurious — though in a more New England style — as Dickens's at Devonshire Terrace or Thackeray's at Palace Green. To Emerson's sense this was a barrier to free intellectual intercourse. "If Socrates were here," he remarked in his journal, "we could go and talk with him; but Longfellow, we cannot go and talk with; there is a palace, and servants, and a row of bottles of different coloured wines, and wine glasses, and fine coats." Certainly the Craigie House was not a domicile in the severe fashion of Concord, and it may well have proved somewhat inhibiting to the full communication Emerson was always searching for. We can only observe that it was as right for Longfellow as the Coolidge House in Concord was for Emerson: his mind functioned freely in it, and what other test can we apply?

If the signs were auspicious for Longfellow's homemaking, they were equally auspicious for his friendships. With his warm and kindly nature, his unfailing amenity, his modesty and gentleness and good spirits, he made friends easily — though, with his underlying reserve, he made few intimates; those he made for life. One of them, a man he had come to know before he settled in Cambridge, was the stout and jovial young professor of Greek, Cornelius Conway Felton, a distinguished Hellenist, who many years later became, to his own sorrow, president of Harvard. Another was Charles Sumner, a handsome and talented young Bostonian, "a glorious youth," as Longfellow described him, who, when Longfellow was new in Cambridge, was lecturing at the Harvard Law School, and whose tumultuous political career lay far in the future. The friendship they formed was intense and lasting, and Sumner, during the early years especially, was in and out of the Craigie House almost as freely as a lodger. A third friendship, though never to the same degree an intimacy, was the friendship Longfellow formed — he could hardly be said to have renewed it — with his classmate at Bowdoin, Nathaniel Hawthorne, whom he had known only distantly in college.

Hawthorne, nevertheless, in his seclusion at Salem, seems to have read *Outre-Mer* with pleasure, and in 1837, probably with a certain effort, he sent Longfellow a copy of *Twice-Told Tales*, accompanying it with a graceful letter and a gesture of friendly feeling. Longfellow, though he had not been asked to do so, proceeded to review the volume in the *North American Review*, observing that a new star had risen in the heavens; and before long the two men were meeting occasionally, dining together in Boston or at the Craigie House, and coming to have great respect for each other as writers and affection as men. At first, no doubt, Hawthorne's extreme shyness and taciturnity puzzled Longfellow, who described him in a letter as "a strange owl," but as time went on, he came more and more to appreciate Hawthorne's quality, and he was very soon calling him, now in his journal, "a grand fellow." They talked at one point of collaborating on a book of fairy tales, and it is well known that Hawthorne passed on to Longfellow the theme of *Evangeline* — a poem which, with already the most sincere admiration for his friend's work, he reviewed with warm enthusiasm in a Salem newspaper. There were dark reaches in Hawthorne's spirit where Longfellow could never have followed him, and "the old, dull pain" that, as he said, "runs through all Hawthorne's writings" was not the trait he prized most in literature. But it did not keep him from feeling the special power of those writings, or from recognizing the "wizard hand" that, as he suggested in his beautiful threnody on Hawthorne, had committed them to paper.

These friendships were an essential element in the happiness which, in spite of everything, Longfellow enjoyed during these years. Still more essential was his marriage. He had fallen deeply in love with Frances Appleton during the summer in Switzerland; after he settled in Cambridge, and saw her from time to time in

Boston, this emotion developed into an absorbing passion. For several years his advances were coolly repelled, and when he published *Hyperion* in 1839, with its too-transparent treatment of their association at Interlaken, Fanny Appleton was embarrassed and at least mildly annoyed. Rejection was peculiarly painful to Longfellow, and his miseries during these years owed much of their acuteness to it. Finally, however, one does not know quite why, Fanny relented, and in the summer of 1843 they were married. No alliance could have been more fortunate. Longfellow's wife was a remarkable woman, as everything, including her letters and journals, indicates — strong-minded without being domineering, sharp and perceptive, sensitive to the arts, and along with these qualities, capable of warm and steady devotion. Longfellow's physical and emotional health was not uninterruptedly good even after his marriage, but at the center of his life was a great happiness, and for nearly twenty years, except for the death of one child, his personal and domestic existence was one of almost pure felicity.

During his first months in Cambridge, while he was adjusting himself to his new duties, Longfellow's literary productivity was in complete abeyance. Yet the beginning of a "second period" for him as a poet did not have long to wait. His new life soon began to liberate impulses that had been enchained for years, and in October, 1837, wishing to send a poem with a bouquet of autumn flowers to Fanny Appleton, Longfellow composed the piece that begins "Spake full well in language quaint and olden" — the piece now entitled "Flowers." He remembered later the great delight he had taken in writing it, "and the bright sunshine that streamed in at the southern windows as I walked to and fro, pausing ever and anon to note down my thoughts." The poem was published a little later in the *Knickerbocker*, but even with this start, though the ice was broken, Longfellow moved forward slowly, and during the whole of the following year he wrote only three or four poems. One of these, however, when it too was published in the *Knickerbocker,* was the poem that was to make his name, not unfamiliar already to readers, resound throughout the nation and beyond with reverberations that were not to die out for many decades. This was the famous, the all-too-famous, "Psalm of Life," which he composed one bright summer morning, we are told, on the blank spaces of a letter of invitation. It was published in October, and now at last Longfellow came to know what not only recognition but the most far-echoing popularity was. A few more poems followed — some of them also called, when they first appeared, "psalms" — and late in 1839 Longfellow felt ready, for the first time, to get out a volume of his own verse. This he entitled, with a hint of the German, *Voices of the Night;* it was made up, rather miscellaneously, of nine new poems, seven poems of his college period, and a group of poetic translations, including again the *Coplas.*

Meanwhile, though he had written rather little verse in these two years, he had gone back to prose fiction; he had by no means, at this stage or even later, settled down to the conception of himself as exclusively a poet. In the fall of 1838 he had begun a book he was to call, quite properly, not a novel but a romance, drawing very directly on his experiences in Germany and Switzerland. With his usual facility, and in spite of inevitable interruptions, Longfellow kept on happily with this work during the winter, and sometime in the spring he finished the book he had decided to call, with perhaps a conscious reminiscence of both Keats and Hölderlin, *Hyperion.* It was published early in the summer, some months before *Voices of the Night. Hyperion* enjoyed at first a mild success of scandal, and when that interest died down, it continued to exercise a gentle spell over many readers for other and better reasons. No doubt this was one of the motives that, ten years later, led Longfellow to go back to prose fiction, now for the last time. The desire to do something with New England life was still present to him, and in 1849 he published *Kavanagh: A Tale,* a kind of short novel with the setting of a Yankee village. It had no great success, even with Longfellow's closest friends, and he never went back to the form.

His literary energies, during that whole decade, had been directed less and less to prose — though even now he wrote a few reviews and literary articles — and more and more to poetry. It was only after *Voices of the Night*, strangely enough, that his genius for narrative poetry began to assert itself, but he had immersed himself too deeply in the ballad poetry of northern Europe not to be stirred by it creatively sooner or later, and in 1841, having evoked a lively response with two ballads on native themes, "The Skeleton in Armor" and "The Wreck of the Hesperus," he published his second volume, *Ballads and Other Poems*. A few years later he was ready to try his hand at narrative poetry on a more ambitious scale — the scale of something like the idyl or the little epic. It was Hawthorne who provided the immediate impetus. Dining with Longfellow one day, along with the Reverend Horace Conolly, a Salem clergyman, Hawthorne persuaded Conolly to repeat to Longfellow the story he had communicated to Hawthorne himself, a few years earlier, of the pathetic separation of two young lovers during the deportation of the Acadians from Nova Scotia. Conolly had wanted Hawthorne himself to write a tale on this theme, but Hawthorne had known at once that it was not in his vein: "there are no strong lights and heavy shadows," as he said, and without these, what could he have made of it? Longfellow, on the other hand, was immediately struck by the pathos and the poignancy of the story; Hawthorne was only too willing to make him a present of it, but it was not until a few years later that Longfellow began work on his Acadian idyl. This was of course *Evangeline: A Tale of Acadie,* and it appeared in the fall of 1847.

Hawthorne, as we have seen, reviewed *Evangeline* in the Salem *Advertiser;* in thanking him for the review, Longfellow thanked him also for resigning the subject to him: "This success I owe entirely to you," he went on, "for being willing to forego the pleasure of writing a prose tale which many people would have taken for poetry, that I might write a poem which many people take for prose."

He was drawn, in these middle years, not only to narrative poetry, but — like so many of his contemporaries, English and American, French and German — to the poetic drama; since his boyhood in Portland Longfellow had cherished a love of the theater, and now that he was lecturing on the European drama, the idea of a play in verse must have thrust itself upon him more than once. In the spring of 1840 he was lecturing to his students on the Spanish drama — on Lope de Rueda, Lope de Vega, Calderón — and reading plays like the greater Lope's *El Mejor Alcalde el Rey*, " a glorious play . . . full of movement and dramatic power, and with a tide of language like a mighty river." Impressionable as he was, Longfellow could hardly fail to be excited to emulation by all this reading, and one day in March he broke out in his journal: "A good idea! Yes, I will write a comedy, — 'The Spanish Student.' " That summer, paying a long visit to his family in Portland, he wrote, apparently with ease, the first draft of a play in verse, taking a hint from one of Cervantes's "exemplary tales"; and though, once *The Spanish Student* was finished, he began to be nervous and apprehensive about its reception, he brought himself to publish it in *Graham's Magazine,* and in 1843, since it had so far been spared any very harsh criticism, it appeared in book form.

A few weeks indeed before the idea of this comedy had come to him, a thought that was to lead even farther had occurred to Longfellow — or rather, for the moment, two thoughts. Late in 1839, considering what he should write next, he questioned himself in his journal on the possibility of a drama on Cotton Mather — "or," he went on, "a drama on the old poetic legend of *Der Arme Heinrich?* The tale is exquisite." Nothing, for some years, came of these ideas, either that of Cotton Mather or that of

"Poor Henry," but two years later a design that was ultimately to include them both formed itself in his mind: "a long and elaborate poem by the holy name of CHRIST; the theme of which would be the various aspects of Christendom in the Apostolic, Middle, and Modern Ages." Thirty years were to pass before this ambitious plan for a sacred trilogy came to full realization, but meanwhile, toward the end of Longfellow's years at Harvard, he succeeded in writing what might be called the middle panel. This was the mediaeval panel, of course, and it did in fact deal with the legend of "der arme Heinrich." After so many years of latency, *The Golden Legend,* as he called it, was at last composed at the turn of the decade and published in 1851.

Meanwhile, during the years since *Ballads and Other Poems,* Longfellow had by no means fallen silent as a writer of short poems, lyrical or narrative. That volume was followed, a year later, by his least characteristic, though not his least sincere, collection. Affected, perhaps, by the very politically minded Freiligrath, and moved by an old conviction of his own, Longfellow, as he lay for some nights sleepless in his berth on the *Great Western,* during a stormy passage homeward in 1842, composed a group of humanitarian poems on the slavery question, and later that year these eight pieces were published in a thin pamphlet as *Poems on Slavery.* Whatever may be the quality of these poems, it took a certain moral courage to publish them — though not a heroic one — at a time when anything approaching Abolitionism was taboo in respectable quarters, social and literary, and Longfellow made enemies by giving them to the world. The radical antislavery leaders, on the other hand, greeted the volume with elation. The vein, however, was not a really natural one to Longfellow, and he came back to much more characteristic themes and styles in the two other volumes he published during his years as a teacher — *The Belfry of Bruges and Other Poems* (1845) and *The Seaside and the Fireside* (1850).

As if, moreover, his literary energies were insufficiently expended, during the forties, on his teaching and writing, Longfellow somehow, and despite his afflictions, found time and strength for a third literary role, the role of anthologist. Two of the anthologies he edited, *The Waif* in 1844 and *The Estray* in 1846, were small unpretentious volumes — made up of some very good and some very bad "fugitive" poems — which could hardly have absorbed much of his leisure; but the third was a really ambitious and arduous undertaking. This was the immense volume entitled *The Poets and Poetry of Europe*. Longfellow appears to have begun work on it in the fall of 1843, after his marriage, and though, during the following months, the condition of his eyes was at its worst, he had the assistance of his wife and of Felton, and the book was published in 1845. Nothing like *The Poets and Poetry of Europe* had ever appeared before, here or in England, and one doubts whether anything like it had ever appeared on the Continent. Made up of translations, some of them Longfellow's own, from the work of nearly four hundred poets, representing the literatures of ten modern languages, this extraordinary anthology is the most tangible monument to Longfellow's achievement as a scholar. It ranges in time from the earliest Middle Ages — from the era of the Eddas and *Beowulf* and *The Cid* — to the nineteenth century and the era of Ugo Foscolo, Lamartine, and Heine, and from the earliest poetry in Italian to the Swedish poetry of Longfellow's own time. With the advantage of hindsight, we can now find many faults in the book — faults of inclusion, of omission, of translation — but we are not likely to exaggerate the genuinely Arnoldian role it played, for some decades, in helping to propagate among American readers "the best that is known and thought in the world."

Silent and apparently sterile as the poet in Longfellow had mostly been during his twenties, there seems never to have been a time when he was wholly forgotten or ignored. When *Voices of the Night* appeared, one reviewer remarked that Longfellow's earliest poems were "already well known to the readers of poetry"; and another declared that some of them had become "thoroughly domiciliated in the national heart." If this was true, Longfellow owed his youthful currency to the fact that so many of his juvenile poems had been reprinted in newspapers and that some of them had very early appeared in anthologies. Perhaps the most widely circulated of these latter was *The American Common-place Book of Poetry* (1831), edited by one George B. Cheever, the Untermeyer of his time. Cheever had included seven of the young poet's pieces, observing in a footnote to one of them that Longfellow's poetry "displays a very refined taste, and a very pure vein of poetic feeling." This was perhaps the first published commentary of a critical sort on Longfellow under his full name, and stale as his language now seems, Cheever was not without a certain perceptiveness at the time.

In any case, this precocious fame was relatively a modest one, and it was not until after "A Psalm of Life" and *Voices of the Night* that Longfellow's immense popularity, and along with it his high standing with many of his fellow writers, may be said to have been launched on its long course. But during the few years that followed, the growth of his reputation as a poet was rapid and phenomenal. The new poems in *Voices of the Night*, said a reviewer in the *North American*, "are among the most remarkable poetical compositions which have ever appeared in the United States." "Nothing equal to some of them," Hawthorne wrote to Longfellow, "was ever written in this world, — this western world, I mean; and it would not hurt my conscience much to include the other hemisphere." Poe, appealing to Longfellow for contributions to *Graham's*, took the opportunity to assure him of "the fervent admiration with which his genius has inspired me." A reviewer of *Ballads and Other Poems* began by remarking that "Mr. Longfellow's poetry has become so generally known, and wherever known, is so universally admired, as to need no aid from the journals of literature."

It is not that there were no discordant voices, no voices of dissent from this chorus; indeed, there was never a time, during his long career as a writer, when Longfellow *was,* as a matter of fact, "universally" admired. Minority judgments were always being expressed; often judiciously, often not. It is well known that Poe, reviewing *Ballads and Other Poems* a year after the letter just quoted, rather inconsistently declared that Longfellow's "conception of the *aim* of poetry *is all wrong*"; and that he still later, in his obsessive way, excoriated Longfellow at length, and more than once, for the literary crime of plagiarism.* It is almost as well known that, voicing what was a pretty general feeling among the Transcendentalists, Margaret Fuller disposed of Longfellow as "a man of cultivated taste, delicate though not deep feeling, and some though not much poetic force." A reviewer of *Evangeline* in the *American Review*, George Washington Peck, could object to the meter of the poem as "equally cold, affected and unnatural," to the style as "not really fine, but tawdry," and to Evangeline herself as "so insipid a creature."

Opinions such as these, however, were always, in the literal sense, minority opinions; and the general consensus both of readers and of critics was almost certainly very close to the judgment that Hawthorne expressed in reviewing *Evangeline* — that Longfellow should be recognized as standing "at the head of our list of native poets." Six editions of *Voices of the Night* were published within the first two years; *Evangeline* went into its sixth edition within three months of its publication; and figures like

---

* The examples of plagiarism Poe cites turn out, for the most part, to be either coincidences or the normal and often distant echoes of one poet by another. As a man, Longfellow was more generous in spirit — and, it should be said, less tormented — than Poe; after Poe's death, he expressed the most genuine admiration for his work, and added: "The harshness of his criticisms I have never attributed to anything but the irritation of a sensitive nature chafed by some indefinite sense of wrong." Howells says, on what authority one does not know, that, while Poe was belaboring Longfellow as a plagiarist, Longfellow was helping to keep him alive "by the loans which always made themselves gifts in Poe's case."

these, or even more dazzling, would be the monotonous tale of all his later volumes. If Hawthorne, moreover, might be thought to be too biased an admirer, a British reviewer of *The Golden Legend* in *Blackwood's*, five years later, could also be cited: "in perfect candour, we must own that, in our opinion, Longfellow at this moment, stands, beyond comparison, at the head of the poets of America." The "eminence in literature" which the Bowdoin undergraduate had aspired to, had come to him in good season and in full measure.

IV

Voices of the Night—and Day

A READER who was familiar with Longfellow's boyish poems, and who opened *Voices of the Night* when it first appeared, would surely have been struck very soon by the tones of a new manner:

> I heard the trailing garments of the Night
> Sweep through her marble halls!
> I saw her sable skirts all fringed with light
> From the celestial walls!

One need not share Poe's exaggerated opinion of these lines—"No poem ever opened with a beauty more august"—to be aware at once of a firmness of tone, a boldness in attack, a freshness of image, that one would have found nowhere in Longfellow's juvenilia. And as this imagined reader read on in the poem, with its rather fine prosopopoeia of Night as a majestic, even mythic, female figure, its delicate rhythmic effects, and its language of alleviation; as he came to the last stanza—

> Peace! Peace! Orestes-like I breathe this prayer!
> Descend with broad-winged flight,
> The welcome, the thrice-prayed for, the most fair,
> The best-beloved Night!—

with its beautiful literary reminiscence, he would surely have felt that he was hearing the voice of a far more mature and a far more distinguishable literary artist. Not that the poem is perfect:

there is a difficulty, to the visual imagination, in reconciling the "marble halls" in which Night dwells, with the "celestial walls" by the light from which her skirts are fringed. But the flaws are observable only on a second look, and one's first sense is of the sustained and hymnic character of the whole.

The poem indeed is called "Hymn to the Night" — Longfellow cannot not have known Novalis's "Hymns to the Night" — and the little volume is pervaded, as its title promises, by this nocturnal symbolism. There had been an anticipation of this in one or two of the undergraduate poems:

> Here rest the weary oar! — soft airs
> Breathe out in the o'erarching sky;
> And Night — sweet Night — serenely wears
> A smile of peace: her noon is nigh.*

But only now is the presence of Night so pervasive as to become a kind of signature:

> The night is come, but not too soon. . . .

> When the hours of Day are numbered,
> And the voices of the Night
> Wake the better soul, that slumbered,
> To a holy, calm delight. . . .

> . . . That a midnight host of spectres pale
> Beleaguered the walls of Prague.

The author of these poems was always to be, in one of his roles, a poet of the Night, or the Twilight; Night was to have for him an emotional significance that the day never quite had. It is not that it ever had for him the profoundly religious meaning it had for Novalis, or the philosophical meaning it had for Hölderlin, or the bitter overtones it had for Poe. Only rarely is it the setting, as it is in "The Beleaguered City," for the spectral and the menacing. Almost always it brings thoughts, as it does in

* "The Venetian Gondolier" (1825).

"Hymn to the Night," of repose, assuagement, release from care. At moments one discerns a longing for unconsciousness, even oblivion, in this poet, that runs strangely counter to other reaches of his feeling.

So strong a wish as this, indeed, is seldom expressed, but one finds it explicit in such a poem as "Curfew," the last poem — a kind of envoi — in *The Belfry of Bruges*. The short, heavy two- and three-stressed lines of "Curfew" have a weary and tolling music like that of the curfew bell itself:

> Dark grow the windows,
>   And quenched is the fire;
> Sound fades into silence, —
>   All footsteps retire.

A book is closed, its contents are forgotten, the hearthstone grows chill, and then,

> Darker and darker
>   The black shadows fall;
> Sleep and oblivion
>   Reign over all.

It is not always, as it is here, the utter *unconsciousness* of sleep that is invoked, but it is almost always a release from "the cares that infest the day." This is the theme of another poem in the same volume, "The Day Is Done"; a poem that, in its tone, its cadences, its imagery, has almost the air of a translation from the German:

> The day is done, and the darkness
>   Falls from the wings of Night. . . .

The poet, in his "sadness and longing" — his *Traurigkeit* and his *Sehnsucht*, so to say — confesses that he wishes a simple lay to be read to him,

> That shall soothe this restless feeling,
>   And banish the thoughts of day.

The poems of the great masters resemble too much "the strains of martial music"; they suggest

> Life's endless toil and endeavor,

and the poet confesses that "to-night I long for rest."

This piece was originally a proem to Longfellow's anthology *The Waif,* the selections in which are mostly of the simple and undisturbing sort he calls for in "The Day Is Done"; but the poem has a modest authenticity of its own. And even when the nocturnal is absent, in these volumes, the strain of the elegiac is likely to be audible. It is so in one of the most successful pieces in *Ballads and Other Poems,* a piece that Hawthorne understandably liked, "The Goblet of Life." The central metaphor here is that of the fennel which wreathes and crowns the cup of existence; bitter as its taste is, when its leaves are pressed into the waters of the cup, it imparts to them a power that, in our darkness and distress, gives "new light and strength." Much of Longfellow's misery during these years must have dictated this curiously astringent poem; the endurance, not the joy, of life is what it enforces:

> I pledge you in this cup of grief,
> Where floats the fennel's bitter leaf!
> The Battle of our Life is brief,
> The alarm, — the struggle, — the relief,
> Then sleep we side by side.

He rarely comes so close to harshness, to an almost Hardyesque harshness, as he does in this poem, but the minor key in which many of these poems are written suggests the plaintive nocturne of some lesser romantic composer. Nothing could be more characteristic of him, on this side, than the melancholy imagery, in another poem, "Afternoon in February," of closing day, a frozen marsh, a dead river, clouds like ashes, snowfall recommencing, and a funeral train passing slowly through the meadows as one hears the dismal pealing of a funeral bell.

There is no wildness of terror or fierceness of anger in this melancholy of Longfellow's, as there is in Poe's or Melville's, and no such dull and continuous pain as he himself saw in Hawthorne's; at its most acute, it never goes beyond a bearable despondency. It could be described as romantic nostalgia of the less passionate and rebellious sort, but it is as far as possible from being a mere literary convention; it was as inherent in Longfellow's temperament as a similar vein of feeling was in Heine's — without, as a rule, the recoil of irony. His sensibilities were tenderer, more vulnerable, more exposed to injury than most men's, even than some poets'; and the inevitable strains of existence — bereavement, frustration, loneliness, or just "causeless" dejection — told on him, especially in these years, with a sharpness that was bound to reflect itself, now and then, in his work.

There was never a time, however, when Longfellow was willing, as some greater and even some lesser writers have been, to yield himself wholly to the evidence of his sensibilities and make a coherent world-view out of his sufferings. His aversion to the tragic was as temperamental as his sensitiveness to pain, and as all mankind knows, or once knew, he insisted from the outset on correcting — one might say, on contradicting — the evidence of his sensibilities by opposing to it a doctrine of earnest struggle, of courageous resolution, of cheerful and productive action. He was encouraged in this by what he had made, morally, of his reading in Goethe —

> Wer immer strebend sich bemüht,
> Den können wir erlösen — *

but if he simplified and diluted what he found in Goethe, as he certainly did, he by no means debased or falsified it. His resolute hopefulness is quite as genuine as his melancholy, only it is the product not of spontaneous emotion but of conscious effort

---

* Whoe'er aspires unweariedly
Is not beyond redeeming.

and self-discipline. Perhaps it is expressed most acceptably in "The Light of Stars," one of the two or three better poems in *Voices of the Night*. In this poem he confesses that in his breast, as in the night, there is no light but a cold and starry one, and especially the light of "the red planet Mars," to which he declares he is giving the first watch of the night. Mars, cold as he may be, is the planet of heroic action, and the poet is determined to accept that stern influence:

> The star of the unconquered will,
> He rises in my breast,
> Serene, and resolute, and still,
> And calm, and self-possessed.

"The Light of Stars" was never one of Longfellow's extravagantly popular pieces, perhaps because there is too nice a balance in it between the confession of suffering and the voice of the resisting will. There was no such balance, and no such expressive metaphor, in "A Psalm of Life" or "The Village Blacksmith" or "Excelsior"; and the slack commonplace of these inferior poems insured their universal currency for many decades.*

They had the appeal of poems that enforce "lessons" — it is Longfellow's own word — and they have repelled more exacting readers, from Poe onward, by their explicit and elementary moralizing. To Poe this meant, as we have seen, that Longfellow's conception of the aims of poetry was *"all wrong"*; that he was utterly mistaken in supposing that the Didactic, as Poe

---

* It is amusing to recall, however, that Baudelaire borrowed some of the language and imagery of "A Psalm of Life" for his sonnet "Le Guignon":

> Loin des sépultures célèbres,
> Vers un cimetière isolé,
> Mon coeur, comme un tambour voilé,
> Va battant des marches funèbres.

But Baudelaire manages somehow to intensify and deepen what he found in Longfellow, and of course with both poems it is the whole context that decides.

said, was a legitimate province for the poet. Poe himself, of course, is all wrong here; there is no reason whatever why the didactic should be ruled out of serious poetry; it has an ancient and august derivation, and freely enough understood, it is a powerful element in much of our contemporary verse. The real objections to Longfellow's didacticism are of another sort. One of them, as Poe was the first but not the last to point out, is that the lesson is usually appended to the poem instead of being implied by it — appended with what Howells calls Longfellow's "quaint doubt of the reader." Even more importantly, Longfellow's moralizing poems fail, either wholly or relatively, because he was not a moralist. His gifts were quite different from that. Nothing, to repeat, could be more sincere than his moral convictions, but they are at second hand; they were not the fruit, as Emerson's (for example) were, of solitary and independent cogitation. He lived by them, as many men have lived by truths they have learned from others; but honorable as they were, they have no intrinsic intellectual interest, and they usually do nothing for his poetry but enfeeble it. All this is only too evident.

Longfellow was obeying a truer instinct when he turned to the equally popular, but for him less treacherous, form of the ballad or short balladlike poem. He had a strain of the genuine folk poet in his make-up — in his unaffected naïveté, his simplicity of mind and heart, his love of rapid and usually pathetic storytelling, and his power of improvisation — for some of these poems were written with as little effort as a folksinger puts into a new ballad on an old and familiar kind of subject. Hackneyed as it is, "The Wreck of the Hesperus" could hardly be surpassed as a literary imitation of the border ballad — for if the subject is native, the style is a perfect pastiche of the English or Scottish popular ballad, of "Sir Patrick Spens" or "The Wife of Usher's Well." It is a poem for the young, of course, without any more under-feeling than the subject itself carries with it, but on its youthful level, it has in it the authentic terror of the sea. So, too, has the equally familiar "The Skeleton in Armor," which is a little triumph of seaworthy narrative verse; the stanza, borrowed from Drayton, plunges ahead with the speed of a vessel in a favoring wind, and the wintry imagery of Northern lands and seas is full of romantic charm — the gleam of the Northern lights, the half-frozen sound, the stars shining on the dark Norway pines, the horsemen drawing up on the white sea-strand, the vessel beating to sea in a wild hurricane. The sea as both a mysterious attraction and a bitter peril is as much Longfellow's as it is Melville's, superior as Melville of course is in power; and a good poem like "Sir Humphrey Gilbert" has the presence in it of the sinister icebergs one recalls from Melville's grimmer poem "The Berg." The "secret" in another vigorous ballad, "The Secret of the Sea," which was suggested by a Spanish folk poem, is that "Only those who brave its dangers / Comprehend its mystery." *

Few poets — as so many readers, including Kipling, have felt — have had a stronger sense of the sea than Longfellow; and the best poems in *The Seaside and the Fireside*, for the most part, are the poems in the section, "By the Seaside," to which both "Sir Humphrey Gilbert" and "The Secret of the Sea" belong. The longest of these is "The Building of the Ship." One regrets that this poem, like some others of Longfellow's, was staled and shopworn almost from the beginning by constant use in school readers and in youthful recitation, for, flawed as it is by some of Longfellow's habitual faults — the too facile family sentiment of one or two passages, for example — it has, to a robust taste that

---

* There is something curiously premonitory of Housman's "The Land of Biscay" in the rhythms of this poem:

> Sails of silk and ropes of sandal,
>   Such as gleam in ancient lore;
> And the singing of the sailors,
>   And the answer from the shore!

can overlook these flaws, a vivacity, a swiftness of movement, and a painterly concreteness of detail, as in an old-fashioned genre-painting or print, that save it from simple banality. The building and the launching of a sailing vessel — what artisan's activity could have had less of the lifelessness of a merely literary symbol for Longfellow, with his memories of a boyhood in Portland surrounded by shipyards and stocks?

To be sure, "The Building of the Ship," as has often been pointed out, owes its particular form to the example of Schiller; "The Song of the Bell" was its literary model. A workmanly process is the unifying symbol in both poems, bell-casting or shipbuilding; and a master workman is the dominant figure in both. Longfellow's political moral, too, the celebration of national Union, is not unlike Schiller's, the celebration of civil orderliness. But if his poem is less a bravura piece than the German poem, if it is metrically less dazzling, it is free from that strain of rather bourgeois smugness, of crass domestic comfort-worship and political stuffiness, that weighs so heavily over "The Song of the Bell." Longfellow's earnest Unionism seems relatively tonic and open-aired, and even his sentimental domesticity — the love of the young workman for the Master's daughter and their wedding, which coincides with the launching of the vessel — has a kind of innocence that keeps it inoffensive. "The Building of the Ship," moreover, has a perfectly real metrical animation of its own, with its hurrying lines of irregular length, its tossing rhythms, and its freely falling rhymes.*

The charm of the poem derives largely from the vividness of the tangible objects and activities in it. It is what Whitman would

---

* Curiously, the coda of "The Building of the Ship" as originally written was a passage of melancholy reflection on the eventual shipwreck of the vessel and the oblivion that overtakes all master shipwrights, however cunning and however dedicated. It was out of harmony with the high spirits of the rest of the poem, as Longfellow seems to have felt, and the present famous conclusion ("Thou, too, sail on, O Ship of State!"), rhetorical as it is, brings the poem to a more powerful end.

call a Song for Occupations — for one Occupation, of course — and it abounds in the materials of construction; the graceful model the Master builds, the timbers he assembles from a dozen regions (chestnut, elm, oak, and "the knarred and crooked cedar knees"), the keel of the ship stretched along the blocks, and its strong skeleton as it gradually emerges ("stemson and keelson and sternson-knee"). Almost as in Whitman, one hears the sound of axes and mallets plied "with vigorous arms," and sees and smells the columns of smoke that wreathe upward from the boiling and bubbling caldron, overflowing with black tar, "heated for the sheathing." A little later one sees the rudder ready to be set in place ("with oaken brace and copper band"), the cunningly carved figurehead, the tall and tapering masts, and the slender spars. In his less intense way, Longfellow had something of Whitman's love for his "faithful solids and fluids."

He had also, what is not characteristic in this sense of Whitman, the feeling of the ghostly; "phantom" is one of his favorite words, and the ghostly is often associated for him with the idea of the sea. The lines about the future service of the figurehead have his stamp all over them:

> On many a dreary and misty night,
> 'Twill be seen by the rays of the signal light,
> Speeding along through the rain and the dark,
> Like a ghost in its snow-white sark,
> The pilot of some phantom bark,
> Guiding the vessel, in its flight,
> By a path none other knows aright!

The tone of the poem as a whole is hearty and confident; it is a daylight poem; but a passage like this, conveying the sense of night and mystery, saves it from an inartistic monotony of effect. The actual building of the ship may be an emblem for Longfellow of cheerful productive effort generally, as, in an afterthought, he made it an emblem of the building of the American Union in particular; but that vigorous motive is at least momentarily counterpointed by the image of the spectral vessel in its flight. To one or two generations the poem may have been tediously familiar, but it deserves not to be wholly forgotten.

So, too, do two or three short poems in "By the Seaside," besides those already mentioned; the group as a whole indicates how much Longfellow's art, on its own level, had matured and refined itself in the ten years since *Voices of the Night*. The least forgotten of these poems, "Seaweed," to be sure, is another flawed success. There is real enough energy in the way in which the oceanic tempest is conjured up in the opening stanzas — the Atlantic storm wind driving the surges, laden with seaweed, upon the land, and then subsiding again until the drifting currents have found repose — but, as so often, the symbolism of the storm wind as a type of the poet's wild emotion is far too heavily enforced in the succeeding stanzas; and, as someone has remarked, the seaweed itself is not a very fortunate symbol of the poet's songs. No such objection can be brought against "Chrysaor," which has the kind of purity and perfection that a tiny masterwork can achieve. Saintsbury thought it the most Browningesque poem of Longfellow's, though, if so, it is not the muscular but the serene Browning of whom one might be reminded. The poem enforces no reflection whatever, but simply, with a curious calm magic, summons up the image of a refulgent star rising at twilight out of the sea like the hero Chrysaor rising from the arms of his beloved Callirrhoë — "forever tender, soft, and tremulous." If the poem suggests Browning, it suggests even more strongly, with its lovely unhackneyed myth, some lapidary poem in the Greek Anthology.

The star in this poem rises over a perfectly tranquil sea. The treacherous and tempestuous sea, on the other hand, lurks in the background of "The Fire of Drift-Wood": the driftwood that is burning on the hearth has come from "the wreck of stranded ships," and it is made to express, but quietly and without strain, the wreckage of the friendship that has formerly united the host and his callers. No note is forced; the scene in the parlor of the old farmhouse near the port is evoked without apparent effort — the sea breeze blowing damp and cold through the windows, the glimpses of the lighthouse and the dismantled fort beyond, the darkness of twilight gradually settling in the room until the faces fade from sight and the gloom is broken only by the voices of host and guests. They speak of an unrecallable past, of what has been but also of what might have been, and of

> The first slight swerving of the heart,
>   That words are powerless to express,
> And leave it still unsaid in part,
>   Or say it in too great excess.

Few poems of Longfellow's have more the character of a small drama, and one composed of materials so apparently slight and evanescent that they might seem to defy expression. The last stanza, as Howard Nemerov has said, "exactly resolves the elements of the poem, and does so without any gorgeous or spectacular fussing":

> O flames that glowed! O hearts that yearned!
>   They were indeed too much akin,
> The drift-wood fire without that burned,
>   The thoughts that burned and glowed within.

Much of Longfellow's shorter verse rises out of purely personal sources — out of private springs of feeling and mood — and much of it, too, rises out of his love of story and legend. This does not mean that he was wholly incapable of what has been called Public Speech, that he was untouched by public issues or unmoved by public wrongs. He was far from being a Shelley, a Heine, a Victor Hugo; but he was a representative American liberal of his generation, hopeful, humane, generous, and idealistic; and there were impersonal "political" questions that for him were productive of vivid personal emotion. "The Building of the Ship" turned into a political poem under the threat of Disunion, and if we can recapture in imagination the ardent nationalism it expresses we shall not be surprised to learn how deeply Lincoln was affected by it when it was recited to him early in the war.

As strong as his patriotism, however, and sometimes in uneasy relation to it, was Longfellow's all but Quakerish pacifism. There was a kind of "ambivalence" here, it is true, in his emotions. For all his personal mildness, Longfellow, as a man of imagination, was quite capable of being stirred and even, in a sense, pleased by the spectacle of violence; there was a strain in him of General Wadsworth or of his uncles in the Navy, and the warlike was not quite simply repellent to him. At the other pole, however, his hatred of violence, his love of the peaceful and the gentle, was even stronger and more characteristic; and he had persuaded himself wishfully, though with a benevolence one must respect, that the barbarous days of war and bloodshed were over, or that at least they were rapidly approaching their historic end.

The early forties, so long after Waterloo and our own War of 1812, were no doubt propitious to such convictions, and Longfellow made them the theme of three poems, two of which appeared in *The Belfry of Bruges* and the third in *The Seaside.**
The most familiar of the three, "The Arsenal at Springfield," is only half successful if only because the anti-war theme is developed so fully in direct rhetorical terms. Yet the poem takes off from a fine image — the burnished gun-barrels at the Arsenal rising to the ceiling like the pipes of a huge and ominous organ — and even if it is true that the comparison began by being Fanny Longfellow's, not her husband's, Longfellow knew what to make of it; the poem has a real force, partly because the

---

* There was a vigorous peace movement in New England at this time, and on the Fourth of July, 1845, the year in which Longfellow wrote "The Occultation of Orion," his friend Sumner made a passionate and highly controversial anti-war address in Boston, "The True Grandeur of Nations."

feminine a-rhymes are so curiously expressive here; partly too
because, in his associative way, Longfellow conjures up his hor-
rid imagery of warfare with an imaginative conviction that
makes war and peace seem to be in genuine tension with each
other:

> On helm and harness rings the Saxon hammer,
>   Through Cimbric forest roars the Norseman's song,
> And loud, amid the universal clamor,
>   O'er distant deserts sounds the Tartar gong.

There is a similar tension, but in its elements a finer one, in
"The Occultation of Orion," another pacifist piece. Myth and
astronomy together are endowed with a kind of grandeur here
that one misses in the other poem; the constellation Orion is
made the symbol of barbaric violence, but it is a splendid violence:

> Begirt with many a blazing star,
> Stood the great giant Algebar,
> Orion, hunter of the beast!
> His sword hung gleaming at his side,
> And, on his arm, the lion's hide
> Scattered across the midnight air
> The golden radiance of its hair.

To counter this warlike metaphor Longfellow finds two metaphors of peace and harmony, the seven-stringed lyre of Pythag-
oras that, towering from earth to the fixed stars, symbolizes
the harmonious music of the spheres; and the serene moon that,
as it moves silently across the sky, occults or blots out — in a
manner that Longfellow knew to be bad astronomy — the constellation of the great hunter:

> And suddenly from his outstretched arm
> Down fell the red skin of the lion
> Into the river at his feet.

Peace and harmony have triumphed over violence, and the strings of the heavenly lyre, echoing a burst of angelic music, proclaim that

> "Forevermore, forevermore,
> The reign of violence is o'er!"

Again the theme is made explicit, but it is made so in a more dramatic and less oratorical manner than in the other poems, and it is not a fatal blemish. How fine, moreover, is the sense of radiance and harmony that, with his language and his imagery, Longfellow creates in this poem!

The third of these pacifist pieces, "Tegnér's Drapa," is also a threnody on the Swedish poet Esaias Tegnér, the mad bishop of Växjö, whom Longfellow so much admired, and whose pious poem, "The Children of the Lord's Supper," he had translated — as well as certain passages from his more masculine *Frithiof's Saga*.* "Tegnér's Drapa" was the first of Longfellow's experiments in a kind of free verse; this was undoubtedly suggested to him by the example of some of the German poets, but its un-rhymed lines, irregular in length, he seems also to have thought, mistakenly, were characteristic of skaldic poetry, which is said, on the contrary, to be rigidly regular. Nevertheless the verse has a vaguely archaic character, and the mythic echoes of the Prose Edda — for Longfellow identifies Tegnér with the slain god Baldr — give it a certain flavor of the heathen melancholy of Ice-landic poetry. But the flavor is faint at best, and after several rather fine verse-paragraphs, the poem trails off in a too-obvious and simplistic inculcation of the pacifist moral.

There is nothing comparable to "The Occultation," or even to "The Arsenal," in Longfellow's other contribution to the political muse, the little group of antislavery poems. They are too largely

---

* In Icelandic poetics, a "drapa" is a praise-poem or eulogy, though Long-fellow seems to have thought, if we can judge from a note in *The Poets and Poetry of Europe*, that the word signified a "death-song."

the product of his conscious and conscientious good will, too little the product of his imagination, to carry full conviction; "his very anger is gentle," as Whitman said, and in some of these poems — "The Quadroon Girl," for example — he falls into a deplorable vein of theatrical sentiment that betrays the unreality of his inspiration. His touch is surer when he can rely on association and picture, as he does in "The Slave's Dream," though even this piece does not rise much above the level of good verse for school-readers and recitation. Yet Longfellow's hatred of chattel slavery was as strong as any such bitter emotion could be to a man of his disposition, and two of these poems communicate it with a certain eloquence. "The Warning," part of which is lifted from his old Phi Beta Kappa poem, makes rather convincing use of the figure of Samson, shorn and bound and blinded, but a menace to the temple of the commonweal; and in "The Witnesses" the vision of the sunken slave-ships on the ocean floor, with their freight of fettered skeletons, has an even greater rhetorical force. But Longfellow had little of the Old Testament wrath in his nature that makes some things of Milton's, and even of Whittier's, vibrate with so contagious a rhetoric; and he did well never to come back to the too-explosive subject of slavery.

It goes without saying, now, that there is much that is facile and flaccid in these five volumes; like most minor poets who have been prolific as well as minor, Longfellow had no clear sense of the distinction between his weaknesses and his real strength. He seems to have taken as much pleasure in some of his inferior poems as in the better ones; he thought "Maidenhood" and "Excelsior" "perhaps as good as anything I have written"; and certainly he published only what he himself thought was worthy of him. His nature was so genuinely sensitive and *gefühlvoll* that, with the best conscience in the world, he could fall a victim to the bad sentimental taste of his age — there is of course a good sentimental taste — and there were subjects that normally betrayed him into the sort of false and misplaced feeling that one finds in Lydia Hunt Sigourney. One of these subjects was childhood ("To a Child"); he is almost always at his feeblest on this theme.* Another treacherous subject for him was that of innocence or simple unstained purity ("Maidenhood"); one need not make light of this virtue in order to find Longfellow's celebration of it painfully wanting in moral complexity or edge. Death, too, sometimes inspired in him a soft and second-rate moral response, not a tragic one ("Footsteps of Angels"); and the fact that he shared this weakness with greater writers of the age — Dickens, Tennyson, and others — does not conduce to greater patience with him.

Both morally and artistically speaking, when such subjects are in question, there is something suspect in emotions that well up so easily as these do, and that express themselves with so little stress or struggle. In general, it was a double-natured gift that the gods bestowed on Longfellow when, as it were in his cradle, they endowed him with the talents of an improvisator. On the one hand, this gift was what enabled him, at his best, to write with a fluency, a speed, and a translucency that are appropriate to his subjects and fully expressive of them. On the other hand, when he is at his second-best or his worst, the gift was clearly a fatal one: "the weakness of his genius," as Paul Elmer More once said, was "an absence of resistance"; and when thoughts or feelings sprang up in him that needed to be resisted, he gave them as free a rein as the thoughts or feelings that could safely be trusted. The almost effortless rapidity with which some of his successful poems were composed did them no injury, but a

---

* One sympathizes with Miss Sturdy, in James's story "The Point of View," who, while speaking of the American cult of children, remarks with some acerbity to her correspondent: "The future is theirs; maturity will evidently be at an increasing discount. Longfellow wrote a charming little poem, called 'The Children's Hour,' but he ought to have called it 'The Children's Century.'"

similar rapidity helps to account for the failure of some others. If "The Wreck of the Hesperus" came into his mind not by lines but by stanzas, this, given the subject, was as it should have been; and many years later "The Saga of King Olaf" lost nothing of its quality through being composed, most of it, in little more than a fortnight. If, on the other hand, the dramatic poem *Judas Maccabæus,* on so difficult a subject, got itself written in twelve days, that fact helps to account for its disappointingness.

For these reasons and others, one could wish away perhaps half the short poems of Longfellow's Harvard years. The rest, unequal as they may be in value, are worth preserving in some ideal anthology of verse of the second order. His art, with some ups and downs, was to go on refining and enhancing itself perceptibly to the very end, but already the poems down to *The Seaside and the Fireside* furnish pretty much the measure of his capacities as a lyrical and narrative poet. There are states of feeling that remain this side of either ecstasy or despair — sadness, weariness, a half-pleasurable fear, elation, the simple apprehension of beauty — that Longfellow could express with a veracity that has nothing in it of falseness or the meretricious. Moods of the weather, seasons of the year, divisions of the day or night — to these external states he was delicately sensitive, and they often become the expressive equivalents of his emotions. The physical *element* of his imagination, as Gaston Bachelard would say, was water, not earth or air or destructive fire, and the sea was for him a symbol that, in its allurement and its menace, had the primordial power of a symbol in a dream. He had something like a genius for narrative poetry — not, to be sure, of the psychologically or philosophically interesting sort, but in the popular and romantic sense — and he could almost always draw, to happy effect, on legend or literary tradition. His sense of form was fallible, but at his best he is an accomplished, sometimes an exquisite, craftsman, like a master in some minor art, a potter or a silversmith; and his command of his materials, at such times — language, meter, rhyme, imagery — though it is not that of a great artist, is wholly adequate to his purposes. It is still to be seen what he could make of larger and more ambitious forms, especially, for the moment, that of poetic drama.

V

Dramatic Poems (I)

THE SPANISH STUDENT is much too fragile and weightless a piece of work to deserve the injustice of labored treatment. It suggests the music of guitars heard, or overheard, on a mild and starlit night, rather than the orchestrated music of comic opera — though it might be remembered that Longfellow's favorite opera was *Don Giovanni*. We can hardly, however, argue that Mozart should have composed the music for *The Spanish Student* as Goethe thought he should have done for *Faust;* Offenbach would have been quite equal to the task. The play has some of the quality of romantic light opera, and if one approaches it in that spirit, one is likely to find that it has a tenuous charm of its own.

In one sense it is a purely "literary" production. Its mere materials — its plot, its devices, its personages — are all bookish, traditional, even worn; they have no relation, naturally, to American life during Tyler's presidency or to modern life generally, and this is part of what accounts for the minor character of the play. Granted this, Longfellow cannot, needless to say, be reproached for drawing his materials from other writers; it is what dramatic poets have done since the dawn of time, and it was mere ignorance on Poe's part that led him to rail at Longfellow for deriving his subject from Cervantes and Middleton. A sixteenth-century subject was what he wanted, and he found it in Cervantes's "exemplary" tale "La Gitanilla" — "The Little

Gypsy Girl" — which Middleton had taken over for the main plot of *The Spanish Gipsy*. It is a variation on the folklore theme of the King and the Beggar Maid: in Cervantes's tale, a young nobleman of Madrid falls passionately in love with a gypsy girl, Preciosa, who dances divinely; he joins her band of gypsies in order to be near her; she turns out to be the daughter, stolen as a baby, of the corregidor of Murcia, a rich man, and Don Juan and Preciosa are at last joined in wedlock with the blessings of the bride's parents.

This is the archetypal plot that Longfellow borrowed, with certain variations — for, with perhaps a reminiscence of the young rogue in *Outre-Mer*, he makes his gentleman-lover a student at Alcalá, and Preciosa's true father is no corregidor but a gentleman who is returning to Spain, doubtless from America, "laden with wealth." Where Cervantes, moreover, is vigorously prosaic and, despite his plot, novelistic, Longfellow is delicate, dreamy, and tender in a wholly nineteenth-century manner: he has more in common with Alfred de Musset than with Cervantes. And indeed the real "source" of *The Spanish Student* is not "La Gitanilla" but, much more personally, Longfellow's own youthful romance with Spain. "The play is thoroughly Spanish in flavor," says Iris Lilian Whitman, and certainly what Longfellow was doing in it, essentially, was erecting a little memorial to those enchanted months he had spent in Spain so many years before. There is nothing in it, to be sure, of the tormented Spain of Ferdinand VII's time; there is everything in it of the Spain that had revealed itself to the romantic vision of the young American traveler.

The reader of the play finds himself at first in a Madrid of poetry — in gentlemen's chambers, in the Archbishop's palace, in the Prado, in the nocturnal streets — for most of the action goes forward at night. And if one leaves Madrid behind, it is to move on to a public square in the village of Guadarrama, or a posthouse on the road to Segovia, or, as if this were *Il Trovatore*, a gypsy camp in the forest at night, where some of the gypsies are working and singing at a forge while, by its flaring light, others are playing at cards, as in a baroque genre-painting. The very last scene is a pass in the Guadarrama mountains from which the city of Seville — "the merest flaw that dents the horizon's edge" — can just barely be made out in the distance. The characters who fill these pleasantly operatic scenes are the immemorial characters of Spanish literature and, as Longfellow saw it, of Spanish life — idle gentlemen and amorous students, proverb-mongering servants in the style of Sancho Panza, gypsies and dancing-girls; clerics, from the great Archbishop of Toledo down to the simple-minded curate of a country village; a comic alcalde, a muleteer, a contrabandista. And all these personages move about to the accompaniment of romantic music, for the strains of a guitar are frequently audible, and the action is often interrupted by light and graceful songs — the most famous of them, "Stars of the summer night," being Longfellow's own, while others ("Ah! thou moon that shinest," for one) he translated from the Spanish.

These songs are of the most diaphanous, and the blank verse of the dialogue, without having much muscle or sinew, is limpid and melodious. (The prose of the comic scenes, though straight out of Elizabethan comedy, is not lacking in vivacity.) And now and then the verse flowers in some fine and fitting metaphor — as it does in a speech by Victorian, Longfellow's young lover:

> Our feelings and our thoughts
> Tend ever on, and rest not in the Present.
> As drops of rain fall into some dark well,
> And from below comes a scarce audible sound,
> So fall our thoughts into the dark Hereafter,
> And their mysterious echo reaches us.

Or in a speech of his in the last scene:

> This is the highest point. Here let us rest.
> See, Preciosa, see how all about us

> Kneeling, like hooded friars, the misty mountains
> Receive the benediction of the sun!

There is the pretty image, so much in the taste of the day, which both Poe and Margaret Fuller liked:

> I will forget her! All dear recollections
> Pressed in my heart, like flowers within a book,
> Shall be torn out, and scattered to the winds!

Almost always these images are suitable to the scene and the persons; only one, in its exaggerated masculinity, seems wholly inappropriate; it is from a speech by Victorian's friend, Hypolito:

> A damsel has ensnared him with the glances
> Of her dark, roving eyes, as herdsmen catch
> A steer of Andalusia with a lazo.

It would be easy to say — and it has been said, by Poe and others — that *The Spanish Student* is essentially lyrical; a dramatic poem, at the best, not a play. And certainly it is comedy that leans toward the songlike rather than toward the vigorously active, tightly woven, Molièresque. But what is dramatic may be freely and even loosely defined, and Longfellow's play in verse has an easygoing dramatic character of its own; some of the scenes — Preciosa's dance before the Cardinal and the Archbishop, the Count of Lara's attack on her in her chamber and Victorian's intervention, the amusing scene in which Hypolito pulls the leg of old Padre Cura — should be effective enough on the stage. One can imagine *The Spanish Student* being very agreeably performed by talented amateurs. But it is true that the play owes its charm not to what is ordinarily thought of as dramatic but to the freshness, the naïveté, the youthfulness of the personal emotion that breathes through it — Longfellow's nostalgic love of the Spain in which he had spent eight romantic months at the age of twenty.

There is a certain unfairness to Longfellow in speaking of *The Golden Legend* independently of the trilogy of which it later became a part.* This was not, moreover, as we have seen, an afterthought; at a very early point Longfellow had conceived the design of a long dramatic poem that should deal with Christianity in three cardinal eras, and when he wrote *The Golden Legend* he thought of it, quite consciously, as the second part of such a poem. He would certainly, in the end, have wanted *Christus: A Mystery* — the title he gave to the trilogy — to be read as a unified whole. Yet in fact it is far from being one; the three parts stand together side by side, but except for the loose unity of the Christian theme, they do little to complement or enhance one another artistically, and one can only, as one contemplates them, agree with Howells that they "are *welded*, not *fused*, together." Longfellow was aspiring to the composition of a very ambitious major poem of a sort for which he was ill equipped. Moreover, the whole design was not completed for twenty years after *The Golden Legend*, and meanwhile the poem is expressive, in a dozen ways, of Longfellow's imaginative life during his later years at Harvard, not of his life in the early seventies. Of two possibilities the less misleading is to consider it by itself.

The play was planned as the mediaeval part of the trilogy-to-be. While he was taking the water-cure at Marienberg, Longfellow had jotted down in his journal a note which indicates that, at least just then, he intended that the first part should embody the virtue of Hope, the second that of Faith, the third of Charity. *The Golden Legend* is the poem of Faith, and its subject is the tale of Poor Henry as Longfellow found it treated in a beautiful courtly idyl of the early thirteenth century, Hartmann von Aue's *Der arme Heinrich*. One easily sees why Longfellow was strongly

---

* The title, *The Golden Legend,* had no association, before Longfellow, with Hartmann von Aue's poem; it is the title Caxton used for his translation of the *Legenda Aurea* ("Golden Legends"), by Jacobus de Voragine, a thirteenth-century collection of saints' lives. Perhaps Longfellow claims too much for the story of Poor Henry by calling it *the* Golden Legend.

drawn to this legend. It embodies not only the virtue of Faith, as many mediaeval subjects do, but that virtue as it is associated with maidenly innocence, a saintly will to self-sacrifice, such as Longfellow was always touched by. Hartmann's poem is a variation on the archetypal Alcestis-theme. His Heinrich, a proud and powerful prince, is stricken with leprosy, and learns from the physicians at Salerno that he can be healed only by the blood of a pure maiden who shall offer herself, Alcestis-like, as a voluntary sacrifice. A small peasant girl in Germany does so offer herself; the two of them journey to Salerno, and the girl is about to be cut to the heart by a physician's knife when Heinrich repents of his cruel selfishness, and she is saved. Prince that he is, he is now humbled in his pride, and makes the little peasant saint his wife.*

It is the simplest, even the starkest, of plots, and Longfellow takes it over with, negatively speaking, little change — except that Heinrich's repellent leprosy is toned down to "a strange, mysterious disease," and Hartmann's eight-year-old peasant girl becomes a more credible fifteen. But while Hartmann's poem has a strong simplicity not only of plot but of form, and limits itself to a single uncomplicated action, Longfellow wished to make his own poem a rather elaborate representation of mediaeval religious life, on its best and its worst sides, with even a glance at mediaeval scholasticism and medical learning. *The Golden Legend* has a certain fullness as a result, at the deliberate cost of a strictly dramatic unity. It abounds in scenes and episodes that help to fulfill Longfellow's purpose but that, in a "regular" drama, would be artless distractions. He was not writing that kind of poem.

If *Der arme Heinrich* suggests a small window of stained glass,

---

*Early in the twentieth century Gerhart Hauptmann wrote a poetic drama, *Der arme Heinrich*, on this same subject; it differs from Hartmann's poem in ways that strongly suggest, on Hauptmann's part, a knowledge of Longfellow's play. (*The Golden Legend* had been translated into German in 1859 and again in 1880.) Hauptmann's play, though not one of his most interesting, shows that the stuff of the legend can be put to admirable dramatic uses.

in pure and primary colors, *The Golden Legend* suggests a softly hued but loosely composed mural, perhaps in a library, in the manner of some nineteenth-century Pre-Raphaelite. What it loses in one kind of unity it gains, without sacrificing another kind, in historical many-sidedness. And the amplifications have often a charm or a liveliness of their own. There are interpolated tales, such as the pretty story of Christ and the Sultan's Daughter, drawn from *The Boy's Wonder-Horn*, which Elsie tells to Prince Henry in an early scene. The journey Henry and Elsie take from the Odenwald to Salerno is as slow and leisurely in representation as if they were in no hurry to arrive at their goal or to come to a resolution. The two travelers pause in Strasbourg, where they listen, in the square before the cathedral, to a lively version of an unseemly open-air sermon, accompanied by the cracking of a whip. In a different vein, they witness, in the cathedral itself, a Nativity play, one of the most successful things in the poem in the way it recaptures the naïve and reverent manner of a true mediaeval "mystery"; some of its tiny scenes — "Jesus at Play with His School-Mates," for example — could hardly be improved on in their imitative quaintness and tenderness.

At the convent of Hirschau in the Black Forest, where Henry and Elsie are lodged, there are comic scenes of an almost Goliardic boisterousness, especially one in the refectory at midnight, where the wanton monks are engaged in a drinking bout or Gaudiolum. But there is also a hushed and prayerlike scene in the scriptorium, where a devout monk is illuminating a manuscript of the Gospel of St. John. As Henry and Elsie later make their way through the covered bridge at Lucerne, Henry, an aristocratic guide, explains to Elsie the macabre paintings of the Dance of Death on its walls, and together they recognize that the bridge itself is an emblem of the passage from life to the afterlife. Halting under a tree at noon, at the foot of the Alps, they watch a band of barefoot pilgrims wending their way slowly through the tranquil landscape. At Salerno, before Prince Henry and Elsie arrive, the comic note is struck again as two theologians engage in a pedantic scholastic dispute over universals, which ends as they "rush out fighting"; they are followed by two scholars, one of whom outlines to the other, a newcomer, the preposterous course of study at the medical school, of which the first three years are "given to Logic alone." The final scene, after Henry and Elsie have returned as man and wife to his castle of Vautsberg on the Rhine, and they stand on the terrace at evening gazing off over the valley, is pitched in a solemn and even elegiac key.

It is not only episodes that Longfellow invents to enrich his picture of the Middle Ages; he very much enlarges also Hartmann's small cast of five characters, and gives himself as much freedom here as Shakespeare, say, in one of his history plays or Schiller in *Wallenstein*. The great minnesinger Walther von der Vogelweide — or Walter of the Vogelweid, as he is called here — appears as a friend of the stricken Henry; he is about to set out on a crusade, and is thus a type both of the faith and of the highest poetry of his age.* A whole series of clerics, good and bad, make their appearance: Friar Cuthbert, the coarse-fibered open-air preacher; the bibulous monks in the refectory at Hirschau; the saintly illuminator, Friar Pacificus; the aged and saddened Abbot Ernestus, who laments the degeneracy of true religion in his age; the traveling scholastic who affixes his hairsplitting theses to the gate of the college at Salerno. And there is the hearty, somewhat Shakespearean Padrone of the vessel that carries Prince Henry and Elsie from Genoa southward to their destination. None of these personages is characterized in more than a very "flat" and two-dimensional manner, and indeed they appear too briefly, one by one, to be at all fully developed. But given Longfellow's intention, they are characterized quite fully

* The figure of Walther fascinated Longfellow, who had included a poem about him ("Walter von der Volgelweid") in *The Belfry of Bruges* and two poems by him in *The Poets and Poetry of Europe*.

enough, with admirable liveliness and sometimes a genuine, if not very savage, satiric humor. They lend to the poem a bustling variety that gives it depth and color.

Only one of the characters whom Longfellow adds to Hartmann's cast appears throughout the poem, and this is the baleful character of Lucifer. There is no Satan in *Der arme Heinrich*, and Longfellow's Lucifer, if we must continue to speak of literary debts, has his origin not in that poem but in *Faust*. It is true that he has the air of a somewhat bowdlerized New England Mephistopheles; he never promises to abet the seduction of an innocent girl, and his language is wholly free from the occasional grossness of Mephisto's; but otherwise his traits are recognizable to readers of Goethe — his cynical humor, his contempt for mankind, his grinning casuistry, his anger when he is baffled. He first appears to Henry not, like Mephisto, in the guise of a traveling scholar, but in the not very dissimilar guise of a traveling physician; and very much in the spirit of Mephisto, gives Henry to drink a potion that he pretends is the Elixir of Perpetual Youth. He is at his comic-cynical best when he later appears as a priest in a village church and, seating himself in the confessional, soliloquizes on the falsity of the confessor's role. We see him again, in the garb of a Carmelite friar among the barefoot pilgrims, chuckling to himself over the opportunities such a pilgrimage affords him "for sowing broadcast the seeds of crime." At Salerno he assumes the disguise of a friar-physician and does what he can to hurry on the sacrifice of Elsie. He is thwarted in the end, like Mephisto, and we learn in an Epilogue that

> . . . since God suffers him to be,
> He, too, is God's minister,
> And labors for some good
> By us not understood!

Does not Mephisto, too, confess that he is

Ein Theil von jener Kraft,
Die stets das Böse will und stets das Gute schafft? *

The irony and the ambiguity of Mephisto's speech, it is true, are simplified and diluted by Longfellow, who was familiar too with Emerson on "the good of evil born," which he also simplified; and the lines in the Epilogue are no more than an expression of his generous but not very philosophical optimism.

In Prince Henry himself there is a dim suggestion of Faust, especially in the first scene. One sees him sitting alone at midnight, in a tower chamber, ill and restless, soliloquizing despondently and longing for rest and peace; it is hard not to be reminded of the first scene in *Faust*. And Henry yields to the seductions of Lucifer very much as Faust yields to those of Mephisto. But in fact he is no more to be compared with Faust than Longfellow is to be seriously compared with Goethe. The legend itself would have kept Henry from developing into a genuinely Faustian character, and in any case one need not remark that Longfellow was quite without the capacity to conceive or to represent a character so complex, so contradictory, so grandiose, so demonic as Faust. His protagonist has little or no force of character, little or no heroic stature; his feebleness, indeed, is the principal defect of the poem, and effectually keeps it, if nothing else did, from attaining the major quality that Longfellow certainly aimed at. Henry *might* have been represented as powerfully and agonizingly torn between faith and faithlessness, and achieving faith as the reward of a desperate struggle. There is nothing whatever of this in the poem; none of the characters, indeed, is depicted as arriving at his faith through any spiritual ordeal, and Henry himself suggests not a mediaeval Titan, but a beautiful, melancholy, somewhat epicene figure, in knightly armor, in some painting by Millais or Burne-Jones.

* Part of that Power, not understood,
Which always wills the Bad, and always works the Good.

Except for his sneering tone, Lucifer is dead right about Henry when he speaks of his

> Weakness, selfishness, and the base
> And pusillanimous fear of death.

He does fear death, to be sure, but his most interesting trait is his vacillation between this fear and the intense *longing* for death. His mysterious malady is a kind of emblem of this diseased wish for oblivion, and when he is healed of it, he has presumably returned to a healthy man's love of life — though, if so, this is not very powerfully represented in that last scene on the terrace at Vautsberg. Meanwhile, in any case, the will to oblivion is almost the first emotion Henry expresses:

> Rest! rest! Oh, give me rest and peace!
> The thought of life that ne'er shall cease
> Has something in it like despair,
> A weight I am too weak to bear!
> Sweeter to this afflicted breast
> The thought of never-ending rest!
> Sweeter the undisturbed and deep
> Tranquillity of endless sleep!

Yet it is the *fear* of death, of course, that induces him, despite his better feeling, to yield to Elsie's insistence on sacrificing herself for him; and as they emerge from the covered bridge at Lucerne, he breaks out in a bitter protest against the mortality that its pictures celebrate. "Why is it hateful to you?" asks Elsie, and he answers:

> For the reason
> That life, and all that speaks of life, is lovely,
> And death, and all that speaks of death, is hateful.

His thoughts of death, however, are obsessive; and in a later scene, as he stands at night on the terrace of an inn at Genoa, gazing out over the sea, he is on the very verge of suicide:

> A single step, and all is o'er;
> A plunge, a bubble, and no more;
> And thou, dear Elsie, wilt be free
> From martyrdom and agony.

Even Elsie seems to offer herself as a sacrifice not only out of a saintly willingness to die for Henry's sake, but out of a somewhat questionable aversion from life. "Better is Death than Life!" she cries —

> Ah yes! to thousands
> Death plays upon a dulcimer, and sings
> That song of consolation, till the air
> Rings with it, and they cannot choose but follow
> Whither he leads. And not the old alone,
> But the young also hear it, and are still.

It is very curious to come upon this suicidal theme in Longfellow's work, which has mostly been associated with other motives. It is expressed, very incongruously, by both Victorian and Preciosa even in *The Spanish Student*, which would not seem to call for these shadows of feeling;* and in *The Golden Legend*, where its presence is more natural, it hovers over the action like a somber cloud. We are confirmed by it in the impression that some of the short poems make on our minds. It is never allowed to carry everything before it, to be sure; in the end, Henry, as in Hartmann's poem, saves both himself and Emily in a revulsion of his better nature; and he is healed not by her blood but by the touch of St. Matthew's bones, which no doubt signify what Tillich would call the Courage To Be. Yet there is something spasmodic rather than resolute in Henry's gesture, and it does not efface the impression of morbidity and weakness that too much of the rest of the poem has conveyed. We end by thinking of Henry as a nineteenth-century romantic melancholiac rather than a haughty and then humbled mediaeval prince. Granted this, however, his figure has an authenticity of its own, and if it fails to provide the

* In Act III, Scenes I and V.

poem with an energetic moral center, it is not without an elegiac and pensive grace.

There is more force of will and firmness of purpose in the heroine, Elsie, than in her princely friend, and it seems to have been Hartmann's little peasant girl, not Heinrich, who awakened Longfellow's imaginative interest at the beginning: "I have a heroine as sweet as Imogen," he noted in his journal, "could I but paint her so." Sweetness, indeed, remains too much her hallmark in the completed poem: she is too largely, like even Imogen, the offspring of a wishful masculine fantasy of purity and goodness, and there is too little of humanity, even saintly humanity, in her make-up. But, thanks partly to the *donnée* of the legend, she exhibits a quiet decisiveness from the outset, steadily bearing down the distressed opposition of old Gottlieb and Ursula, her parents, and refusing to yield to Henry's own protests. She is as much his guide on the journey to Salerno, though in a different sense, as he is hers. And it is she, rather than Henry, who gives utterance to what is presumably the intellectual significance of the poem:

> Faith alone can interpret life, and the heart that aches
> 　　and bleeds with the stigma
> Of pain, alone bears the likeness of Christ, and can comprehend its dark enigma.

She is the New England, indeed the Unitarian, counterpart of Gretchen in *Faust;* but she is even purer and holier than Gretchen, and in spite of the relative moral energy she manifests, she has hardly substance enough to become a type of the Eternal Womanly.

The agreeable impression of movement and variety *The Golden Legend* gives, its freedom from bareness and monotony, arises partly, as we have seen, from the frequent changes of setting and the multiplicity of the human figures. But it also arises from the resourceful variety of the forms of verse in which Longfellow develops his subject. No doubt this too was a hint from *Faust,* but if so Longfellow was wise to take it. Another poet might have cast the whole poem in blank verse; Longfellow casts rather little of it in that meter. This sprang at least in part from his feeling that his own blank verse was "very heavy and slow"; it was on this account that he rewrote the first scene, originally in that form, and put the blank verse into rhyme. Our own feeling is likely to be that, when he writes such verse, he is sometimes not so much heavy and slow as too melting, fluent, and nerveless. Yet even his blank verse can take on a melancholy gracefulness which keeps us from regretting that he did not entirely eliminate it from the poem. Surely it is the appropriate form, for example, for Walter of the Vogelweid's soliloquy as he leans over the parapet of Henry's castle at sunset:

> The day is done; and slowly from the scene
> The stooping sun up-gathers his spent shafts,
> And puts them back into his golden quiver! . . .

There are a few other passages in this form, but on the whole Longfellow did well to keep their number down, and to write most of the poem in other meters.

The most frequent of these is the octosyllabic verse, rhyming not in couplets but irregularly, which he was familiar with in Scott and Byron, and which he himself always wrote with naturalness and ease. In *The Golden Legend* his octosyllabics seem peculiarly expressive, in their grave and gentle movement, of the sober feeling that pervades so much of the poem:

> It is the sea, it is the sea,
> In all its vague immensity,
> Fading and darkening in the distance!
> Silent, majestical, and slow,
> The white ships haunt it to and fro,
> With all their ghostly sails unfurled,
> As phantoms from another world
> Haunt the dim confines of existence.

In the comic passages, this four-stress line takes on, with the freedom of extra light syllables, a sprightly, speechlike, jocular rhythm that suggests what is called *Knittelvers* in German poetry, and indeed, again, it was probably Goethe's example that inspired Longfellow here. Like Goethe, he may well have felt that this "doggerel," as it is sometimes called without derogation, was appropriate to his mediaeval theme:

> It makes a peculiar atmosphere,
> This odor of earthly passions and crimes,
> Such as I like to breathe, at times,
> And such as often brings me here
> In the hottest and most pestilential season.
> To-day, I come for another reason.

It is verse such as this that helps to give the humorous scenes their genuine brightness and lightness.

Longfellow's interest in experiments in verse has largely been forgotten; in his own time he was occasionally rebuked for it, and a British reviewer of *The Golden Legend* scolded him for his "besetting sin of experiment." This reviewer had in mind, partly, the very long, weary, eight-stress line that appears just once, in the scene on the road to Hirschau already quoted from ("Faith alone can interpret life . . ."); here is another couplet:

> All the hedges are white with dust, and the great dog under
>   the creaking wain
> Hangs his head in the lazy heat, while onward the horses toil
>   and strain.

It is said that no English poet before Longfellow — and later Swinburne ("March: An Ode") — had used such a meter, and indeed it would, if maintained for more than thirty lines or so, become intolerable; in this scene of noontide heat and ambling movement on horseback, it has a real suitability. But what probably exasperated the reviewer in *Blackwood's* still more than these octameters was the passages written in a verse of which both the line-lengths and the rhyming are irregular:

> Lo! over the mountain steeps
> A dark, gigantic shadow sweeps
> Beneath my feet;
> A blackness inwardly brightening
> With sullen heat,
> As a storm-cloud lurid with lightning.

This is from the Epilogue; in the Prologue Longfellow discards even rhyme and writes in a kind of free verse:

> Shake the casements!
> Break the painted
> Panes that flame with gold and crimson;
> Scatter them like leaves of Autumn,
> Swept away before the blast!

The trochaic rhythm of this keeps it from being entirely "free," but in Elsie's tale of Christ and the Sultan's Daughter, as in "Tegnér's Drapa," there is no metrical regularity of any kind:

> And at midnight,
> As she lay upon her bed,
> She heard a voice
> Call to her from the garden,
> And, looking forth from her window,
> She saw a beautiful youth
> Standing among the flowers.

It cannot be said that the verse of this passage is anything but toneless and dull, as the language too is, but the verse of both the Prologue and the Epilogue have a certain flexibility and liveliness, and one respects Longfellow, in any case, for his willingness to break, now and then, with the conventions of English verse.

The poem is diversified, too, by lyrical passages — the rhymeless Evening Song that Elsie and her family sing together, and the Latin drinking songs that the monks of Hirschau sing at their Gaudiolum. The seven little scenes of the Nativity play at Strasbourg are written in a series of stanzaic forms; these are so startlingly mimetic in the way they reproduce the verse of the genuine miracle plays as to suggest, fancifully and for the moment, a transmigration into Longfellow's person of the soul of some "York" or "Chester" poet. Herod, in "The Slaughter of the Innocents," rants thus:

> Potz-tausend! Himmel-sacrament!
> Filled am I with great wonderment
>   At this unwelcome news!
> Am I not Herod? Who shall dare
> My crown to take, my sceptre bear,
>   As king among the Jews?

And Longfellow adds this stage direction: *"Here he shall stride up and down and flourish his sword."* If Longfellow's ventriloquism sometimes proved a treacherous gift, it stood him in good stead in the writing of this miracle play. In general, the metrical virtuosity he exhibits in *The Golden Legend* has much to do with its vitality.

The poem has little intellectual interest: Longfellow was not in the slightest degree a philosophical poet, and Goethe's often-quoted remark about Byron — "When he thinks, he is a child" — applies much more truly to him. In that sense, he arouses expectations that he cannot fulfill; we are bound to approach a poem on such a subject and on such a scale in the hope that its theological and ethical implications will be freshly and deeply explored — and *The Golden Legend* badly disappoints us. If we are looking for dramatic power or psychological depth, we are equally disappointed. What we find instead is a poem in dramatic form that evokes, with undeniable charm and delicacy of color, the Middle Ages as they could be apprehended by a sensitive and erudite nineteenth-century mind; not perhaps the "real" Middle Ages, in the most rigorous historical sense, but a poetic version of them that, for imaginative veracity, challenges comparison safely with most other versions in the nineteenth century. Samuel Longfellow quotes Ruskin as saying that in *The Golden Legend* Longfellow had "entered more closely into the temper of the Monk, for good and for evil, than ever yet theological writer or historian"; and even if we cannot quite subscribe to this Ruskinian superlative, we can agree that something real in the temper of the monk — as well as of the prince, the poet, the peasant — comes through in Longfellow's treatment. It is decidedly the most successful part of the trilogy.

VI

Acadian Idyl

ONE EASILY sees why Longfellow, given the quality of his imagination, was attracted at once by the Acadian story that Conolly, in Hawthorne's presence, related to him. Uninviting as it seemed to Hawthorne, the story had a whole group of elements that recommended it immediately to the very different mind of his friend. The chief of these was the motive that had already, in *Der arme Heinrich*, appealed to him so strongly in the figure of Hartmann's little peasant girl — self-forgetful devotion and saintly loyalty, especially on the part of a girl or woman. When Conolly had finished his tale, we are told, Longfellow remarked: "It is the best illustration of faithfulness and the constancy of woman that I have ever heard of or read." It was a primordial motive, to be sure, as the Hebraic figure of Ruth and the Greek figure of Penelope are enough to attest; but clearly it had a deep personal value, too, for Longfellow, with his dependence on the devotion of woman; it had a value, too, for his woman-oriented culture. There was never any question for him which of the two lovers was to dominate the poem: the male lover, whose constancy in fact must have been as heroic as his sweetheart's, plays a distinctly secondary role from the beginning; he is the *object* of loyalty — and of search — and not its active participant; and a sardonic imagination might even feel that Gabriel Lajeunesse, in his passivity and elusiveness, is unconsciously fleeing from Evangeline rather than seeking her out. Certainly he is no dominating and aggressive Odysseus, any more than Evangeline is a merely steadfast and long-waiting Penelope; and the poem, in itself and in the popular imagination, is hers, not Gabriel's.*

In any case, the note of feminine faithfulness is struck unambiguously at the very outset in a direct and quasi-epical announcement of the theme:

Ye who believe in affection that hopes, and endures, and is patient,
Ye who believe in the beauty and strength of woman's devotion,
List to the mournful tradition, still sung by the pines of the forest;
List to a tale of Love in Acadie, the home of the happy.

The symbol of this faithfulness, which is itself made to symbolize a still deeper spiritual faith, is the compass-flower of the prairie which the Jesuit father points out to Evangeline — the flower whose leaves are turned to the north as steadily as a compass and which thus becomes an utterly dependable guide, amid the pathless prairie, to the traveler. It is true that there is a certain passivity in this flower-symbol, and that, in spite of her domination of the poem, what characterizes Evangeline herself is less a tragic vehemence of will than, as the lines just quoted indicate, a capacity for passive endurance and a long-suffering patience. Toward the end we are told that

Patience and abnegation of self, and devotion to others,
This was the lesson a life of trial and sorrow had taught her.

It is what imparts to *Evangeline* its particular Longfellow character of delicate and rather feminine pathos, and deprives it of the true heroic strain. But pathos of this sort is a genuine poetic effect,

---

* A descendant of Hawthorne, Manning Hawthorne, and a grandson of Longfellow, H. W. L. Dana, collaborated some years ago on a useful monograph entitled *The Origin and Development of Longfellow's "Evangeline"* (1947).

and it is felt and expressed so purely, so appropriately, here as to escape the charge of sentimentality.

The story, moreover, as it was told to Longfellow, involved not only the idea of constancy but the idea of a search — and, indeed, of a wandering, a wandering much longer than that of Odysseus. It was an ancient and irresistible theme, and it appealed at once to the traveler in Longfellow, as well as to that in his readers. "His bride," Conolly had said of the hero, "set off in search of him, — wandered about New England all her lifetime." New England, indeed! That admirable section of the country proved far too restricted a scene for Longfellow's ranging imagination, and in fact Evangeline never, so far as we hear, sets foot on the soil of Maine or Massachusetts, of New Hampshire or Connecticut. Some of the real Acadians, as everyone knew, had wandered — after what they called "le grand dérangement" — as far from their native place as Louisiana, and had founded communities there in a congenial Roman Catholic ambience; this historical fact was Longfellow's excuse for broadening his canvas to the vast proportions of a "diorama" — he had seen Banvard's Moving Diorama of the Mississippi in Boston while he was at work on the poem — and for enriching *Evangeline* with some of the manifold landscape associations of the historic American drive toward the West and the South. The rivers are naturally important here, as they were in reality, and as they always were to Longfellow's imagination; and one sees Evangeline, with her companion exiles, floating down the Ohio in a boat, past the mouth of the Wabash, and then, like a more decorous Huck Finn, down the Father of Waters itself and into its far-ramifying lakes and bayous. Later she searches for Gabriel on the prairie — whither Longfellow follows Cooper and Bryant in fancy — and spends many months at a Jesuit mission on the western slopes of the Ozarks. The forests are not forgotten, though they figure less than one might expect in an American poem: we have a glimpse of Evangeline, obeying the summons of a rumor, searching for her lover on the banks of the Saginaw River in the heart of the Michigan forest. In the end she is found, for the first time, in a city, the city of Philadelphia — the only locale in the poem that Longfellow himself had ever visited. Meanwhile, *Evangeline* has drawn vitality not only from the ancient theme of the wandering but from a peculiarly American footlooseness.

The wandering, moreover, is not only a movement in space, is not only geographical, but is also an exile, with all the emotional and historic connotations of that word; and we cannot doubt that Longfellow's feelings were deeply affected by the fact, or that it helps to account for the universal popularity of the poem. The cruel "derangement" of the Acadians by the British was the essential setting of the story, but, aside from the archetypal appeal of the theme, Longfellow was certainly conscious of a particular model here. He had been lecturing to his classes on *Hermann und Dorothea*, and even translating passages from it for their benefit; and he could not have failed to be aware that the pathos of Goethe's domestic idyl depended in part on the poet's use of a still more recent exile — the driving from their homes of people on the German border by the armies of the French Revolution — as the setting for his *gutbürgerlich* tale. Despite the possibilities, however, there is little or no patriotic bitterness in Goethe's poem; and there is the minimum of humanitarian indignation in *Evangeline*. The misery of the Acadians, herded together at night on the sea beach, while the smoke and flames of their burning homes and barns rises skyward, is rendered in the true and touching elegiac manner; but the brutality of the English troops — save for the one moment when a soldier strikes Basil the blacksmith on the mouth and knocks him down — is instinctively muted and minimized. Indignation was an emotion Longfellow could feel strongly as a man, but not one that he could usually express with great conviction as a poet; and one understands Whittier's sensible judgment that it was a good thing Longfellow, and not he, had written *Evangeline*: "If I had attempted it," he said, "I should

have spoiled the artistic effect of the poem by my indignation at
the treatment of the exiles by the Colonial Government."

He would certainly have spoiled this particular poem, which
depends so much, for its emotional tone, on the melancholy of
exile and so little on the iniquities of oppression; again, like the
antislavery poems, *Evangeline* is quite wanting in Hebraic-
prophetic wrath. It is largely wanting, too, despite its subject, in
effects of violence, raw hardship, or fear. The pervasive mood of
the poem is one of tranquillity, mildness, and peace; not the agita-
tion of action and danger so much as the hush of revery. Everything seems to have taken place at a great distance, a great many
years ago, and to be seen through a soft haze of dreamy nostalgia
— not close at hand in a populous poetic Present. Much of the
action, as usual with Longfellow, occurs at night, by moonlight,
or at sunset; and if full daylight is invoked, it is likely to be the
hot soporific light of noon, as it is in the beautiful scene in which
the tired wanderers moor their boat on the beach of an island in
the Atchafalaya, where the air is faint "with the odorous breath
of magnolia blossoms"; and lie down to slumber beneath the
boughs of a great cedar, hung with trumpet-flowers and grape-
vines. In the early cantos of the poem, it is understandable that
Longfellow should wish to communicate the fullest possible sense
of the bucolic "peace and contentment" in which the inhabitants
of Grand-Pré, so soon to be hounded from their homes, spend
their innocent lives; understandable that he should have made the
descent of the English troops take place during the tranquil days
of the Summer of All Saints, or Indian Summer:

> Now recommenced the reign of rest and affection and stillness.
> Day with its burden and heat had departed, and twilight de-
>   scending
> Brought back the evening star to the sky, and the herds to the
>   homestead.
> Pawing the ground they came, and resting their necks on each
>   other,

And with their nostrils distended inhaling the freshness of
    evening.
Foremost, bearing the bell, Evangeline's beautiful heifer,
Proud of her snow-white hide, and the ribbon that waved from
    her collar,
Quietly paced and slow, as if conscious of human affection.

Never was Longfellow's inspiration more Latin than it is in this
passage, and no doubt he was fully aware of the hovering presence of Vergil, the Vergil of the *Eclogues* and the *Georgics,*
when he wrote it; aware, too, no doubt, how far he fell short of
the ultimate distinction of Vergilian pastoral. The idyllic strain of
pastoral, in any case, was clearly dictated by the dramatic demands of the opening cantos; but, except for the stormy scene in
the church at Grand-Pré, when the commander of the English
troops reads to the assembled men of the village the royal order
of transportation, there is little of the tumultuous, of the unquiet,
in *Evangeline* — less even than in *Hermann und Dorothea.*

This is true of the action, and it is true too of the natural
setting, despite the possibilities it might have offered for another
emotional treatment. The fierce hostility of nature, of which
other American writers have made so much, is only at moments
suggested, while its painterly beauty, its picturesque charm, is
constantly evoked. Sometimes it is evoked at the expense of pho-
tographic reality, too. Longfellow himself had never visited Nova
Scotia, and Paul Lieder pointed out long ago that the famous
description of the environs of Grand-Pré in the prologue — the
primeval forest, the pines and hemlocks bearded with moss, the
rocky caverns of the neighboring ocean — has very small literal
truthfulness to the mild, rather flat, and unforested scenery of the
Basin of Minas, but is a rewriting in hexameters of Longfellow's
description of the Swedish countryside in an essay on Tegnér he
had published a decade earlier:

    Almost primeval simplicity reigns over this Northern land, —
almost primeval solitude and stillness. You pass out from the gate

of the city, and, as if by magic, the scene changes to a wild, woodland landscape. Around you are forests of fir. Overhead hang the long fan-like branches trailing with moss, and heavy with red and blue cones. . . . Anon you come forth into a pleasant and sunny land of farms.

This quiet and heavily wooded Swedish landscape lent itself to Longfellow's poetic purpose far more suitably than the actual scene would have done. And so of the Mississippi: the treacherous river of Mark Twain, with its shifting currents, its deadly fogs, its snags and sand bars and towheads, appears as a majestic and almost benevolent stream in *Evangeline* — flowing among green islands on which cotton-trees nod their shadowy crests, and opening out at times into broad lagoons where "silvery" sand bars are visible beneath the waters. The moon rises as the exiles sweep into the Bayou of Plaquemine:

> Lovely the moonlight was as it glanced and gleamed on the water,
> Gleamed on the columns of cypress and cedar sustaining the arches,
> Down through whose broken vaults it fell as through chinks in a ruin.

There is a certain suggestion of terror in the prairie landscape to which Evangeline moves on — in the sense one has of the savage tribes wandering over it and "staining the desert with blood," as well as in the fine image of the vulture circling and sailing over it, "like the implacable soul of a chieftain slaughtered in battle." But again it is the beauty of the prairie rather than its fearfulness that dominates:

> Spreading between these streams are the wondrous, beautiful prairies;
> Billowy bays of grass ever rolling in shadow and sunshine,
> Bright with luxuriant clusters of roses and purple amorphas.*

* In his scene-painting of the prairie Longfellow depended a good deal on a book by Colonel John Frémont, *The Exploring Expedition to the Rocky Mountains, Oregon, and California,* which he had been reading just

And the city, humanly speaking, proves to be quite as benevolent as the river and the prairie have been. When, in the last canto, Evangeline reaches Philadelphia, she finds it a city of pure friendliness, filled with a Quaker spirit of equality and brotherhood that recalls to her the simple world of her Acadian girlhood. Even the pestilence that descends upon the city — no doubt, to be literal, one of the yellow-fever epidemics of the 1790's — is conjured up with none of the ghastliness of the plagues in Lucretius or Ovid or, for that matter, in the Philadelphia novels of Brockden Brown. Horror of a too explicit sort would have jarred irremediably on the emotional unity of *Evangeline,* which, to repeat, is not that of bitterness and terror but that of idylism, nostalgia, and a melancholy tenderness.

A reviewer in the *American Review* found Evangeline herself an insipid creature and, with his dislike of the whole poem, he might well have found Gabriel Lajeunesse even more so. Certainly if we are looking for either a heroic largeness or a novelistic roundness of characterization in them, we shall be badly let down. Yet they have, on the whole, as much largeness and as much roundness as they need in a poem that is neither heroic nor novelistic. *Evangeline* suggests a minor poetic form, not the epic, and it suggests a more archaic literary form than the novel. It is enough if the tenderness and the tenacity of the lovers' devotion to each other — for, after all, Gabriel does prove constant — are made credible, as they are; enough if the two of them move through the poem not as realistic lovers of the mid-eighteenth century in the colonies, but as figures of the frankest romanticism, dimly outlined, quietly moving, grave and gentle, and speaking hardly at all. Gabriel's father, the blacksmith Basil Lajeunesse, has enough choler and enough heartiness to give him a certain definition, but it is no more than that; and Evangeline's

---

before he wrote this passage. Basil Lajeunesse, by the way, was the name of one of the men in Frémont's party, "one of our best swimmers," apparently a Canadian *voyageur.*

father, the prosperous farmer Benedict Bellefontaine, who dies of heartbreak on the sea beach during the night before the deportation, is a figure of pure pathos. The minor characters — René Leblanc, the old notary; the gentle priest, Father Felician; Michael, the gay fiddler; the priest of the Jesuit mission; the pathetic Shawnee woman whose husband has been slain by the Comanches — fill in the human scene pleasantly and rescue it from the bareness that might so easily have impoverished it.

It was a happy thought, moreover, on Longfellow's part, to avert the monotony inherent in so simple a story by the familiar but here very suitable device of the tale-within-a-tale. The subject itself, involving the lives of very simple people, lent itself naturally to any color he might wish to give his narrative by drawing upon the resources of folklore — the folklore that, like Scott and Irving and the German writers, he had long found so appealing. René Leblanc, the notary, draws all the children of the village to him with his tales of the loup-garou or werewolf, of the white Létiche or ghost of an unchristened child, of the oxen in the stable that speak on Christmas Eve. To the older people, alarmed by the injustice that may soon be done to them, the notary tells, not very relevantly, the story of the Thieving Magpie — of which Rossini had long since made an opera — to demonstrate that, however unjust men may be, God is always just. These were folktales of French, or at least European, derivation, but Longfellow's mind was already turning toward the folklore of the Indians; and charmed as he was by the books of Henry Rowe Schoolcraft, he represents the bereaved Shawnee woman, in *Evangeline*, telling such tales as that of Mowis, the bridegroom of snow, and of the fair Lilinau, who was wooed by a phantom — tales which he had found in Schoolcraft's richly packed volumes, *Oneóta* and the *Algic Researches*. The presence in *Evangeline* of this subordinate strain of the primitive and the uncanny enhances its dreamlike quality in a minor but unmistakable fashion.

No one seems to have found fault with this, but plenty of readers and critics at the time protested vigorously, as plenty have done since, against the metrical form in which Longfellow chose to cast his poem. This was of course the very controversial form of the allegedly classical hexameter. No really successful English poem had yet been written in this form, though experiments with it had been made ever since Elizabethan times; and while Longfellow was writing *Evangeline*, he came upon a translation, in *Blackwood's*, of the last book of the *Iliad* in hexameters, which struck him as admirable. "This is the only way to translate Homer," he remarked in his journal, anticipating Matthew Arnold's view by several years. "It gives at least some idea of him." He was already well along in his own poem, however, and the impulse to write it in hexameters had come to him not from any English writer but from the German poets, especially from Goethe's *Hermann,* and from Esaias Tegnér. The article he had published on the Swedish poet in 1837 had been mainly a detailed account of Tegnér's long poem of the Viking age, *Frithiof's Saga,* certain passages from which he had translated, by way of illustration, in at least an approximation to the very various metrical patterns of the original. One of these passages had been in hexameters, and Longfellow had not shrunk from the attempt to reproduce them:

Three miles extended around the fields of the homestead, on
    three sides
Valleys and mountains and hills, but on the fourth side was the
    ocean.
Birch woods crowned the summits, but down the slope of the
    hillsides
Flourished the golden corn, and man-high was waving the rye-
    field. . . .

Whatever the quality of the Swedish hexameters may be, Longfellow was clearly fumbling uncomfortably with their English equivalents; yet this did not deter him, three or four years later, from tackling another poem of Tegnér's, the sentimental village idyl Longfellow called "The Children of the Lord's Supper," which was in the same form. He had gained something in facility with this translation, but — perhaps it is the sweetish piety of the original that is to blame — the verse is essentially lax and invertebrate. There is more metrical vigor in "To the Driving Cloud," a short poem of Longfellow's own, on an Indian subject, which appeared in *The Belfry of Bruges* just before he set to work on *Evangeline:*

> There thou chasest the stately stag on the banks of the Elkhorn,
> Or by the roar of the Running-Water, or where the Omaha
> Calls thee, and leaps through the wild ravine like a brave of
>   the Blackfeet!

A constant difficulty with the measure in English is illustrated by the weak first foot of the second line, but thanks partly to the sonorous proper nouns — "Omaha" being accented on the second syllable — and partly to such strong spondaic endings as "Elkhorn" and "Blackfeet," "To the Driving Cloud" has, as Longfellow himself felt, a strength one would not have anticipated from the earlier experiments. One line is as good, in itself, as perhaps we have a right to expect of the English hexameter:

> Stalked those birds unknown, that have left us only their footprints.

Even here, if we are haunted by the thought of the classical hexameter, we have to pretend that "us" is a strong syllable and "their" a weaker one than it is, and *Evangeline* abounds in similar demands on tolerance. Similar demands, that is, if we make the mistake, like so many readers of the poem, of imagining that English hexameters are legitimate only so far as they approximate closely the measures of Homer and Vergil. They can never, for familiar reasons, really be the English equivalents of the Greek or Latin hexameters, and it is open to any classically trained reader to reject them all, out of hand. If we feel no disposition to be so

sweeping, we can concede that the so-called hexameter has sometimes been used agreeably in English, that it pleases partly by its
more or less indefinite reminiscence of the classical measure, and
that it is pedantry to think of it as anything more than a possible
English line that sometimes lends itself, as the German line also
does, to pleasant poetic effects. It is not likely ever to be used
again by serious poets, but in England, in the mid-nineteenth century, it gave an attractive character to such poems as Clough's
The Bothie of Tober-na-Vuolich (where it has a loose-limbed
but rather athletic quality) or Kingsley's *Andromeda* (where it is
firmer and more sculpturesque) or Hawtrey's translation of a
passage in Book III of the *Iliad* (which Matthew Arnold so much
admired). *Evangeline* antedated all these poems, and perhaps it
helped to awaken a transitory interest in the form.

In any case, it stands or falls, from this point of view, not on
the correctness of its hexameters, classically speaking, but on their
intrinsic charm and their appropriateness to its inner character.
When we read *Evangeline* in this spirit, we are likely to feel that,
at its most successful, the verse has a kind of grave, slow-paced,
mellifluous quality, like a slightly monotonous but not unmusical
chant, which is genuinely expressive of its mournful and minor
theme. Matthew Arnold was as just as he often was when he said
that "the merit of the manner and movement of *Evangeline*, when
they are at their best, is to be tenderly elegant; and their fault,
when they are at their worst, is to be lumbering." They are
likely to be lumbering when Longfellow writes not from natural
sympathy but from the necessities of the subject, as he does in
the address of the English commander to the assembled men of
Grand-Pré — which, moreover, is a far too faithful paraphrase of
the address actually delivered by Colonel John Winslow, as Longfellow found it in Haliburton's history of Nova Scotia:

> "You are convened this day," he said, "by his Majesty's orders.
> Clement and kind has he been; but how you have answered his
> kindness,

Let your own hearts reply! To my natural make and my temper
Painful the task is I do, which to you I know must be griev-
ous. . . ."

The verse, as Longfellow writes it, simply does not lend itself
to stern public pronouncements; luckily Winslow's speech is the
only passage of just this sort in the poem, though the pacifying
speech of Father Felician, which immediately follows it, is equally
halting. Longfellow's hexameters are most successful in passages of
melancholy and pathetic inaction (as in the scene on the sea
beach in Part the First), or of a moonlit mysteriousness (as in
the scene in which Evangeline wanders out into Basil's Louisiana
garden in the "magical moonlight"), or of landscape or seascape
charm (as in the very first and very last lines of the poem). He
appears to have gained in sureness of touch as he went on with
Evangeline; one of the most "tenderly elegant" passages occurs in
the second canto of Part the Second, one of the later cantos to be
written. It is that in which Longfellow evokes, in a manner so
different from Whitman's, the song of the mockingbird in a
thicket beside the Atchafalaya:

> Then from a neighboring thicket the mocking-bird, wildest of
> singers,
> Swinging aloft on a willow-spray that hung o'er the water,
> Shook from his little throat such floods of delirious music,
> That the whole air and the woods and the waves seemed silent
> to listen.
> Plaintive at first were the tones and sad: then soaring to madness
> Seemed they to follow or guide the revel of frenzied Bac-
> chantes.
> Single notes were then heard, in sorrowful, low lamentation;
> Till, having gathered them all, he flung them abroad in derision,
> As when, after a storm, a gust of wind through the tree-tops
> Shakes down the rattling rain in a crystal shower on the
> branches.

This is less strangely mimetic, and less poignant, than the "aria"
of the mockingbird in "Out of the Cradle Endlessly Rocking,"

but in spite of some weak first feet and weak trochees in mid-line — thanks of course to the sensitive diction as well as to the hexameters ("wildest," "delirious," "plaintive," "revel," "lamentation," "derision") and to the expressive simile in the last lines — the passage demonstrates how delicately and flexibly the verse can adapt itself to Longfellow's representational purpose.

As if to prove to himself that he had done well to choose this measure for *Evangeline*, Longfellow amused himself, when he had finished the canto, by translating the passage on the mocking-bird into pentameter couplets:

> Upon a spray that overhung the stream,
> The mocking-bird, awaking from his dream,
> Poured such delirious music from his throat
> That all the air seemed listening to his note.
> Plaintive at first the song began, and slow;
> It breathed of sadness, and of pain and woe;
> Then, gathering all his notes, abroad he flung
> The multitudinous music from his tongue, —
> As, after showers, a sudden gust again
> Upon the leaves shakes down the rattling rain.

The intention of self-parody is evident enough, and doubtless it is all that is needed to explain the dullness of these "heroic" couplets — the like of which Longfellow never wrote earlier or later — but it is hard to resist the feeling that hexameters were "intrinsically" better suited to the effects Longfellow wished to achieve.

In spite of his habit of improvisation, he had taken greater pains with *Evangeline* than with anything he had yet written; he had by no means dashed it off, as he was later to dash off "The Saga of King Olaf," but had labored over it, when leisure permitted, for a year and three months. "*Evangeline* is so easy for you to read," he once said, "because it was so hard for me to write." No doubt his desire to give the pseudo-classical verse its greatest possible finish had much to do with this difficulty: he had submitted the manuscript to his Hellenist friend Felton for his metrical corrections, and seems to have followed them all, faithfully. He had cut out some passages for reasons of his own, reasons that are not always obvious: did he do well to omit the following lines, originally in the first canto, from the passage describing the youthful play of Gabriel and Evangeline together?

> Often in summer they strayed by the ocean, and searching for
>   sea-shells,
> Ankle-deep in the sheeted tide, and then like the beach-birds
> Chased the sibilant wave as slowly it slid down the shingles.

The lines themselves, it is true, are extremely sibilant, but surely they are suitably expressive as a result, and they are pleasant also as picture. However this may be, there can be no dispute over Longfellow's revision of the very end of the poem. As he first wrote the final line, one February evening, it was a weak one:

> While the great sea without reëchoes the mournful tradition.

The next morning, we are told, he canceled this line and substituted for it, with only a slight alteration, the familiar lines from the prologue — lines which Paul Elmer More once called "hexameters . . . as sonorous and rhythmical as any in the language":

> While from its rocky caverns the deep-voiced, neighboring
>   ocean
> Speaks, and in accents disconsolate answers the wail of the
>   forest.

This reiteration, at the end, of two lines from the opening passage brings the poem to a subdued musical conclusion, turning the fancy away again from the long-suffering human figures and back to the ocean beside which they had first appeared — the ocean that, nevertheless, as its disconsolate accents suggest, has been in a "pathetic" sympathy with them all along.

VII

A Romance and a Tale

OUTRE-MER had been the record of those charmed years Longfellow had spent in France, Spain, and Italy during his first travels in Europe as an open-eyed and ardent young pilgrim. The little book had ended, except for an epilogue, with some hurried and rather perfunctory notes on his journey to Vienna and a visit to the castle of Greifenstein. Perhaps through some momentary weariness, he had given over the attempt to write about his months in Dresden and Göttingen; but now, in the late thirties, settled in Cambridge, he was possessed by the desire to turn to a similar literary account those later experiences, during his second sojourn abroad, in Heidelberg, in Switzerland, in the Tyrol. *Outre-Mer* had abounded in the sense of all that was appealing to the imagination in the Latin, the Mediterranean cultures. Now it was the turn of Germany and the North, and *Hyperion* was to be the record of those more mature, more overcast, but hardly less impassioned travels among Germanic scenes and the expressions of the Germanic mind.

It, too, like *Outre-Mer*, was to be a sketchbook of a sort, but of a somewhat more ambitious sort. Longfellow called it a "romance," and given the poverty of our critical vocabulary, the word will do as well as any other. The Germans themselves would perhaps call it a *Reisenovelle*, a travel-tale, or even a *Wanderroman*, a novel of journeyings; and the form may have been suggested to Longfellow, at many removes, by *Wilhelm Meister's*

Apprenticeship or *Wilhelm Meister's Wanderyears* or, on a much more modest level, by a novella like Tieck's "A Summer Journey." *Hyperion*, at any rate, was not to be a mere portfolio of sketches but a piece of prose fiction with the benefit of a plot; the most tenuous of plots, to be sure, hardly more than substantial enough for a short story, but one that would serve as the airy scaffolding of a Sentimental Journey — a series of impressions of travel, drawings of "characters," incidental episodes, and as many digressions on literary and other subjects as he might wish to indulge in. It is a frankly loose-jointed and leisurely form, and Hawthorne, who admired *Hyperion*, perhaps recalled this form, twenty years later, when he came to write *The Marble Faun*, as Howells, who also admired it ("the lovely romance of 'Hyperion' "), may have recalled it, still later, when he came to write *Their Wedding Journey*. Poe rather missed the point when he objected that *Hyperion* was "without design, without shape, without beginning, middle, or end." It is certainly wanting in that severe unity of "effect" which Poe held to be the essential virtue of a short tale, but Longfellow was not aiming at any such result, and the shapeless shape of *Hyperion* has a legitimacy of its own.

The title may have been suggested to Longfellow by that of Hölderlin's then little-known epistolary and philosophical novel, but if so, this was a risky borrowing, and the rather grandiose mythic reference is far less suitable to Longfellow's slight romance than it was to Hölderlin's profoundly Hellenic one. The title merely indicated, Longfellow wrote to a friend, that "here is the life of one who in his feelings and purposes is a 'son of Heaven and Earth,' and who though obscured by clouds yet 'moves on high.' " This is tall talk as applied to Longfellow's pleasant young protagonist, and he would have seemed to claim less if he had called the book — as he wrote to Greene later, one hopes humorously, he might have done — by the appalling, but less pretentious, title, "Heart's Ease, or the Cure of a Morbid Mind." It matters very little; but "Heart's Ease," et cetera, would at least have indicated that the book was held together morally by the "lesson" Longfellow had also been preaching a few months earlier in "A Psalm of Life" — the lesson that a man may triumph over glooms and repinings "in constant, steady, cheerful endeavors, always willing and fulfilling, and accomplishing his task."

So Paul Flemming, his hero (the name was also that of a seventeenth-century German poet), observes to his Heidelberg friend, the young German Baron von Hohenfels. Flemming is a very American youth of a certain type — serious, intense, high-minded, a little humorless and prudish, but sensitive and imaginative, and above all, like one of James's young Americans — Clement Searle or Caroline Spencer — homesick for Europe, especially for the European past. He has been plunged into grief by some ill-defined bereavement, and is wandering about the Continent in the hope of distracting his mind from his sorrow. At a hotel in Interlaken he becomes acquainted with Mary Ashburton, a charming young Englishwoman traveling with her mother — again the situation is amusingly Jamesian — goes for walks with her in the environs, discusses art and poetry with her, and promptly falls deeply in love. Flemming's passion — like Longfellow's for Fanny Appleton — is unrequited, and when he realizes this, he leaves Interlaken broken-hearted. After recovering from a fever in Salzburg, however, he wanders on to Saint Gilgen, and there, on the walls of a little chapel, he sees a memorial tablet bearing an inscription that makes a deep impression on him:

> "Look not mournfully into the Past. It comes not back again. Wisely improve the Present. It is thine. Go forth to meet the shadowy Future, without fear, and with a manly heart."

In his own heart he finds an echo of this robust wisdom, and resolves henceforth not to lean on others, "but to walk self-confident and self-possessed," "to live in the Present wisely, alike forgetful of the Past, and careless of what the mysterious Future [may] bring." From that moment his strength returns to him, his thoughts revert to America, and he makes up his mind to turn his steps homeward. "Henceforth be mine a life of action and reality!"

There can be no doubt that some such resolution had a serious personal meaning for Longfellow, or that it is morally praiseworthy; in an abstract kind of way it is not very different from Wilhelm Meister's resolution at the end of his apprenticeship; but as it is embodied in *Hyperion* it hardly rises above earnest commonplace. We have never been given the slightest clue to the concrete form Flemming's resolution might take after returning to his energetic country; in what tangible and practical manner he might "improve the Present"; and this, among other things, deprives the romance of any true moral solidity, fictionally speaking. The real interest of *Hyperion*, only too obviously, lies not in the moral action, but in the divagations of one sort or another — they bulk too large to be called digressions — that make up the staple of the book. It was a great age of travel literature, not in the heroic Elizabethan sense, but in a more personal and impressionable one; and what doubtless most attracted Longfellow's readers at the time was *Hyperion*'s character as a pleasantly fictionalized guidebook. Americans were taking more and more to European journeys — Emerson was reproaching them, at about the same moment, for doing so — and whether as a substitute for actual travel or a reminder of it, *Hyperion* gave them an agreeable sense of moving about among the *Sehenswürdigkeiten* of the Rhine valley, the Alps, the Tyrol — the Rhine itself, the Rhone glacier, Mont Blanc at sunrise, the Jungfrau as seen from the Furca Pass, the ancient castle at Heidelberg, or the Franciscan church at Innsbruck.*

* This guidebook strain in Longfellow, which comes out also in such poems as "The Belfry of Bruges" and "Nuremberg," is amusingly parodied in a poem of John Betjeman's, "Longfellow's Visit to Venice (To be read in a quiet New England accent)."

Not that Longfellow proves himself, here any more than in *Outre-Mer*, a descriptive writer of great power; side by side with the great writers of this kind — with Ruskin, let us say — he is meager and hasty. He relies, for his effects of romantic wandering, not so much on sustained pieces of landscape painting or architectural evocation, as on his general genial movement from place to place by stagecoach or on foot; on his stops at inns with picturesque names, the White Horse or the Rheinischen Hof or the Golden Ship; and indeed, to a considerable extent, on the mere suggestive charm of the storied place-names themselves — Andernach, Bingen, the Odenwald, the Valley of Lauterbrunnen, Saint Wolfgang. The whole narrative is bathed in so sunny and ingenuous an atmosphere of vagrant nostalgia that the mere name of a village or a lake, a river or a mountain, is enough to set the fancy vibrating pleasantly, if not with much sonority. And so of the glimpses one is furnished of "real" life in Germany and Austria; they never draw one's eye to the reactionary realities of the thirties — the censorship, the repression, the political imprisonments — any more than similar glimpses in *Outre-Mer* draw one's eye to the Italy of the early Risorgimento. Longfellow's personal sympathies were entirely with the radicals of Young Germany and the revolutionaries in Italy, but to have struck that note in *Hyperion* would have been to shatter its poetic unity irremediably. This is not true of such scenes as that of a "Beer-Scandal" at a student's tavern in Heidelberg, or an Aesthetic Tea at a rich banker's house in Frankfort, or the funeral of a child in the churchyard of Saint Gilgen. There is a certain riotous vivacity, or mild social satire, or rustic pathos in scenes like these; and this was the Germany and Austria that a sentimental pilgrim like Paul Flemming would have responded to, not those of Metternich or Frederick William III.

Much more than to these rather set pieces of social description, however, *Hyperion* owes its undeniable, and even now appreciable, flavor and color to its pervasive and almost obsessive literariness. Longfellow, when he wrote it, was still living in the first glow of his enthusiasm, his *Begeisterung*, for German literature, and *Hyperion* is the engaging memento, like a giftbook or album, of his love affair with the German mind. No one before him, in this country, had plunged so eagerly into those romantic waters, or come up with so rich a haul of literary impressions; and he poured them out, in *Hyperion*, with a youthful prodigality. No doubt he was rifling his own lectures at Harvard when he did this, but if so, his stylistic sense saved him from an obvious error; he does not merely thrust passages from his lectures, like inorganic lumps of commentary, into the structure of his narrative. The literary talk in which the book abounds is always, and with real naturalness, worked into the fabric of the whole.

Much of it has kept its pristine brightness. At the table d'hôte of the Rheinischen Hof in Mayence, Flemming encounters a fat gentleman from Baireuth who proves to have been a friend of Jean Paul Richter's, and an animated dialogue ensues between the two of them on the subject of this, in both their estimations, incomparable author. Strolling about in Frankfort, Flemming and his friend the Baron carry on a conversation about Goethe which, in its give-and-take of enthusiasm and skepticism, reflects amusingly the division in Longfellow's own mind, still, at the time he wrote *Hyperion:* Flemming puts forward all the rather stuffy reservations on the subject that Longfellow was ultimately to discard. At the Golden Ship in Salzburg, as Flemming lies abed recovering from his fever, his traveling companion, the eccentric Englishman, Berkley, entertains him by talking, and talking very well, about E. T. A. Hoffmann, whom he had frequently seen in Berlin society. He even reads aloud to his sick friend a tale of Hoffmann's, the "Musical Sufferings of John Kreisler," in a particularly spirited translation of Longfellow's own. Earlier than this, at Interlaken, Flemming had held forth to Mary Ashburton, during one of their earnest colloquies, on the beauties of the German language and the charm of German poetry, and had improvised for her benefit translations from such poets as Uhland and Salis — "The Black Knight," "The Castle by the Sea," "The Song of the Silent Land." We might now wish that Flemming — and Longfellow — had preferred Novalis or Hölderlin to these forgotten, or almost forgotten, small poets; but there is a disarming exuberance, nevertheless, in his manner of extolling them.

On the strength of such talk as this, and other utterances, Longfellow is entitled to a small but secure niche in the history of our literary criticism. His critical writing, it is true, like his lecturing, is frankly subjective, appreciative, affirmative; his general literary *principles* are the commonplaces of romantic aesthetics, and his taste, fine as it often was, often too went sadly astray. At his best, however, he wrote sensitively, warmly, and imaginatively, like the poet he was, about the writers who delighted him. His most trustworthy resource as a critic was, like Lamb's and Hazlitt's, his command, in characterization, of metaphor and the evocative: his critical remarks abound in the kind of expressive imagery that conveys, without labored exposition, the special quality of the writer he is dealing with. Jean Paul's thoughts, for example, says the man from Baireuth, "are like mummies embalmed in spices, and wrapped about with curious envelopments; but within these the thoughts themselves are kings." The Englishman Berkley, attempting to convey to Flemming his sense of the demonic in Hoffmann, avers that when he reads him, "it is with me as when in the summer night I hear the rising wind among the trees, and the branches bow, and beckon with their long fingers, and voices go gibbering and mocking through the air." To turn away from *Hyperion* for a moment, Longfellow, in the preface to *The Poets and Poetry of Europe*, speaking of the inadequacy of all translations of poetry, remarks that they "do not always preserve the rhythm and melody of the original, but often resemble soldiers moving onward when the music has ceased and the time is marked only by the tap of the drum."

It is characteristic of his criticism to express itself not only in metaphor but in metaphor that depends for its appreciative effect on allusions and references that are charming in themselves, as when, in the same anthology, he remarks of German folksongs: "Among their thousand sweet and mingled odors criticism often finds itself at fault, as the hunter's hounds on Mount Hymettus were thrown off their scent by the fragrance of its infinite wild-flowers." But it is not only in his criticism that Longfellow's mind habitually reveals its natural grain through metaphor and allusion: his prose in general sparkles with imagery and reference, fanci-ful, pretty, sometimes witty, sometimes inapt, but almost always delightful in itself. The prose of *Hyperion* owes its pleasantness, to a considerable extent, to this rococo ornament. Longfellow does not always eschew the mildly grotesque: Flemming's friend the Baron, remarking on the tenacity with which a fixed idea can root itself in the mind, observes that such an idea is "like the watchman's wife, in the Tower of Waiblingen, who grew to such a size, that she could not get down the narrow staircase, and when her husband died, his successor was forced to marry the fat widow in the Tower." This ornamental imagery is usually lit-erary and associative, but sometimes it is unexpectedly un-bookish and "native," as it is when Flemming, wishing to express his feeling that philosophical speculations are often aimless and anticlimactic, compares them to "those roads in the Western for-ests of my native land, which, though broad and pleasant at first, and lying beneath the shadow of great branches, finally dwindle to a squirrel track, and run up a tree!"

Allusiveness curls itself about the structure of Longfellow's prose like the floriated or foliated scrolls of arabesque decoration. At times this allusiveness is in questionable taste, as it is when we are told, much too majestically, that Mary Ashburton's beautiful figure passed before Flemming's vision "like the form of Beatrice through Dante's heaven." But as a rule it is innocent enough, and it seems inexhaustible. The Baron von Hohenfels is said to resemble, both in person and character, Harold the Fair-Hair of Norway in the Icelandic death-song of Regner Hairy-Breeches (Ragnar Lodbrók). The landlord of the hotel at Interlaken reminds Flemming of the innkeeper in *The Golden Ass* "who had been changed by magic into a frog, and croaked to his customers from the lees of a wine-cask." Weak minds that come to terms too easily with the passions they cannot control, are compared to the Byzantine emperor Isaac Angelus, who made a treaty with the heathen Saladin and tried to purchase the Holy Sepulchre for gold; and those dull persons who are deaf to the voice of local association, even on great battlefields, are said to resemble "the old grammarian Brunetto Latini" — Dante's teacher — who "met on the plain of Roncesvalles a poor student riding on a bay mule." In this florescence of imagery and allusion Longfellow's prose suggests the practice of the English romantic prose-writers, Lamb, De Quincey, Carlyle. He may be less weighty, but he is not less prodigal, than they.

He gives variety to the slender narrative of *Hyperion* not only in these ways but, as in *Outre-Mer*, by the tales and legends that are scattered along the ambling course of the story. These are often agreeable in themselves, and Longfellow exhibits a real skill in adapting the manner of the telling to the character of the teller. The young daughter of the landlady at Salzig, rowing Flemming across the Rhine, tells him, in her ingenuous way, the story of the two castles of Liebenstein and the Sternenfels which tower above them; and there is a similar naïveté in the manner in which the innkeeper's grandmother, in another village, relates to him the pious tale of the Christ of Andernach. In a wholly different vein, one that suggests Poe rather than the folktale, is the story Flemming tells Mary Ashburton, in an attempt to touch her heart, of the student Hieronymus who comes upon the Fountain of Oblivion in the deepest solitude of the Black Forest, and sees in the limpid depths of the Fountain "the great City of the Past, with silent marble streets, and moss-grown walls, and spires uprising with a wave-like, flickering motion." The City of the Past, in which Hieronymus beholds, as Longfellow loved to do, the scenes and the friends of his boyhood, is a less uncanny version of Poe's City in the Sea. Quite unlike this pretty piece of romantic allegory is the curiously affecting story told to Flemming and Berkley, as they sit by a fountain at Saint Wolfgang, by the mad monk Brother Bernardus. He has been converted from Romanism, he tells them, by his intense studies and meditations — converted to a vision of the one true Church that shall unite all peoples; he insists that he has been called by the Spirit to journey to America as Minister Extraordinary of Christ, and there to begin his great work of reform. The insane calm and circumstantiality with which Brother Bernardus tells his story ring so true as to suggest that Longfellow was drawing upon some actual encounter.

In spite of his ambitions for it, *Hyperion* is at best a slight and imponderous book, and in some stretches the thinness of the air makes one breathe in gasps; but it keeps its modest place as a minor classic thanks to the infectiousness of its Europe-cult, the youthful vitality of its literary enthusiasms, and the attractiveness of its incidental tales. *Kavanagh*, which Longfellow wrote a decade later, is even slighter and more imponderous than *Hyperion;* one feels that the merest puff from the lips of criticism would shatter it, and indeed it seems to have proved to Longfellow himself that prose fiction was not, for him, a mode worth pursuing any further. Yet it was written, as he said, *con amore,* and an indulgent criticism will find, even now, elements of tenuous, but not merely imaginary, interest in it. We can hardly, it is true, go along with Emerson, who, incredibly, thought *Kavanagh* "the best sketch we have seen in the direction of the American novel," or even with Hawthorne, who thought it "a most precious and rare book, as fragrant as a bunch of flowers and as simple as one flower." Yet, with a little effort, we can see why it pleased both of them, as we can see why, twenty years later, Howells could speak of its "delicate truthfulness." It *has* a certain veracity, just as it has a certain faint and flowerlike fragrance.

It is the fragrance of American pastoral. Like the stories of the local colorists which began to appear some time afterward, *Kavanagh* is an elegy on the old-fashioned village life of New England that was already, when he wrote, beginning to recede into oblivion, though Longfellow felt this before it had become a commonplace. Fairmeadow is a Yankee village of the old order, perhaps in Maine; quiet, sleepy, isolated, innocent, and, despite its occasional outbursts of contentiousness, essentially sound. It does not have long to preserve these virtues uncontaminated. The Grand Junction Railroad is opened through the town, destroying its "rural quiet and seclusion," and the inhabitants, visited every day by this "ogre," become restless, excited, and ambitious. When Arthur Kavanagh comes back after an absence of three years, he finds Fairmeadow completely transformed from a simple village to "a very precocious town." Like Sarah Orne Jewett's Dunnet, forty years later, though less memorably and less poignantly, it has sold its birthright for a mess of progress.

Kavanagh is far less rich in local substance than *The Country of the Pointed Firs*, but one recognizes the author of "The Bald Eagle," nevertheless, in the genuine and gentle humor with which some of his village types are sketched. The voice of Dickens, it is true, is at times somewhat too audible, as it is in the person of the little taxidermist, Moses Merryweather, "Dealer in Singing Birds, foreign and domestic," or in that of Hiram A. Hawkins, dealer in English linens and carpets, who has changed his name to H. Adolphus Hawkins, and goes in for the composition of morbid verses. Yet even these individuals are not wholly untrue to village life, and other characters are unmistakably authentic — the loud-voiced cheerful doctor, the harsh-tongued and embittered Calvinist pastor (who is dismissed), Mr. Wilmerding, the young butcher (who weighs babies as well as meat in his scales), or Sally Manchester, a maid-of-all-work, "a treasure, if you can get her," whose disposition is not sweet, "but, as is sometimes said of apples by way of recommendation, a pleasant sour." In a quite different and unhumorous style is the sketch of the dignified and affable old judge, Cecilia Vaughan's father, "somewhat bent by his legal erudition, as a shelf is by the weight of the books upon it"; he may be a portrait-from-memory of Longfellow's grandfather.

There is also, and more conspicuously, a village schoolmaster, Mr. Churchill, a sort of Spoon River character long before Masters; a man of letters manqué, dreamy and poetic, who contemplates the writing of a great Romance, but is hindered by the vexatious routine of schoolteaching, by the demands of a growing family, and still more by his own feebleness of will, from ever finishing or indeed even beginning it. He makes the mistake, however, as Arthur Kavanagh sadly tells him, of supposing that the true themes of romance lie in the blue distance and not underfoot, close at hand, in the next street. Mr. Churchill recognizes this, but accepts even the fact of frustration and failure manfully. He is a stout-hearted Longfellow character, as we should expect, not a defeated village poet in Spoon River or Winesburg, Ohio.

He is a credible type in a New England village, and with his quaint literary erudition, his fanciful humor, and his ineffectual rebelliousness, he is characterized with a certain roundness. So much can hardly be said for Arthur Kavanagh, who gives his name to the title. Scion of an ancient Roman Catholic family in Maine, trained at a Jesuit college in Canada, he has weaned himself away from Romanism by what must be the most painless spiritual process in literature, and like Brother Bernardus — of whom he is, in this particular, rather strangely a copy — has arrived at the conception of a "union of all sects into one church universal." His preaching at Fairmeadow is so benevolent, so liberal, as to inspire the suspicion, in his predecessor's mind, that his views are "nothing better than rank Arianism and infidelity"; but these views are apparently so mildly enunciated that they arouse no protest in his congregation. Kavanagh, indeed, is not a realized character, but a mere projection of Longfellow's generous, though extremely misty, theological ideas.

One chapter in *Kavanagh*, however, is written with a good deal more animation than any of the churchly passages — a chapter in which Longfellow exhibits a greater knack for literary satire, at broad and rather mordant caricature, than, in spite of the Aesthetic Tea in *Hyperion*, one would have guessed him to have. He had taken sides in the debate that raged throughout the forties between the partisans of literary nationalism and the partisans of universalism.* As if he had forgotten the patriotic and youthful ardor of his commencement oration, he had joined forces with the traditionalists of the *Knickerbocker*, and arrived at the view that, in literature at least, nationalism is a shallow delusion. He was never at his best in dealing with general ideas, and in fact he was so rootedly American that he could feel no need to flaunt his literary loyalty. For the moment, and with no serious consequences to his work, he lined himself up with the universalists. Certainly some members of the nationalist party had made spectacles of themselves.

Their humorless and tasteless bombast is what Longfellow is satirizing in the twentieth chapter of *Kavanagh*. He probably had in mind a certain Cornelius Mathews, editor of a magazine called *Yankee Doodle*, in sketching the figure of the brash Mr. Hathaway who arrives one day to pester Mr. Churchill — for the minister has, after all, written for periodicals — to contribute to a new magazine he proposes to launch and thinks he will call "The Niagara." "In a rather florid and exuberant manner," this person declares that what we need is a national literature "commensurate

* The story of this debate is fully and interestingly told by Perry Miller in *The Raven and the Whale* (1956).

with our mountains and rivers, — commensurate with Niagara, and the Alleghanies, and the Great Lakes"; a national epic to correspond to the size of the country; a national drama "in which scope enough shall be given to our gigantic ideas"; in short, "a national literature altogether shaggy and unshorn, that shall shake the earth, like a herd of buffaloes thundering over the prairies!" He describes to the long-suffering Mr. Churchill the work he is now engaged upon, a great national drama the scene of which is laid in New Mexico and in which cock-fighting seems to play a conspicuous role.* He recommends to the schoolmaster the work of a certain poet named Honeywell, whom Nature made "with her shirt-sleeves rolled up," and who "succeeds equally well in the plaintive and didactic style of Wordsworth, and the more vehement and impassioned style of Byron."

If Mr. Hathaway's rhodomontade is a parody of Cornelius Mathews — and even, by anticipation, of Whitman — Mr. Churchill's rejoinders are an unintentional parody of the universalists, so tepid are they, so stale in thought, so peppered with exasperating half-truths. Who wished, even in 1849, to be told that literature is "rather an image of the spiritual world, than of the physical," or that what is best in the great poets is not what is national in them but what is universal, or that, if we are simply "natural," we shall be sufficiently national? In making the schoolmaster a mouthpiece for such views, Longfellow made him, for the moment, a complacent bore. This did not keep him from dashing off a spirited caricature in his representation of Mr. Hathaway. And there is literary amusement, too, in the figure of the young lady poet Clarissa Cartwright, who descends upon Mr. Churchill one day — fixing upon him "the full, liquid orbs of her large eyes" — with an appeal to him to read and criticize her poems. These works are

---

* Only a year or two earlier Longfellow himself seems to have projected a Mexican drama, to be called "Don Serafin, or The Marquis of the Seven Churches," with scenes in the cockpit and the circus! If he meant this seriously, which seems unlikely, he was parodying himself in *Kavanagh*.

contained in a large manuscript bound in crimson velvet, and the poetess explains to Mr. Churchill that she hopes to publish them in a volume to be entitled "Symphonies of the Soul, and other Poems." The original of Clarissa Cartwright had descended upon Longfellow himself a few days before he wrote this passage.

Kavanagh owes such vitality as it has to elements like these, and not at all to its flimsy and sentimental plot. This plot involves two young female friends, the fair, delicate, oversensitive Alice Archer and the ardent Cecilia Vaughan, who are, according to Longfellow, "in love with each other." Their relations might have formed a study in what James spoke of as "those friendships between women which are so common in New England," and which he dramatized so veraciously in *The Bostonians*. But there is so little human reality in either Alice or Cecilia — they are observed at such a gingerly distance and characterized so diaphanously — that they cannot be compared for a moment with Olive Chancellor and Verena Tarrant. They both fall in love, somewhat improbably, with the soulful Arthur Kavanagh, but since he is unaware of Alice's rather unearthly passion for him, and has an eye only for her friend, he proposes to Cecilia and is accepted. This is the signal, according to the code of fictional sentiment, for Alice to fall into a decline, to waste away rather picturesquely, and before long to expire. Arthur and Cecilia are married, after Alice has been laid away in a lonely grave, and set out on a journey to Italy and the East, where Arthur hopes to inspire in other hearts "the desire and prophecy that filled his own, — the union of all sects into one universal Church of Christ." Nothing could be more nebulous than this project, and it is left hanging idealistically in the air. The main action of *Kavanagh* is wholly without fictional solidity or serious truth. Longfellow had some but not most of the specific gifts of the novelist, and *Kavanagh*, despite the pleasure he took in writing it, seems to have taught him this. Very fortunately, on the whole, he was done with prose fiction for the rest of his literary life.

In the thirteenth chapter of *Kavanagh* we are told that Mr. Churchill is in the habit of recording in pencil, on the panels of an old white pulpit in his study, the thoughts that have come to him in his meditative moods. Two or three pages of these thoughts follow, couched in single sentences or very brief paragraphs of an aphoristic or epigrammatic sort. A few years later, in getting out a collected edition of his prose writings, Longfellow gathered together in a section called "Drift-Wood" a number of his fugitive critical essays and, along with them, another small collection of thoughts to which he gave the familiar title "Table-Talk"; this was composed of notes like Mr. Churchill's. Many years later, after his death, Samuel Longfellow included still a third selection from Longfellow's notebooks in his *Final Memorials* of his brother. No one would expect to find in Longfellow's Table-Talk the profundity one often finds in Coleridge's or the intellectual radiance one finds in Emerson's journals. But these unpretentious jottings of his have a quality of their own, a dimmer and milder but authentic quality of delicate allusiveness or of metaphoric fancy; and a few of them may be worth quoting here:

> Translating the first line in the Divine Comedy is like making the first move in a game of chess; nearly every one does it in the same way.

> Many critics are like woodpeckers, who, instead of enjoying the fruit and shadow of a tree, hop incessantly around the trunk, pecking holes in the bark to discover some little worm or other.

> Authors, in their Prefaces, generally speak in a conciliatory, deprecating tone of the critics, whom they hate and fear; as of old the Greeks spake of the Furies as the Eumenides, the benign Goddesses.

> Rather cheerless is the aspect of our early history. The stern old puritanical character rises above the common level of life; it has a breezy air about its summits, but they are bleak and forbidding.

In the mouths of many men soft words are like roses that soldiers put into the muzzles of their muskets on holidays.

So innate and strong is the love of liberty in all human hearts that, even against our better judgment, we instinctively sympathize with criminals escaping from prison.

Love makes its record in deeper colors as we grow out of childhood into manhood; as the Emperors signed their names in green ink when under age, but when of age, in purple.

The tragic element in poetry is like Saturn in alchemy, — the Malevolent, the Destroyer of Nature; but without it no true Aurum Potabile, or Elixir of Life, can be made.

More and more do I feel, as I advance in life, how little we really know of each other. Friendship seems to me like the touch of musical-glasses, — it is only contact; but the glasses themselves, and their contents, remain quite distinct and unmingled.

Our passions never wholly die; but in the last cantos of life's romantic epos, they rise up again and do battle, like some of Ariosto's heroes, who have already been quietly interred, and ought to be turned to dust.

VIII

The Middle Years

THE SEVEN years that followed Longfellow's retirement from Harvard were the happiest of his life — happier even, on the whole, than the three years of his first stay abroad, when he was often lonely and homesick. The years from forty-seven to fifty-four were a kind of genial late summer for him, a mellow Fructidor, in which every force seemed to coöperate with every other to content and fulfill him. Was he not free at last from the prison of academic duties, free from the grind of the classroom and the shoulder-pack of administration? Could a marriage, moreover, have been happier or better than his and Fanny Longfellow's? Could he have been more fortunate than he was — he who had so tender a feeling for childhood — in the presence and the devotion of his own five children, Charles, Ernest, Alice, Edith, and Annie Allegra? None of his friendships had failed him: Hawthorne, it is true, during most of these years, was absent, in England or Italy; Sumner, who had become a senator in 1851, was more and more engrossed in the antislavery struggle, and in Washington much of the time; Felton became president of the University in 1860, and died two years later, worn out with his fruitless labors. But Longfellow kept in steady touch with all these, and with such other old friends as George Greene, Sam Ward, Louis Agassiz, and Tom Appleton; and there were new and younger friends — James Russell Lowell, Charles Eliot Norton, James T. Fields — with whom his friendship became al-

most as warm as it had been with some of his contemporaries.*
Recognition as a writer, besides, could hardly have been more
complete than Longfellow's was, by this time, or less successfully
challenged; and just materially, thanks to his literary rewards and
his wife's fortune, his life was as easy and as free from pinch as
that of any American writer has ever been. Things went on at the
Craigie House in their settled, spacious, mostly untroubled way;
and after 1850 the family took more and more to spending the
summers at Nahant, on the rocky shore north of Boston, where
Longfellow could be within sight and hearing of the sea — of its
tides, its wash against the rocks, its dreamlike calms, its restful
monotony, and, in spite of that, its infinitely changing aspects, of
which he never tired.

Happy as these years were, however, it would be a falsification
to represent them as merely placid. For one thing, even now,
Longfellow was not wholly free from the old physical torments,
neuralgia and eyestrain and the like, that had always betrayed the
imperfect serenity of his "buried" life. And on the public level
the deepening tensions of the fifties, the intensifying violence of
the sectional conflict, did not fail to inspire in him the most painful emotions, though temperamentally he could not express these
emotions in his work or throw himself into the active struggle.
He never wrote an "Ichabod" or a "Speech on Affairs in Kansas"
or a "Beat! Beat! Drums!" but, silent as he might be outwardly,

---

* Longfellow had become acquainted with George Washington Greene,
a grandson of General Nathaniel Greene, in Marseilles in 1827, when they
were both in their first youth; they traveled together in Italy and became
lifelong friends. Howells, who saw Greene occasionally as an elderly man
at the Craigie House, thought he resembled an old Italian house-priest in
manner, "gentle, suave, very suave, sooth as creamy curds, cultivated in
the elegancies of literary taste, and with a certain meek abeyance." Samuel
Ward, who called the poet "Longo," was a New York financier and man of
the world, a cousin of Greene's and a brother of Julia Ward Howe's.
Thomas G. Appleton, Mrs. Longfellow's brother, was another man of the
world and a famous Boston wit. It was he who said, of the statue of Horace
Mann in front of the State House, the work of a female sculptor, that it
should have been called "Mann, by Woman."

he felt as passionately about these questions, in his way, as Whittier or Emerson or Whitman did. Webster's Seventh of March speech, in 1850, had seemed to him a "most abominable" one, and the Fugitive Slave Law he believed was fit only to be broken. When, in 1851, Thomas Simms, an escaping Negro, had been arrested in Boston and sent back to slavery, though Longfellow took no part in the attempt to rescue him, he broke out in his journal: "This is the last point of degradation. Alas for the people who cannot feel an insult!" Unlike the conservatives of Boston and Cambridge, he had been in full sympathy all along, and not merely on friendly grounds, with Sumner's "extremism" in the struggle against slavery; and when Preston Brooks made his murderous attack on Sumner on the floor of the Senate, Longfellow exclaimed in a letter to his friend that he had no words to write to him about "this savage atrocity." Three years later, he declared that the day on which John Brown was hanged was a great day in our history, "the date of a new Revolution, — quite as much needed as the old one."

Longfellow's feeling for the Union had always been deep and strong, but he came to believe, as of course most men in the North did, that the Union was not worth preserving at the cost of endless concessions to the South; and in the fall of 1860 he felt that the election of Lincoln was nothing less than "the redemption of the country." "I hope," he wrote a little later, when some of the Southern states were on the verge of secession, "the North will stand firm, and not bate one jot of its manhood. Secession of the North from freedom would be tenfold worse than secession of the South from the Union." War, he had always been convinced, was "an infernal thing," but the Civil War, when it came, seemed to him "not a revolution, but a Catalinian conspiracy," and he had reconciled himself to the military struggle two or three months before the attack on Fort Sumter: "It is now too late," he wrote, "to put the fire out. We must let it *burn* out." Yet such convictions did not keep him from suffering deeply, during all the early months of 1861, from the dreadful sense of approaching catastrophe, and when hostilities finally came he was doubtless torn between a certain exultation and a profound sadness.

Distressed as he had been by these national disasters, Longfellow had not allowed them to distract him from the work he was now freer to do than he had ever been, and within a few weeks after he had given his last lecture, he was busy with another ambitious poem. No subject had haunted his imagination over a longer period than that of the Indians; an Indian fight had been the subject of his first boyish poem, "The Battle of Lovell's Pond," and, as we have seen, several of his undergraduate pieces had dealt with the tragedy of that race. He had pored over Heckewelder's book on the Indian tribes of Pennsylvania, and, like Cooper, had been much affected by it. The first consequence of this reading was a kind of dramatic debate with a classmate during his junior year — an "English Dialogue between a North American Savage and an English Emigrant" — in which Longfellow had played the sympathetic role of the savage, Metacomet or King Philip. He had certainly read Irving's essay, "Traits of Indian Character," and he wrote King Philip's role in the grave and highly figurative style that Irving, as well as others, had imitated ("The rivers run with blood, but never, never will we suffer the grass to grow upon our war-path"). In the fall of his second year at Harvard he had been much excited by a kind of powwow of Sauk and Fox Indians, including the great Black Hawk himself, on the Boston Common, with their war-clubs, bears' teeth, and buffalo scalps; and in 1849 he had entertained at his house a good-looking young Ojibway chief and poet named, somewhat gutturally, Kah-ge-ga-gah'-bowh, and heard him lecture in Boston, in his chief's costume, ramblingly but gracefully, on the religion, poetry and eloquence of the Indian.* The reading of

* Hiawatha, who, so far as he can be localized tribally, is also an Ojibway, is "young and tall and very handsome."

Schoolcraft, as we have seen, had had an effect on *Evangeline*, and the idea of a long poem on Indian life and lore was probably latent in Longfellow's mind for some years before it came to realization.

What seems to have crystallized this intention was his reading, in the summer of 1854, of the great Finnish folk epic, the *Kalevala*, in German translation. The "virus of suggestion," as James would say, was planted in his mind by this reading. "I have at length," he noted in his journal, "hit upon a plan for a poem on the American Indians, which seems to me the right one, and the only. It is to weave together their beautiful traditions into a whole." And, with the *Kalevala* before him, he added fatefully, "I have hit upon a measure, too, which I think the right and only one for such a theme." A day or two later he set to work on this poem — "Manabozho," as for a few days he considered calling it; "Hiawatha," as he soon came to think of it, less correctly but more euphoniously. He worked steadily and happily on it during the summer at Nahant, took it up again the following winter, and finished it late in March. It was published as *The Song of Hiawatha* in the fall of 1855, and immediately became the object of perhaps the most extravagant praise and the most extravagant detraction Longfellow had yet experienced.

The detraction gave him pain, hypersensitive as he was to critical censure, but this was overbalanced by the immense popularity of the poem and by tributes from other writers whom he respected — Emerson, for one, who, though he had no great regard for the Indians, wrote to Longfellow that he found *Hiawatha* "very wholesome; sweet and wholesome as maize." Only a few months later Longfellow had turned to another undertaking. A friend of his, Emmanuel Scherb, a German poet, had suggested to him the idea of a poem on the persecution of the Quakers by the New England Puritans; seventeenth-century New England seems already to have been a preoccupation of Longfellow's during these years, and before long he began, not a poem, but a tragedy in prose which he called at first "The Old Colony" and later "Wenlock Christison." For some reason, perhaps because the prose dialogue gave him trouble, Longfellow was dissatisfied with this play after he had finished it, and although, in the summer of 1860, he had a few copies set up in type with the title of "The New England Tragedy," he was never to publish it in this form.

Meanwhile, he had begun another play on a New England subject, not this time a tragedy but a kind of comedy. One of Longfellow's ancestors on his mother's side had been John Alden, a member of that small band of Separatists who had founded the colony of Plymouth. There was a traditional story of Alden's having undertaken to woo his future wife, Priscilla Mullins, not on his own behalf but on that of the bashful Miles Standish; and this mildly humorous incident was the subject of his play. Again, however, he seems not to have been contented with his dramatic treatment of it, and a year later, having set it aside for a time, he went back to the theme, rewrote the play in the form of what he called "a kind of Puritan pastoral," a narrative poem in hexameters, and published it as *The Courtship of Miles Standish* in the fall of 1858. All this while he had been publishing short poems in the magazines — *Putnam's*, the *Atlantic*, and others — but not since *The Seaside and the Fireside* had he made a collection of them; now, included in the *Miles Standish* volume were more than a score of such pieces under the group title "Birds of Passage." As time went on, Longfellow fell into the way of using this pleasant title ("Birds of Passage, Flight the Second," and so on) for groups of short poems included in the same volume with longer ones.*

Drawn though he was, during the late fifties, to the New England past, it was not in Longfellow's nature to limit his poetic life to the history of his own country: he moved back and forth,

---

* "Birds of Passage" is the name of a poem originally included in *The Seaside and the Fireside*, but Longfellow later used it as a proem to the lyrical poems in the *Miles Standish* volume.

as we have seen, between his native culture and the European in
an alternation as natural and effortless as that of the tides. The old
Norse world, among others, the world of the sea-kings and the
great earls, never lost its claim on his imagination; and when,
early in 1859, he was struck by the thought that a very good
poem might be made out of the life of King Olaf, who converted
the North to Christianity, he turned back to the *Heimskringla,* the
history of the Norse kings that Snorri Sturlason, the Icelandic
chieftain, had written in the thirteenth century, and especially
to that part of it called "King Olaf Tryggvason's Saga." This re-
reading confirmed him in his enthusiasm for the subject, and during the month of Lincoln's election — when his mood was one
of almost bellicose elation — he composed a series of balladlike
cantos about the contentious Olaf, one each day, that, with a few
later additions, were to make up his own "Saga of King Olaf." It
might have made an attractive small book in itself, and perhaps
Longfellow had some such plan in mind, but a dreadful stroke fell
upon him before he could have carried it out, and "The Saga of
King Olaf" did not appear until three years later, when it was included as the Musician's Tale in *Tales of a Wayside Inn.*

George William Curtis once told Howells that, one summer day
in 1861, he had been driving past the Craigie House with Dr.
Holmes, and that the latter had said he trembled to look at the
house, "for those who lived there had their happiness so perfect
that no change, of all the changes which must come to them,
could fail to be for the worse." It was a strangely premonitory
thought. Only a short time later, that perfect happiness was destroyed by a peculiarly cruel and shocking blow. Fanny Longfellow, sitting one day in the library before an open window,
dropped some burning wax, or perhaps a lighted match, on her
summer dress, and in a moment she was wrapped in flames.
Though Longfellow, awakened from a nap in his study nearby,

attempted to put out the flames by throwing a small rug about her, she was already too terribly burned to be saved, and on the following day she died. Longfellow himself had been so badly burned about his face and hands that he was unable to attend her funeral at Mount Auburn three days later. It was the anniversary of their wedding day.

The blow was an almost mortal one, and for months Longfellow lived in a continuous agony of grief. At first his mind wandered, and he feared that he would go mad. He told Felton that he dreaded to recover from the pain of his own injuries, for then he would have to take up "the great burthen," and did not know how he should carry it. When another visitor expressed the hope that he might be enabled to bear his cross patiently, he answered in his anguish, "*Bear* the cross, yes; but what if one is stretched upon it!" It was a mystery to him why he did not die, but like many men before and since, he did *not* die even of a draught that might well have seemed lethal. As time went on, his native firmness of spirit, together with his constitutional resilience, brought about a slow, wavering, and always imperfect recovery, though even in the spring of 1862 he could write to Freiligrath that it was very difficult for him to build up again his shattered life: "It crumbled away," he said, "like sand." He was never able to speak freely of his loss even to his closest friends, and in his verse he could speak of it only indirectly, as he did in such poems as "Palingenesis," "The Bridge of Cloud," and, nearly twenty years later, "The Cross of Snow."

For months he was quite unable to apply himself to work of any difficulty, but he gradually realized that if he was to go on living, it was imperative that he should have recourse to the healing powers of intellectual labor. Fortunately an uncompleted task lay ready to his hand. More than twenty years earlier, in *Voices of the Night,* Longfellow had published a translation of four passages from the *Divine Comedy* — parts of four cantos of the Purgatorio — and in 1843 he had written to Freiligrath that he had translated altogether sixteen cantos of that canticle. It had been work of the most congenial sort, for Dante had long been a passion with him, and he loved the task of translation in general. Some years had passed, however, and it was only in the early fifties that he had found the right moment for resuming the work, but then he had done so, and in the year before his retirement he had completed the whole of the Purgatorio. There for some years the matter rested, but now, painfully unoccupied as he was, the thought came to him that he might take up again his unfinished Dante, and early in 1862 he settled himself to the therapeutic task of translating the Paradiso. In spite of his misery, the work went with Longfellow's accustomed fluency; for days at a time he translated a canto every day, and the Paradiso was finished before the year's end. By April, 1863, he had translated the whole of the Inferno, too, and the entire *Comedy* was at last completed.

Or rather a first draft of it — for Longfellow had become, if indeed he had not always been, a perfectionist in translation, and he had no sooner finished the Inferno than he set about the task of revising the whole *Comedy*. He began by having it set up in type so that he might work with proof sheets, and at some time in 1864 he had the happy thought of calling upon two of his friends, Lowell and Norton, both of them, like himself, erudite Danteans, to meet with him on Wednesday evenings and give him the benefit of their instructed criticism. It was the beginning of a long and happy association. Other friends took part in these sessions from time to time, Greene and Howells and Fields; but Lowell and Norton were the regulars, and the meetings of the Dante Club soon became a kind of literary scholar's wish-dream. Longfellow would begin by reading aloud a single canto, and then his friends, comparing his version with the original, would discuss the various readings, consider the real meaning of obscure words and phrases, seek for the most exact English equivalent of Dante's expressions, and praise or protest with complete

freedom and amiability. Longfellow's sweetness, his amenable-
ness to criticism, his modesty, were unfailing, though Howells
says that, when he could not accept a suggestion, "the passage
had to go as he said." At about ten o'clock the discussion would
come to an end, and host and guests would sit down to a supper of
cold turkey or a haunch of venison, a salad, and appropriate wines.
In 1867 the whole process was finished, and Longfellow's *Divine
Comedy* was published in May. The Club as such no longer met,
but a decade and a half later, at a meeting at Longfellow's house,
the Dante Society sprang from its ashes.

Meanwhile, a few months after he resumed his work on Dante,
Longfellow had begun work on a poetic plan that was to keep
him pleasantly occupied, off and on, for some ten years. This
was the series of tales in verse within a narrative frame, like Boccaccio's or Chaucer's, which were to be known as *Tales of a
Wayside Inn.* Some such design had been in Longfellow's mind
for many years; already in 1846 he had jotted down in his "Book
of Suggestions" the scheme of a group of tales told by emigrants
crossing the Rocky Mountains — "The Indian's Tale," "The
Trapper's Tale," and the like. This was a pretty infelicitous inspiration: one hardly sees Longfellow telling stories successfully
through the lips of trappers and *voyageurs;* and the scheme was
fortunately abandoned. Now, in 1862, a far more promising
conception occurred to him; now it was to be a group of friends
— cultivated men whose characters were to be suggested by actual acquaintances of Longfellow's — gathered together in the
parlor of an ancient rustic hostelry, the Red Horse Inn at Sudbury, on an autumn evening, and beguiling the time by telling
one another stories. "The Saga of King Olaf" became one of
them, and there were six others. *Tales of a Wayside Inn* was published in 1863; it was so popular, and writing of this sort was so
agreeable to Longfellow, that a second and then a third series
proved irresistible, and they were published in 1872 and the following year in *Three Books of Song* and *Aftermath.* In 1867 he

published, for the first time since his wife's death, a collection of short poems; it was called *Flower-de-Luce*.

Early the next year he had gone back to his unsatisfactory tragedy about the Quakers; the subject of persecution "for cause of conscience" had continued to haunt him, and now, in another effluence of energy — "it took hold of me," he said, like "a kind of possession" — he rewrote it entirely in verse in something like ten days. The play was still called "Wenlock Christison." Almost immediately Longfellow set to work on a play dealing with a closely related subject, that of witchcraft in New England, which he had long had in mind, and so completely was he by this time master of his subject that this play too was written in hardly more than a few days. He called it "Giles Corey of the Salem Farms," and the two plays together were published in the fall of 1868 under the common title *The New England Tragedies*. Two or three years later he meditated a third play that might have formed a trilogy with these two; it would have dealt with the Moravians at Bethlehem, and Longfellow hoped that it might "harmonize the discord of the New England Tragedies." But it is hard to see how the peculiarly pacific existence of the Moravians could have lent itself to dramatic treatment, and nothing came of the thought. Nor is it clear that, when he published *The New England Tragedies*, Longfellow conceived of them as belonging to the larger trilogy which was still incomplete.

He had now, as he approached his sixtieth year, become an almost legendary figure; in the popular mind, the Poet *par excellence*, the very incarnation of song and story, and to many of his fellow writers our own equivalent of Tennyson or Victor Hugo. His appearance itself had taken on that vatic or bardic character by which he is mostly remembered. Of course it had not always been so. One of his teachers at Bowdoin recalled Henry Longfellow simply as an attractive boy, slight but erect in figure, with abundant chestnut hair, expressive blue eyes, a clear blooming complexion, and well-bred manners; and even in his thirties Julia Ward was struck by his remarkably fresh and youthful appearance, which she later said he long preserved. As a man in his forties Longfellow had acquired a more mature and commanding look, mild and self-effacing as he normally was; and a Newport bookseller thought he looked more like a sea captain than a poet. Samuel Lawrence's crayon portrait of the fifties, which William Winter thought his best likeness, confirms this impression. The strong, vigorously outlined, clean-shaven face has no hint of mere mildness in it, and the masterful poise of the head, the alertness of the eyes, and the firm line of the lips, full and sensitive as they are, do indeed suggest a nature capable of command. A few years later, because of his burns, he could no longer shave, and was forced to let his beard grow; his hair and his beard were more and more streaked with gray and then turned quite white, and at length his appearance took on the air of eminent and indeed noble old age. Björnstjerne Björnson, struck by something almost iconographic in his look, and remembering an old Norse phrase, "the White Christ," spoke of him as "the White Mr. Longfellow." In his air of "immovable serenity and of a benignity which has learned to condone all human sins," Higginson thought that only Turgenev, of all the distinguished writers he had known, approached Longfellow; and for the Abbé Casgrain of Quebec, Parkman's friend, he was the embodiment in appearance of an elder-day bard or sage: "It is thus," he said, "that Ossian, Baruch, or Camoens is represented."

The Abbé Casgrain was undoubtedly familiar with Longfellow's work, at the very least with *Evangeline* in French translation; long before this — from early in the forties — Longfellow had begun to be the beneficiary, or the victim, and not only the practitioner, of the translator's arduous art. He is said to be, however, like Byron, relatively easy to translate, and one can believe that this is so: his language — limpid, uneccentric, free from all "obscurity," and not exploitative of the more special traits of English or American speech — has in itself a kind of international linguistic character, like some Esperanto for poets; and, at any rate, the business of translating him into most of the literate languages had gone on apace. Beyond the bounds of America or Great Britain, thousands, perhaps tens of thousands, came to know him as the author of *Evangelina* or *Die Brautwerbung des Miles Standish, La Légende Dorée* or *Zlota Legenda, Il Canto di Hiawatha* or *Sangen om Hiawatha, Longfellow's Gedighten* or *Alcune Poesie di Enrico W. Longfellow.* An admirer in China sent the poet a translation of the "Psalm of Life" into Mandarin Chinese on a fan. This was probably the most decorative of all translations of his work; probably the most eminent of all his *translators* was Baudelaire, who paraphrased the first canto of *Hiawatha*, "The Peace-Pipe," as "Le Calumet de Paix," in sonorous Alexandrines, rhyming in six-line stanzas, that make Longfellow sound startlingly like Alfred de Vigny or Victor Hugo:

> Or Gitche Manito, le Maître de la Vie,
> Le Puissant, descendit dans la verte prairie,
> Dans l'immense prairie aux coteaux montueux;
> Et là, sur les rochers de la Rouge Carrière,
> Dominant tout l'espace et baigné de lumière,
> Il se tenait debout, vaste et majestueux.*

Baudelaire quite properly calls his version an imitation, not a translation, and even these few lines make it clear that he is far

---

* This is of course the French equivalent of the only-too-familiar lines:

> On the Mountains of the Prairie,
> On the great Red Pipe-stone Quarry,
> Gitche Manito, the mighty,
> He the Master of Life, descending,
> On the red crags of the quarry
> Stood erect, and called the nations,
> Called the tribes of men together.

In Longfellow, needless to say, Gitche Manito does not "dominate all space," and he is neither "bathed in light" nor "immense and majestic": this is French romantic rhetoric, and it is splendid in its kind.

from slavishly literal. Probably, in any case, no other American writer except Mark Twain has been translated so widely or so often as Longfellow.

It was one of the consequences, and sometimes one of the penalties, of Longfellow's universal fame that, during all these years and to the end of his life, the Craigie House was the resort of an endless succession of visitors, both distinguished and obscure, both fellow countrymen and callers from abroad. Hardly an English man of letters, traveling in America, failed to pay his respects to this most beloved of American writers, and often they were entertained at meals. Dickens, on his first trip to this country, had been given "a bright little breakfast" — the brightness of which seems not to have been dimmed by the presence of "the Unitarian pope," Andrews Norton — and the two young writers struck up a lifelong friendship. Such men as Trollope, Charles Kingsley, Wilkie Collins, and Monckton Milnes arrived on Brattle Street as a matter of course. When Dom Pedro II, Emperor of Brazil, was traveling in this country, not officially but privately — like a modern Haroun al Raschid, said Longfellow — he expressed his desire to dine with the poet, and rather imperially named the persons — Emerson, Lowell, and Holmes — whom he wished also to have invited. Perhaps the most unlikely visitor, from our point of view, was the Russian anarchist Mikhail Bakúnin, who had escaped from Siberia a few months earlier and, having made his way eastward across the Pacific, en route to Europe, had reached the northern United States, and came to call at the Craigie House. He stayed so long, Ernest Longfellow tells us, that he had to be invited to lunch; "Yiss," he answered, "and I will dine with you too" — as he did. He may have proved a somewhat fatiguing guest — his vehemence was notorious — but Longfellow seems to have been charmed by him, and describes him in his journal as "a giant of a man, with a most ardent, seething temperament."

These were distinguished visitors, but they did not outnum-

ber the succession of simple, often touching, and sometimes af-
flicting callers, mostly Americans, who came to constitute a serious problem for Longfellow, but who were invariably received
with courtesy and consideration — though some of them belonged in that category of "books, bores, and beggars" which
even he came to count as one of the principal vexations of daily
life. Fortunately his humor was usually equal to the occasion, and
he could describe some of his guests with characteristic good nature. There was the Englishman who remarked that, in other
countries, you know, we go to see ruins and all that — "but you
have no ruins in your country, and I thought I would call and see
you." There was the young Westerner who asked Longfellow
how old he was, and when the poet answered "Seventy," re-
joined, "I have seen a good many men of your age who looked
much younger than you." A German woman, with a strong accent, called to talk with him about "The Building of the Ship,"
which she was planning to read in public, and which she called
"The Lunch of the Sheep." As he was standing at the front
door one August morning, a woman in black came up to him
and inquired whether this was the house in which Longfellow
had been born; when he explained that it was not, she went on to
ask, "Did he die here?"

His correspondence, too, had assumed appalling proportions,
and his kindness was too genuine to allow him to turn a deaf ear
to any of it. Most of the appeals he received, of course, were requests for his autograph, sometimes for *quantities* of autographs
to be sold at benefits and the like; perhaps there were not many
appeals, however, though there was one, for "your autograph in
your own handwriting." Many of these demands came from people who wished Longfellow to read and criticize their manu-
scripts, like the man in Maine who had written an epic poem on
the Creation, and had "done up" the six days' work "in about six
hundred lines." Other appeals were for original poems; a stranger
in the West put in an order for two poems "on friendship, or a

subject like that, for the album of a young lady who is a very particular friend"; he also directed Longfellow to "send the bill
with the articles." Still other requests were for information; one
correspondent wrote: "Please inform me whether or not your
feelings were in sympathy with your immortal thought when you
wrote the poem of the 'Bridge.'" Fortunately he was able to
smile at such oddities as these, and probably to return a kindly
answer, but countless hours of his time were consumed by these
demands on his amenity, and he suffered from the thought that
they were hours which he could have devoted to his own work
and which would never return. On the whole, however, he suffered patiently and philosophically.

It was now, in the late sixties, almost twenty-five years since
Longfellow had revisited Europe in actuality; in memory and
imagination he had never ceased to revisit the scenes of his
youthful wanderings *outre-mer;* they hovered before him con-
tinually, mingling with the images that kept coming to him in his
European readings, and taking on more and more, no doubt, the
mysterious vividness of scenes and images in a dream. Thoughts
of going abroad for a fourth journey came to him frequently, and
friends in Europe kept urging him to make such a trip. But actual travel, with all its inconveniences and fatigues, had come to
seem to him more and more formidable; and he put off a European journey from year to year with an almost pleasant regretful-
ness. Now, however, seven years after his wife's death, his family at length prevailed on him — he was just over sixty — to let
them lead the way for him, and in the spring of 1868 he set
out for England with Ernest and his new wife, the three girls,
two sisters, a brother, and Tom Appleton. His stay abroad on
this fourth visit was to last eighteen months, months during which
he revisited England and Scotland, Paris, Switzerland, and Italy,
but — perhaps because he could not bear to — not Spain.

It was of course no longer a passionate pilgrimage, as his first journeys had been; it was an old-age revisitation, reminiscent, backward-turned, low-pitched, and, except outwardly, melancholy; and it had no important effect on anything he was yet to write. The rich and plethoric England of the sixties, the garish France of the Second Empire, even the new and energetic Italy of achieved unity — these can have said little to a poet of Longfellow's romantic sensibility, and perhaps they often repelled him. Moreover, he was not now an obscure young scholar, as he had been during his first and second visits, nor merely a very well-known poet, as he had been in 1842, but a writer of immense celebrity, who would have been, as everyone recognized, the American Poet Laureate if there had been such an office, and he had to pay a price for this eminence in the acceptance of conspicuous public honors and social hospitality. He was touched and gratified by all this, of course, but there was too little vanity, even too little amiable vanity, in his nature to make such recognitions anything but onerous as they occurred, and he was undoubtedly relieved when he could escape from them.

Soon after their arrival in England, the honorary degree of LL.D. was conferred upon Longfellow in the Senate House at Cambridge "in the presence of a large concourse of spectators"; a year later the degree of D.C.L. was conferred upon him at Oxford. In London Queen Victoria expressed a desire to see Mr. Longfellow, and he was summoned to an audience with her at Windsor; he called, a few days later, by request, on the Prince of Wales. Albert Bierstadt, the American painter, gave a great dinner in his honor, attended by "several hundred" celebrities, including Gladstone, who paid an eloquent tribute to the guest of honor. Pleasanter, or at least easier, than these occasions was a visit at Gadshill, with Dickens, an old friend, who had been in America the year before. At Farringford, on the Isle of Wight, he passed "a couple of delightful days" with Tennyson, who read "Boadicea" to him at midnight. Of the younger *avant-garde* — of Rossetti or Swinburne or Meredith — he caught not a glimpse, and their own indifference to his presence can be taken for granted.

Later in the summer the party moved on to Switzerland, where their stay at Interlaken must have abounded in intense memories for Longfellow. In Paris, that fall, he made little effort to meet and talk with fellow writers; is it easy, indeed, to imagine Longfellow conversing relaxedly, at a *dîner Magny*, with Flaubert or Gautier or Taine, or listening without discomfort to their un-Cantabridgian talk? He did, however, go to call on Sainte-Beuve, whose work he admired, in the rue Montparnasse, and when he asked his host — they were speaking of Chateaubriand and Lamartine — which of the two seemed to him the greater, Sainte-Beuve replied, "Charlatan for charlatan, I think I prefer M. de Lamartine." One evening, too, Norton took him to dinner to meet Ruskin, who happened to be in Paris, and who surprised him by the quiet gentlemanly way in which he gave vent to his extreme opinions. To Ruskin, for his part, Longfellow seemed "a quiet and simple gentleman," but "strangely innocent and calm." He had a respect for Longfellow's work, however, and there was later some correspondence between them. He and Norton, said Ruskin, were the two Americans he had known and loved best.

The winter was spent in Rome, where the party put up at a hotel on the site of Sallust's villa. One evening the artist G. P. A. Healy, who was painting Longfellow's portrait, took him to call on Liszt at his rooms in the abandoned convent of Santa Francesca, the composer welcoming them at the doorway with a lighted candle held high above his head and casting its rays on his very striking features. Liszt later set to music the Prologue to *The Golden Legend*. But Rome was depressing to Longfellow, to whom it seemed a beleaguered city, bombarded by new ideas but holding out against them, "and living on old shoes." He could no longer revel ingenuously in Rome as he had done forty years earlier.

In the spring they moved southward to Naples, spent a night on their way with the Benedictines at Monte Cassino — Longfellow sitting and conversing with a young monk, before a wood fire, late into the night — and made a trip to Amalfi, where he dreamed of the ancient wharves and quays now lying fathoms deep beneath the sea. He later wrote poems about both these places, one of which, "Monte Cassino," has a genuine charm. Three weeks were spent tranquilly at Sorrento, where they stayed at the Villa Nardi, looking out rather spectacularly on the Bay of Naples, and where, as they were being rowed back one day from Capri, Longfellow was delighted by their six lusty oarsmen, who sang at the tops of their voices "O Pescator del' onda" but pronounced it "O Pescator di Londra." In April they started north again, spent a few more weeks in Switzerland and England, and sailed for America in August, 1869. At the end of the month Longfellow found himself with joy back at the Craigie House. He was rarely to leave the environs of Boston again.

The trip, whatever its tediums or disappointments, proved to have been a refreshing parenthesis for Longfellow, and early the following year, with the vigor of a man half his age, he was busily at work once more. In January he began a second series of Wayside Inn tales, and a little later prepared a second and enlarged edition of *The Poets and Poetry of Europe*. The writing of stories in verse had become a happy form of expression for him, but beyond that, in the years since *The Golden Legend*, his mind had become more and more absorbed in the form of poetic drama, and this was his principal preoccupation in the early seventies. The great purpose, as it was for him, of producing a sacred trilogy, had never faded from his mind; he had perhaps begun to feel that *The New England Tragedies* might constitute its third "movement," but however that may have been, he was ready to begin at last on a first part, and in the fall of 1870 he was launched upon a poem dealing with the life of Christ. "The subject of the Divine Tragedy," he wrote the following winter, "has taken entire possession of me, so that I can think of nothing else." At the end of January the poem was finished, and late in 1871 it was published as *The Divine Tragedy*. The long-cherished design was now, in fact, complete. *The New England Tragedies*, the first of which he re-entitled "John Endicott," were definitely to be included; and after writing an Introitus as a prelude to the whole, two Interludes to serve as bridge-passages, and a Finale, Longfellow was at last ready, in 1872, to publish *Christus: A Mystery*.

Soon after finishing *The Divine Tragedy*, Longfellow had begun a third series of *Tales of a Wayside Inn*, but this was not to be finished for another year, and meanwhile, late in 1871, he turned back to a subject for tragedy that had first occurred to him twenty years earlier — another Biblical subject, this time from the Apocrypha. The "collison," as he called it, between Hellenism and Judaism, as it is recorded in the book of Maccabees, struck him as a genuinely tragic theme. The mother of the seven sons in II Maccabees seemed to him "the Jewish Niobe," and her death, following upon that of her sons, "the deepest and noblest tragedy." This was in 1850, and now, perhaps because the subject had germinated for so many years in his mind, he wrote the verse tragedy of *Judas Maccabæus* in the space, extraordinarily short even for him, of twelve days. It was published in *Three Books of Song* in the same year as *Christus*.

On the very day on which he finished *Judas* Longfellow noted in his journal: "A new subject comes to my mind, — Hagar and Ishmael." The Ishmaelite theme, of course, was one that had been dear to the heart of romantic writers, both in Europe and here, and it is curious to see Longfellow, for whom the figure of the Outcast had not been characteristic, turning so late as this to the familiar archetype. He was doubtful about the plan from the first, indeed, and though he wrote two scenes of such a play, he soon abandoned the subject for one that was to prove incomparably more congenial. This was the subject of the Hero as Artist, as Carlyle might have put it, and the artist in question, Michelangelo, was the one who, more than any other, had fascinated the imagination of the romantic era. Emerson, for whom he embodied the highest expression of the artist's power, had lectured on him many years earlier; and Longfellow was to live with the subject for much of the rest of his life. He felt the difficulty of the material from the beginning: "I shall have," he wrote, "as hard a time in casting this statue as Benvenuto [Cellini] had in casting his Perseus," but the difficulty did not dishearten him; he wanted, he said, "a long and delightful occupation," and though he wrote a first draft within a few weeks, he was in no hurry to publish or even to finish the poem, and in fact he never did publish it. He kept it by him during the next decade, retouching it from time to time, adding and rejecting scenes, and thinking of it to the end as a fragment. *Michael Angelo: A Fragment,* indeed, was not published until the year after his death.

The subject of Hagar and Ishmael was not the only one Longfellow had considered for a time and then abandoned: his mind, indeed, had always been singularly fertile in ideas of a literary sort, and his Book of Suggestions abounds, as Hawthorne's notebooks do, in plans that were never carried out — in his case, mostly, plans for plays either in verse or in prose. Almost always it is easy to see why these projects came to nothing, and Longfellow usually exhibits an admirable self-knowledge as an artist in what he rejected, if not always in what he carried out. Can we much regret that he got nowhere with his projects, in the forties, for a play about La Rochefoucauld and for a trilogy, no less, on the reign of Louis XIV? The period of the Roi Soleil seems to have fascinated him, perhaps on some principle of contrariety, but can one imagine his dealing with it dramatically in any but the most inadequate manner? And so with that other idea for a drama, one on Machiavelli, which was to have demonstrated "the folly and ugliness of opposing expediency to principle" — a subject for Melville, perhaps, but hardly for Longfellow.

Sometimes it is less evident that we should rejoice at his having abandoned an idea; one is less certain of this as regards the idea for a play on Vittorio Alfieri, the great Italian tragic poet, which was to have illustrated "the force of will and the power of a fixed purpose" as well as "the need man has of Liberty." Alfieri's dedication to the idea of freedom might have furnished some fine passages, though the intellectual rigor and tragic intensity of the author of *Oreste* seems, on second thought, to put him somewhat beyond Longfellow's reach. On the other hand, one does rather regret that he failed to write at least one of the plays in a trilogy he planned when he was still teaching at Bowdoin: it would have dealt with "the evil deeds done in the world by the supposed agency of the fairy personages," and would have included plays on Paracelsus, the Salem witches, and slavery. The second of these, without the fairies, ultimately became "Giles Corey," but the other two plays were never composed; surely it is just as well that Longfellow gave up the idea of a dramatic poem on slavery, which would certainly have gone wrong, but might not a fairy-tale play in verse about Paracelsus, in the spirit of Tieck or La Motte Fouqué, as Longfellow would have treated it, have had a considerable charm? Very possibly, but on the whole his unrealized plans of work do not inspire in us any very acute sense of loss.

IX

Indian Edda and Puritan Pastoral

REMARKING ONCE, many years ago, that "immortality often attaches itself to the bad as firmly as to the good," I. A. Richards went on to say that "Few things are worse than *Hiawatha* or *The Black Cat, Lorna Doone* or *Le Crime de Sylvestre Bonnard*"; and yet, he implied, each of them has achieved immortality. Whether or not all these works have in fact proved to be undying, *The Song of Hiawatha* has survived at least as a byword, and in the mind of criticism Richards's judgment of it is probably universal. Whatever fame the poem may enjoy is probably that Miltonic "bad eminence" which, as he said, accounts for the presence in anthologies of so many dubious favorites. And even in Longfellow's time the poem, or at least its reputation, inspired similar feelings of repugnance in the bosoms of some other writers. "How I loathe Wishi-Washi," said Rossetti, "— of course without reading it." Even a reading of it, the chances are, would not have mitigated Rossetti's loathing — might even have intensified it. In any case, it has become more difficult with *Hiawatha* than with any other work of Longfellow's to see the object "as in itself it really is" — to see it thus for better or for worse. Parodists, including Lewis Carroll, began at once to produce this effect, and it is now a task of almost unique difficulty to read the poem without preconceptions and with an ideal openness to persuasion.

Yet, if only for its interest as a historical curiosity of taste, the effort is worth making. The poem was not only phenomenally popular but it was admired by other writers, both here and abroad, whose discrimination we are bound to respect. One reason for this is worth specifying: whatever his success in the task, Longfellow was attempting an interesting experiment, and one that had not been made before. The Indian, of course, had already figured for decades in our literature; the subject, in a general way, may be said to have become hackneyed. Yet it had been viewed in only a few of its aspects. For the poets, the Indians of their time were appealing almost solely for the pathos of their fate, as members of a doomed and tragic race; in his undergraduate poems and in "To the Dying Cloud" Longfellow himself had contemplated them in this light. Writers of drama and fiction had used certain historical Indians, Pocahontas or Philip or Pontiac, as leading personages, and had usually presented them in a light both heroic and melancholy. Cooper, more than any other writer, had given a kind of classical form to this convention, which, being rooted on one side in reality, was not a *mere* convention; and the Indian of historic times — the Mohican, the Huron, the Pawnee — had assumed a mythic largeness of stature in the figures of Chingachgook and Uncas, of Magua and Hard-Heart.

What none of these writers, not even Cooper, had done, except in the most incidental way, was to interest themselves in the Indians' own mythology; in what had already begun to be called the "folklore" of this primitive race, the tales and legends inherited from a remote, ante-historic past, and preserved for generations in the form of oral tradition. This, and not the prowess of splendid savages or even the tragedy of their passing, was what now fascinated Longfellow. Having pored over Heckewelder and Catlin and especially Schoolcraft, he finally, as we have seen, hit upon the idea of a long poem that should bring together, in at least a loose unity, a group of genuine traditional tales centering in the figure of a genuine culture-hero. It was the reading of the

Kalevala that had begotten this idea — the reading of that folk
epic which had been so brilliantly knit together, only a few years
earlier, by a man of genius, the Finnish country doctor Elias
Lönrott, out of the scores of lays he had taken down by dictation
from the lips of elderly *laulajat* or singers, at a time when the
songs seemed about to be lost forever. Unlike Lönrott, Longfellow had not gone among the people themselves to collect his
legends, but he had read them, with the eye of a poet, in the collections other men had made, and he saw how full of a wild
beauty they were.

Most of the lays or "runes" of the *Kalevala* had centered in the
Titanic figure of a Finnish culture-hero, Väinämöinen, "old and
steadfast," who had some of the traits, not many, of a Prometheus
and, since he was a great minstrel, more of the traits of an Orpheus too. In Schoolcraft's volumes Longfellow had come upon
the figure of an Indian Väinämöinen, an Algonkian demigod
named Manabozho, whom Schoolcraft had confused with the historical Iroquoian statesman, Hiawatha or Hayó-went'ha ("very
wise man"), and who, under either name, struck him as the ideal
protagonist for his poem.* Manabozho had been sent down
among men by the Great Spirit in the character of a wise man or
prophet, as the "instructor of the tribes in arts and knowledge,"
and a whole cycle of tales about his benefactions, his exploits, his
prowess, had come into being; Longfellow's self-chosen task was
to select among them, translate them into his own imaginative
terms, and make a coherent poem of them. This is what he did in
Hiawatha.

He felt under no obligation to be literal-mindedly faithful to
what he found in his sources, and his young prophet proves to be
a highly selective version of Schoolcraft's Manabozho, to say

---

* Schoolcraft's mistake was a not unnatural one; after the death of the historic Hayó-went'ha, traditions had begun to accumulate around this person,
and the Iroquois peoples themselves came to identify him with a much more
primitive culture-hero of their own, Tarenyawago.

nothing of the Manabozho that later and less inhibited writers have put on record. The "real" Manabozho was a benefactor, it is true, who taught his people how to hunt, to trap, to make axes and arrowheads, and to cure diseases; but he was a bafflingly primitive and many-sided character in the Algonkian myths, who revealed himself to be not only wise and benevolent but mischievous, conceited, treacherous, and malignant. These latter traits were nothing to Longfellow's purpose, and Hiawatha retains only those traits of Manabozho, mingled with those of Hayó-went'ha, which suited his ideal purpose. There is little, though there is something, of the mere savage in him. He is sent among men primarily as a peace-bringer, a "Deliverer of the nations" from their endless wars and bloodshed; the sectional bitterness of the fifties haunted Longfellow's mind, one imagines, as he wrote, and Hiawatha's principal role is to bring peace and harmony out of discord and dissension. This he succeeds in doing, and although, in his human aspect, he is presumably an Ojibway (or Chippewa), he woos and marries a Dacotah maiden for the sake of cementing the peace that prevails between the two peoples. And in his characteristic benevolence he is admirably equipped for his role as peacemaker. There is a touch of Channing in Hiawatha, as Van Wyck Brooks once said; but was there not, also, in all human probability, a *touch* of Channing in Hayó-went'ha, even in Manabozho, and in the sages and statesmen of more than one Indian tribe?

If "primitive" means only savage, bloodthirsty, and fierce, then Longfellow's Hiawatha is a romantic caricature of the real culture-hero of primitive peoples. And in truth he has not only little of the arrogance of Prometheus or the occasional ruthlessness of Väinämöinen or the malicious cunning of Manabozho, but little of their Titanism, their gigantism, their vague, vast, ageless superhumanity. This "trim, immaculate figure," as Christabel Fiske described him, is essentially human in his proportions, despite his magic resources; eternally young, slender, graceful, and kindly. It is true that he fights with and slays the sinister Manito, Megissogwon; that he kills the great sturgeon, Mishe-Nama, which has swallowed him, by striking its heart with his fist; and that, in his anger at Pau-Puk-Keewis, he allows his hunters to club to death the beaver into which the Storm-Fool has transformed himself. But there is nothing demoniac in his wrath or very convincing in his heroic prowess; he remains a Deliverer, not a great warrior or hero. This does not keep him from having, in another sense, a credibly primitive quality, any more than it kept Longfellow himself, in spite of his gentility and erudition, from having, as Howells said, "somewhat of primitive, of elemental, in him." Hiawatha is not the Savage as Devil — the savage of the Puritans — or the Noble Savage of Cooper or the Heroic Savage of Melville; he has to be called something like the Gentle Savage. The point — one might even say the joke — is that, despite the Indian-haters, there is almost as much truth in this version of the primitive type as in the more theological, the more misanthropic, or the more epic. Schoolcraft, whose wife was part Chippewa and who had lived for years among Algonkian Indians, recognized this in his letter to Longfellow about the poem.

The Indian, he said, must be treated as he is — "a warrior in war, a savage in revenge, a stoic in endurance, a wolverine in suppleness and cunning," but also "a humanitarian in his kindness," "as simple as a child, yet with the dignity of a man in his wigwam." In this light Hiawatha is a poetically stylized but not a falsified version of the American Indian — just as, in their dark and embittered way, Brockden Brown's or R. M. Bird's versions are. What appears in his portrait is not cruelty or vengefulness or cunning, but a primitive stateliness, resourcefulness in invention, intrepidity, gravity, tenderness, and the love of friends. He teaches his people how to raise corn, how to clear the streams of obstructions, how to use picture-writing, and how to cure diseases by the use of herbs and simples. He does not teach them how to make axes and arrowheads, as Manabozho did, and he does not take delight in trickery or deception. He engages in no tribal warfare, he does not torture captives, he does not normally take vengeance on his enemies. Schoolcraft, nevertheless, felt that Longfellow had redressed a balance in the poetic treatment of the Indian that had been tipped too far on the other side.

If we can regard Hiawatha indulgently in this milder light, he has a minor but genuine imaginative truth not merely to Indian but to human reality. He is a composite product — the image of an Indian prophet conjured up by a sensitive nineteenth-century imagination, with its own freshness and naïveté, which had steeped itself in the somewhat expurgated legends that the early ethnologists had brought together. It is a familiar literary phenomenon, after all; what else than this, in kind, and on their perhaps higher level, are Scott's Crusaders or Flaubert's Carthaginians or William Morris's Vikings? Hiawatha has less robustness than some of these, but he has a quasi-primitive veracity of his own — a childlike seriousness, an archaic ingenuousness, that ring perfectly true to one aspect of primordial human experience. He is charming as a small boy listening wide-eyed to Nokomis's legends of the comet, the moon, and the rainbow, and learning to speak with the birds and beasts. He is engaging as a youthful demigod, like Herakles or the Polynesian Maui, with his superhuman fleetness of foot and strength of arm, and even with his much-parodied mittens — those mittens with which, in a recognizably magic way, he can smite the rocks asunder. There is another quality, lighthearted and humorous, in his laughing disdain for the pike and the sunfish that rise to his bait when what he is aiming at is to catch the great sturgeon, the King of Fishes. There is still another quality, a solemn one, in his praying and fasting for seven days and nights in the forests "for profit of the people," and in his repeated wrestlings with the beautiful youth, Mondamin, the Corn Spirit. And a much sterner note is struck when, during the long winter of intense cold and famine, Minnehaha lies dying of hunger and fever, and Hiawatha sets out grimly to hunt for game. "In that bitter hour of anguish," he cries out to the Master of Life for the gift of food, and his cry of desolation echoes through the vacant, snow-mantled forest. Something of the genuine terror of primitive existence resounds in this cry of his.

Something of the primitive response to bereavement, too, the wildness of its protest, echoes in Hiawatha's heartbroken lament for his beloved friend, Chibiabos, the musician. Chibiabos has neglected Hiawatha's warnings and, setting out on a hunt, has run out on to the frozen surface of the great lake, and been dragged down to his death in its icy waters by the Evil Spirits. Hiawatha, when he hears this, sends forth such a wail of grief that even the bison pause to listen.* Chibiabos is only one, but he is the chief, of Hiawatha's Friends, though in the Ojibway tales he is only Manabozho's brother; and in their relationship Longfellow evokes something of the primitive tenderness of friendship of which Melville had found examples among the Polynesians and had dramatized in the love between Ishmael and Queequeg. Chibiabos, alas, "brave as man is, soft as woman," is a gracile and almost effeminate character side by side with Queequeg, but he also serves the purpose in the poem of embodying the primitive music-maker, like Orpheus or Väinämöinen; he holds not only the warriors and the women but the brook, the bluebird, and the squirrel silent with his singing. At Hiawatha's wedding feast he sings two songs, one of which ("Onaway! Awake, beloved") is straight out of Schoolcraft's prose in *Oneóta,* but if it derives from a genuine Indian love song, it has suffered prettification at the hands of Schoolcraft first and then of Longfellow, and Chibiabos, with his "accents sweet and tender," is closer to Longfellow himself than, say, to the shaggy old minstrel Väinämöinen.

---

* Hiawatha, curiously enough, laments the death of Chibiabos "seven long weeks," but later mourns for Minnehaha only "seven long days and nights." Leslie Fiedler would see in this, with a certain justice, something characteristic of the American cult of primitive man.

There is a truer strain of the archaic in that other friend of Hiawatha's, Kwasind, the very strong man, who as a boy, like some other heroes of legend, Beowulf and others, gives no promise of his future prowess, but is idle, listless, and queer, never playing with other children, never fishing or hunting, and in winter cowering over the firebrands in the wigwam.* Kwasind's father and mother, as well as the other youths, are full of a savage contempt for the lazy lad, but Hiawatha has a truer insight and loves him for his very strength and — with a touch that suggests, not the two young Ojibways, but Longfellow himself and Sumner — "for his strength allied to goodness." Kwasind bides his time, like Beowulf, and when his strength is ripe, exhibits it in a fine, careless, almost contemptuous manner, clearing a brooklet of the great tree trunks that impede it, tearing an immense rock from its foundation and pitching it into the swift waters of the Pauwating, and at a later time plunging beneath the swirling rapids of that river and catching a beaver that has taken refuge under water. Kwasind is almost perfectly invulnerable, but not quite, and just as Baldr could be slain only by the mistletoe, Kwasind can be slain only by the cone of a pine tree dropped upon his head. The small, mischievous Puk-Wudjies, the envious Little People, who suggest some of Sumner's enemies, fear and hate Kwasind, and plot to destroy him. This they do, clustered together on the red rocks that overhang the sluggish Taquamenaw as the Strong Man floats downstream in his canoe on a hot summer afternoon, falling asleep in the heat of the sun and offering his skull as a target to his malignant little foes. It is one of the finer mood-evoking passages in the poem.

Manabozho, in the Algonkian tales, is a great and often a heartless trickster as well as a benefactor. Longfellow purges Hiawa-

---

*For a long time, says the poet of *Beowulf*, that hero was spurned as worthless by the Geatish warriors:

> Slack and shiftless the strong men deemed him,
> profitless prince.

tha of all such traits, as we have seen, but he knew how true they were to the spirit of primitive storytelling, and he transferred them to a full-fledged and purely mischievous trickster, whom he also found in Schoolcraft, Pau-Puk-Keewis, "the handsome Yena-dizze" or Idler, also known as the Storm-Fool. Like Lemminkai-nen in the *Kalevala* or Loki in the Eddas, Pau-Puk-Keewis is an incarnation of the primitive spirit of mischief. It is true that he is wanting in the heroic sexual prowess of Lemminkainen and the murderous malignancy of Loki, but he has, like them, much of the childlike and often childish mischievousness of the archetypal trickster, and he adds a dimension of naïve humor to the poem that enhances its truth to Indian reality.* Full of vivacity is the tale of his dancing, in all his Ojibway finery, at Hiawatha's wed-ding feast; full of boisterous humor is the tale of his teaching all the men of the tribe to play games of hazard, and with his superior cunning beating them out of their last deerskin shirts and belts of wampum; full of a crueler feeling is the tale of his wantonly slaughtering the birds, Hiawatha's Chickens, by tens and twenties, for sheer love of destruction. Pau-Puk-Keewis alone arouses real anger in Hiawatha, and the story of his pursuit by the outraged hero and his hunters, while he transforms himself, with the pro-tean resourcefulness of Manabozho, into a beaver, a brant, and at last a serpent, is told with a brio that Longfellow had not found in his source.†

There is less animation in the figure of Iagoo, the great boaster,

---

* If Pau-Puk-Keewis is also free from any association with obscenity — speaking excrements, speaking sexual parts, and the like — this is the result not of Longfellow's expurgation but of Schoolcraft's, and it is only in such later compilations as Stith Thompson's *Tales of the North American Indians* that we find these traces of Algonkian Rabelaisianism.

† The brilliant costume Pau-Puk-Keewis wears at the wedding feast — deerskin leggings, buckskin moccasins, plumes on his head, a fan of feathers in his hand, a doeskin shirt fringed with ermine — must have been inspired by some of George Catlin's charming portraits of real Chippewas and others in his *Manners and Customs of the North American Indians* — by the por-trait, for example, of the Chippewa On-daig, "a young man of distinction, in an extravagant and beautiful costume."

"the marvellous story-teller," who never hears of an adventure
but he himself has had a greater one, and whose name becomes a
byword among the people for his boastfulness; he is a rather pale
version of the archetypal Boaster, and the tales he actually tells
are not inflated tales of his own prowess but charming stories
such as the legend of Osseo, the Son of the Evening Star, which
Longfellow took from *Algic Researches*. Uncannily close to the
quality of primitive life, however, is the character of old Nokomis, Hiawatha's grandmother, who tells the small hero her cos-
mological tales of comet and moon, prods him later into taking
vengeance on Mudjekeewis for the ravishing of her daughter We-
nonah, tries to dissuade Hiawatha from taking a wife outside the
tribe, but in the end mourns for the dead Minnehaha with a shrill
wail of grief:

> "Wahonowin! Wahonowin!
> Would that I had perished for you,
> Would that I were dead as you are!
> Wahonowin! Wahonowin!"

Nokomis, though there is little savagery in her make-up, moves
through the poem with much of the venerableness of an aged
Ojibway crone. Only Minnehaha, among these characters — the
only personage Longfellow invented — rings wholly or almost
wholly false to primitive life; she has the meek submissiveness of
a savage bride, no doubt, but she is another in the list of Longfellow's wishful wife-images, and it is impossible to believe that
her skin is red or her hair long, straight, and black. Even when
she "blesses" the cornfields by walking around them naked in
the darkness of night, Minnehaha does not communicate the feeling, at once gross and solemn, of a primitive fertility rite.

Strains of this sort, indeed, are almost entirely absent from the
poem, as Christabel Fiske observed perceptively many years ago.*
The awe of primitive man in the presence of natural forces, his

* In "Mercerized Folklore" (*Poet-Lore*, 1920), perhaps the best essay on
the poem anywhere.

dread of their destructiveness, the wariness with which he approaches them — these emotions are rarely expressed in *Hiawatha*, partly because they are so imperfectly revealed in Heckewelder or Schoolcraft. Mudjekeewis, Hiawatha, Kwasind feel little need, as primitive men normally do, of wheedling or placating the powers or the creatures which they propose to overcome or to petition. On the contrary, Mudjekeewis taunts the Great Bear with his cowardice in a disdainful speech (which Longfellow, it is true, lifted from Heckewelder); and when Hiawatha appeals to the birch, the cedar, the larch, the fir, and the hedgehog for materials with which to build his canoe, he does it with a certain lordliness. It is true that there is something of the genuine primitive shudder in Hiawatha's encounter with the powerful magician Megissogwon, a malignant spirit of disease and death, who has to be approached through a stricken landscape of black pitch-water, with fiery serpents coiling and playing on it like monsters in some archaic stone-carving. But Hiawatha approaches Megissogwon not cautiously but fearlessly, challenging him defiantly and hurling taunts at him; the young hero's magic shirt of wampum is an emblem of his really invulnerable might. Minnehaha shudders with terror at the two ghostly visitors, Famine and Fever, when they enter the wigwam on that dreary winter day, and Hiawatha, desperate for once, rushes forth into the empty forest for game. But this is the only moment at which the wild helplessness of primitive life is sharply felt.

Granted this — granted that, for the most part, the non-human forces of nature do not inspire much dread in the human characters — Longfellow does succeed in conveying some sense of the intimacy that primitive man feels between himself and the natural world, his blurring of the line between the human and the animal, and even of the line between the human and the inanimate. No writer before him, dealing with the Indians, had struck quite this note of free and easy interchange between human beings and beasts, birds, and fish — kindly, here, as a rule, not hostile, but for this too there is warrant in anthropology. The poem abounds in "helpful animals" and "helpful birds," and small and unformidable as most of them are, they have much of the naïve charm of creatures in a fairy tale — the rabbit who, "half in fear and half in frolic," begs the small Hiawatha not to shoot him; the obliging little hedgehog who gives Hiawatha of his shining quills for his canoe; the frisking, chattering squirrel Adjidaumo, who helps Hiawatha in the belly of Mishe-Nama; the screaming and flapping seagulls who set him free from Mishe-Nama's jaws; and the woodpecker who comes to his assistance in the combat with Megissogwon. The beavers who give refuge to Pau-Puk-Keewis, the brant who change him into one of themselves, have a similar willingness to be of assistance to human beings; and though we hear little or nothing of the more predatory animals of the American forest — the fox, the panther, the wolf — we get a lively sense of the hopping, scampering, swimming, flying life of the forest and the lake.

There was a freshness, too, when Longfellow wrote, and an appeal to the primitivizing fancy, in the local legends and the pourquoi-stories, as they are sometimes called, that he wove with such skill into the substance of the poem. They sometimes have a more primordial quality than the helpful beasts. A great rock in the Sault Ste Marie is the rock that Kwasind flung there when the other young men taunted him with his idleness. The sand dunes of Lake Superior were heaped along its shores by the whirlwind that Pau-Puk-Keewis stirred up in his frenzied dance at Hiawatha's wedding feast. The flecks and shadows on the moon are the body of an old woman whom her grandson, an angry warrior, threw against it. The woodpecker got its tuft of crimson feathers when Hiawatha, grateful for its assistance, stained its head with the blood of Megissogwon. In a somewhat different vein, but often beautiful or at least pretty, are the nature myths that Longfellow retells from Schoolcraft and others — the myth of Kabibonokka, the North Wind, fierce and freezing, who is worsted by Shingebis, the diver, and the blazing fire in Shingebis's lodge; the myth of Shawondasee, the South Wind, and the dandelion maiden with whom he falls in love; the winter-and-spring myth of the old man Peboan, in his lonely lodge, who is visited by a beautiful youth, Segwun, and under his bland influence fades away and is turned into the Miskodeed, the first flower of springtime.

There is no recondite symbolism in these myths or legends as Longfellow retells them; if there is any symbolism, it is perfectly transparent, and Longfellow saw in them no such suggestiveness for romantic allegory as Melville, in *Mardi*, saw in his Polynesian myths and legends. They lack a certain resonance as a result, a certain penumbra of emotion or intellectual meaning. But Longfellow's mind was both more and less "primitive" than Melville's; he delighted in these traditions simple-mindedly for their own sake, and as a result they have, in his handling of them, a clarity of shape, an unambiguous freshness, which they would have lost in the handling of a greater poet. This points to a defect in the poem, but the defect is not without its compensations, and between them they signalize the weakness and strength of *Hiawatha* as a whole. There is another aspect, too, in which its qualities and its defects may be viewed. There was next to no *negative* strain in Longfellow's cult of the primitive; it was not — as it was with most writers in his time — the reverse of any deep loathing he may have felt for civilization or progress, and when, at the end of the poem, the Black Robe chief, the Jesuit priest, arrives with his message of salvation through the Cross, the episode is felt, and intended to be felt, as expressing the promise of a better and happier future. There is thus no painful complexity, no rich contradictoriness, in what Longfellow does with primitive life, and this keeps *Hiawatha* from having the intensity one finds in the work of more passionate men like Thoreau or Melville or even Cooper. The compensation is that it has a greater simplicity of truth to some aspects of primitive life.

Was it a fatal mistake for Longfellow to pitch upon the meter that he thought the only right one for what he called his "Indian Edda"? Many readers thought so at the time, and probably such readers as the poem has today — in English they must be countable by the half-dozen at best — would subscribe to that view with virtual unanimity. It is not only the meter, of course, but the trick of reiteration, especially at the beginning of lines —

> Came the warriors of the nations,
> Came the Delawares and Mohawks,
> Came the Choctaws and Camanches,

and so on, for seven lines in all — that has affected so many readers as laughable; but it is the meter that has been the real sticking-point. Is it not as hopelessly monotonous and even maddening as a primitive drumbeat, without the excuse that no better instruments are available to civilized composers? It is a painful question to any reader who cannot forswear the modest pleasure-giving quality of the poem as a whole. Does this quality simply survive in spite of the meter? — for a poem need not be utterly shipwrecked even by an infelicitous pattern.

The question of value aside, for the moment, the origin of the measure is well known. Anton Schiefner, the German translator of the *Kalevala*, had made a point of imitating in German verse the traditional meter of Finnish popular poetry, the so-called trochaic tetrameter, and of imitating, too, the reiterative devices that are characteristic, after all, not only of Finnish but of much other archaic verse:

> Alsobald schwang Wäinämöinen
> Beide Füsse auf die Heide,
> Auf das meerumspülte Eiland,
> Auf die baumentblösste Fläche.
>   Weilte darauf manche Jahre,
> Lebte immerwährend weiter
> Auf dem Eiland ohne Worte,
> Auf der baumentblössten Fläche.

> Dachte nach und überlegte,
> Hegt' es lang in seinem Haupte:
> Wer das Land ihm wohl besäen,
> Wer den Samen streuen sollte? *

The genius of the Finnish language is said to make of this short-breathed measure a medium of great, though primitive, expressiveness. But the genius of the German language is presumably a very different divinity, and Schiefner's tetrameters have only a limited flexibility. Nevertheless they struck Longfellow as quite peculiarly fitting in a poem on so primordial a subject, and he seems soon to have found himself writing their English equivalents with his usual fluency.

Fluency, indeed, if nothing better, can only too easily be acquired in the writing, or even the improvisation, of *Hiawatha* verses, and the measure has, at its best, a very restricted usefulness — too restricted, on the whole, for a poem so long as *Hiawatha* is. Trochaic verse, familiarly enough, cannot be long sustained in English without monotony, and the shortness of this particular line is another heavy handicap, as some of the translations of the *Kalevala* into English painfully demonstrate. They also demonstrate, however, that it is not easy to rival Longfellow in the resourcefulness with which, in spite of everything, he handles this unpromising measure. Its mechanical regularity, as he writes it, has been somewhat exaggerated. There are not always

---

* The English of these lines, as translated by W. F. Kirby, is as follows:

> Then did Väinämöinen, rising,
> Set his feet upon the surface
> Of a sea-encircled island,
> In a region bare of forest.
>   There he dwelt, while years passed over,
> And his dwelling he established
> On the silent, voiceless island,
> In a barren, treeless country.
>   Then he pondered and reflected,
> In his mind he turned it over,
> "Who shall sow this barren country,
> Thickly scattering seeds around him?"

four thumping accents, no more and no less, in every line, and
the fall of the accents itself is shifting and variable. Lines such as
the following do not have the insistent regularity of drumbeats:

> With the bárk of the réd wíllow.
>
> Over them he strétched his ríght hánd.
>
> Thréw their clóaks and shírts of déer-skín.
>
> Gázing with hálf-ópen éyelíds.
>
> Wár-crý of the Líttle Péople.

And in some of the verse-paragraphs there is an appreciable fluc-
tuation from line to line:

> Slowly o'er the simmering landscape
> Fell the evening's dusk and coolness,
> And the long and level sunbeams
> Shot their spears into the forest,
> Breaking through its shields of shadow,
> Rushed into each secret ambush,
> Searched each thicket, dingle, hollow;
> Still the guests of Hiawatha
> Slumbered in the silent wigwam.

This is not a very "strong-wing'd music," to be sure, but in their
plaintive, flutelike way the lines have an expressive melodious-
ness, and the vowel and consonant music — the music of the liq-
uids, the nasals, the open vowels — is not without a dreamy grace.
   The rhythms of a poem cannot, as a matter of fact, be divorced
from its language and rhetoric, and the charm of the passage
just quoted depends of course not mainly on its metrical delicacy but much more on the atmospheric suggestiveness of the
words — "simmering," "dusk," "coolness," "shadow," "slumber"
— and on the suppleness of the phrasing. Yet the rhythms, as always, respond to the authority of the language, and so it is
throughout the poem. The monotony always latent in the short
trochaic lines obtrudes itself whenever Longfellow forces it to

serve a purpose beyond its reach or whenever his own spontaneity flags; it is felt least, and even forgotten, when he writes out of his most natural feeling. There is something perfunctory in the more formal speeches — Gitche Manito's address to the assembled tribes, Hiawatha's soliloquy on the need for picture-writing, the Black Robe chief's sermon at the end — and the rhythms, as well as the language, turn flat and dull as a result. There is usually not much metrical energy or vigor of language in the narration of violent action — Hiawatha's combats with Mudjekeewis, Megissogwon, and Mondamin; and when softness of sentiment takes over, as it does in the story of Hiawatha's wooing, the meter grows slack and the language pale.

Both the meter and the language come to life, and the poem frees itself from mere monotony, when the action is playful, innocent, or *märchenhaft*, or even when it is violent if the violence is half sportive. The tale of Hiawatha's fishing is told with a vivacity that springs in part from the light, quick rhythms of the verse — the fishes and the seagulls are especially full of life — and in the description of Pau-Puk-Keewis's dancing there is a fine kinetic sense of choreographic movement, slow at first, then accelerated, and finally whirling. So with the hunting of Pau-Puk-Keewis; the verse keeps pace with the swift, unflagging movement of the flight and pursuit, and the mannerisms of style fall away almost completely.

This is even truer of the passages in which the moods of external nature — of languor or drowsiness, stillness or hush, even grimness — are in harmony with the emotions of the human figures. The most genuine feeling in the poem is the feeling that is reflected back from the landscape or the season or the time of day, and the verse is capable of expressing this without deflation. There is something Japanese, as Christabel Fiske observed, in the grotesquerie of the scene in which Hiawatha, sailing in his canoe at night over the black pitch-water, approaches the lair of Megissogwon:

> All night long he sailed upon it,
> Sailed upon that sluggish water,
> Covered with its mould of ages,
> Black with rotting water-rushes,
> Rank with flags and leaves of lilies,
> Stagnant, lifeless, dreary, dismal,
> Lighted by the shimmering moonlight,
> And by will-o'-the-wisps illumined,
> Fires by ghosts of dead men kindled,
> In their weary night-encampments.

Night, and the *frisson* of the sinister supernatural, play a minor but, from the point of view of light and shade, essential role in the poem, not only here but in the canto in which, during the long nights of that ferocious winter, the ghosts of two dead women sit cowering in the shadows of Hiawatha's wigwam, springing up only to seize in their spectral hands the choicest portions of the food Nokomis serves. The ghostliness of this is finely rendered, and there is an austere beauty in the winter itself, as there always is in Longfellow.

Yet night and winter figure less than other times of day and other seasons. It is spring when Hiawatha withdraws into the woods for his Fasting and wrestles with Mondamin, and it is spring when Iagoo brings the first news of the coming of the white man. More expressive of the feeling of the poem, however, than either winter or spring is summer or autumn. No reader fails to feel that, somehow, an Indian Summer softness and drowsiness pervades the whole of *Hiawatha*, little as the season itself figures in any literal sense. It appears only once, indeed — in the canto of the Four Winds, when the lazy South Wind, Shawondasee, smokes it into being:

> From his lips the smoke ascending
> Filled the sky with haze and vapor,
> Filled the air with dreamy softness,
> Gave a twinkle to the water,
> Touched the rugged hills with smoothness,

> Brought the tender Indian Summer
> To the melancholy north-land,
> In the dreary noon of snow-shoes.

It is an Indian Summer poem, and it is also a late-afternoon or sunset poem. The sunsets abound in the feeling of romantic landscape painting.* The setting sun is sometimes seen as a beautiful bird, a flamingo, dropping into her nest at nightfall, and sometimes as a more purely mythical bird:

> Can it be the sun descending
> O'er the level plain of water?
> Or the Red Swan floating, flying,
> Wounded by the magic arrow,
> Staining all the waves with crimson,
> With the crimson of its life-blood,
> Filling all the air with splendor,
> With the splendor of its plumage?

It is into a summer sunset that Hiawatha takes his final departure, sailing westward across the great lake in his magic canoe. Just before this there has been a leap, which most readers are unlikely to notice, from the primordial to the historical, from the epoch of culture-heroes to the seventeenth century and the arrival of the French missionaries. Longfellow regretted this: "The contact," he said, "of Saga and History is too sudden." The point troubled him unduly; the contact of saga and history has often, in fact, been sudden enough, and even at the end of the *Kalevala* the ancient Väinämöinen takes his departure, also in a magic boat, when a sinless child is born in a manger to the virgin Marjatta, and saga is suddenly plunged into a kind of history. Hiawatha, in any case, is a Departing Hero, whose return, like that of Arthur or the Aztec Quetzalcoatl, he himself hints at as he speaks to his people:

---

* A sunset by Thomas Moran, the romantic landscape painter, was used as an illustration for *Hiawatha* in some of the editions of Longfellow's poems.

"Many moons and many winters
Will have come, and will have vanished,
Ere I come again to see you."

Meanwhile, he enjoins them to listen to the words of wisdom
that the priests will speak, for they too, in their turn, have been
sent by the Master of Life. He then stands on the shore of the
lake waving farewell to his people, steps into his birch canoe, and
shoves it into the water:

> And the evening sun descending
> Set the clouds on fire with redness,
> Burned the broad sky, like a prairie,
> Left upon the level water
> One long track and trail of splendor,
> Down whose stream, as down a river,
> Westward, westward Hiawatha
> Sailed into the fiery sunset,
> Sailed into the purple vapors,
> Sailed into the dusk of evening.
> And the people from the margin
> Watched him floating, rising, sinking,
> Till the birch canoe seemed lifted
> High into that sea of splendor,
> Till it sank into the vapors
> Like the new moon slowly, slowly
> Sinking in the purple distance.

With such deeply felt passages in our ears, we are inclined to feel
that, on the whole, in spite of its lapses, there are a good many
things worse than *The Song of Hiawatha*.

Even now Longfellow had not done with the Indians; they
reappear in *The Courtship of Miles Standish*, only now they are
not legendary prophets and singers, boasters and tricksters, but
historical Wampanoag Indians, such as the settlers of Plymouth
had encountered in all their solid actuality on the shores and in
the woods of Massachusetts. As a result, they are seen not

through an Indian Summer haze of poetic primitiveness but with a certain harshness of "realism." They are seen, as a matter of fact, as if through the eyes of the Pilgrims themselves, and if that is a distorting medium, it is clearly the right one for this poem. There is one friendly Indian, the well-remembered Hobomok, and at least one of the Plymouth men, the Elder, William Brewster, speaks up mildly for the savages. But to Miles Standish they are simply "red devils," as they seemed, or came to seem, to the colonists generally; and, except for Hobomok, the Indians in the poem, Wattawamat and Pecksuot and the others, are of the sinister order, "naked down to the waist, and grim and ferocious in aspect"; and they bring not peace but a rattlesnake skin filled with arrows. Friendship is in their looks when Miles Standish and his little band come upon them in their encampment, "but in their hearts there was hatred." They are cunning, crafty, boastful, and full of insult; and Captain Standish is so enraged by their taunts that he leaps upon Pecksuot and plunges a knife into his heart: the savage falls "with his face to the sky, and a fiendlike fierceness upon it." The colonists do not lag much behind the Indians in their fierceness, and the head of Wattawamat, slain by a bullet when he refuses to flee, is proudly exhibited on the roof of the fort at Plymouth: "All who beheld it rejoiced, and praised the Lord, and took courage."

In these rather surprisingly grim incidents, Longfellow is idealizing neither the Indians nor the colonists; for the moment he is closer to Cooper or even R. M. Bird than to Freneau or Lydia Maria Child. Yet grimness is not the predominant tone of *The Courtship;* that strain is sounded for the sake of deliberate musical contrast. "A kind of Puritan pastoral" is what Longfellow meant the poem to be, and what, with its prevailingly silver-gray hue, it is. When, at the end, John Alden, after their wedding, leads Priscilla, mounted on a white bull, homeward through the woods, accompanied by their simple and sober fellow Pilgrims, the little procession seems

> Like a picture . . . of the primitive, pastoral ages,
> Fresh with the youth of the world, and recalling Rebecca
>   and Isaac.

Calvinist Plymouth may seem like a curious setting for pastoral, in any strict sense, and in the role of shepherds and shepherdesses, William Brewster, Miles Standish, and Priscilla Mullins would have been oddly cast. Longfellow was of course not using the word in any such literal sense; the "pastoral" quality of the poem derives from the pleasant remoteness of the scene, its rather agreeable physical bareness, the extreme simplicity of the manners represented, and the theme of innocent youthful love. To nineteenth-century city-dwellers, with their railroads and magnetic telegraphs and steamboats — and their sectional conflicts, here in the United States — Longfellow's Plymouth must have seemed at least vaguely Vergilian.

It is far enough from Hawthorne's seventeenth-century Salem or Boston. But this is not the moral tragedy of colonial Massachusetts; it is the quiet domestic comedy, and though far less searching in its truth, it has an unpretentious truthfulness of its own, as the letters and diaries of the period suggest. The Spirit of Comedy was never less boisterous or lower-keyed than it is in *The Courtship;* the poem not only does not evoke "thoughtful laughter," but it can hardly be said to evoke laughter at all; at the best, a quiet smile. What calls forth the smile is the ancient humor of cross purposes, and John Alden, paying court to Priscilla on behalf of Miles Standish, is a Vicarious Suitor of the comic, not the tragic, sort — a slightly ridiculous Calvinistic Tristan. Blond, blue-eyed, "with delicate Saxon complexion," like Saint Gregory's famous Angles, he is no more virile a figure than Prince Henry or Gabriel Lajeunesse; the real John Alden, a master-cooper who helped to found the town of Duxbury, can hardly have been so unaggressive as Longfellow's timid young hero. Yet in the acuteness of his self-reproach, in his exaggerated feelings of guilt, there is a genuine truth to the Calvinist type:

"Truly the heart is deceitful, and out of its depths of corruption,"

he soliloquizes,

> "Rise, like an exhalation, the misty phantoms of passion;
> Angels of light they seem, but are only delusions of Satan.
> All is clear to me now; I feel it, I see it distinctly!
> This is the hand of the Lord; it is laid upon me in anger,
> For I have followed too much the heart's desires and devices."

The young woman he is in love with is an appreciably stronger character, as Elsie and Evangeline had been. It is true that Alden compares Priscilla sentimentally to a Mayflower, "modest and simple and sweet," and this is what Longfellow himself doubtless intended her to be; but she proves to be somewhat more interesting than that. She has been left alone by the deaths of her father, mother, and brother during that first terrible winter at Plymouth, but she is, as Miles Standish says, "patient, courageous, and strong," and one sees her characteristically as she sits cheerfully at the spinning wheel in her solitary cottage, feeding the spindle with carded wool and singing to herself "the grand old Puritan anthem," the One Hundredth Psalm. Patient and virtuous as she is, however, she is by no means a merely meek sufferer, and she has enough spirit to protest, with some temper, against the offensiveness of Standish's using an intermediary to woo her; to protest, too, against poor Alden's tactlessness. Her momentary archness, in her too-famous question to John, is trying; but in her slight and sketchlike way, Priscilla has a touch of the feminine freshness and independence that James was later to reveal in some of his young New England girls, Mary Garland or Gertrude Wentworth.

There is more robustness of humor in the figure of Miles Standish, who is represented neither romantically, as the valorous knight of patriotic tradition, nor contemptuously, as the "Captaine Shrimpe (a quondam Drummer)" of Thomas Morton's satirical poke, but in a pleasantly comic light as a very kindly version of the Braggart Soldier. His favorite author is Julius Caesar, whose *Commentaries* he knows by heart, and between whom and himself he likes to hint at parallels:

"Better be first, he said, in a little Iberian village,
Than be second in Rome, and I think he was right when he said it."

He finds significance in the fact that Caesar, too, like himself, had fought in Flanders, but he amusingly forgets himself for a moment when, after retelling a story of Caesar's intrepidity in a military crisis, he adds:

"That's what I always say; if you wish a thing to be well done,
You must do it yourself, you must not leave it to others!" —

and then, with hardly a pause, appeals to John Alden to serve as his emissary to Priscilla. When Alden repeats his own words, the Captain can only protest that, though the maxim is a good one, it must be used discreetly; one must not "waste powder for nothing." There is none of the breadth of true caricature in the sketch of Miles Standish, but neither is there any of the strain and falsity of bad caricature. This is Longfellow's own idiosyncratic humor, too, not Irving's or Dickens's.

The hexameters of *The Courtship* are looser, more relaxed, more frequently trochaic, and less sonorous than those of *Evangeline;* sometimes, in their colloquial ease, as in the lines above, they are merely jejune, and sometimes they are painfully prosaic:

Latticed the windows were, and the window-panes were of paper,
Oiled to admit the light, while wind and rain were excluded.

Yet they, and the language, are rarely so inert as this, and *The Courtship* has a sharp tonality of its own — to which the verse and the language of course contribute — somewhat reminiscent of the "primeval" opening and close of *Evangeline*, but quite un-

like its luxuriant and subtropical middle passages. It is the tonality of the Massachusetts seacoast when the wind is from the east,
the rather bleak landscape washed with a gray mist, and one sees

> the steel-blue rim of the ocean,
> Lying silent and sad, in the afternoon shadows and sunshine.

The landscape of the poem itself is Puritanic, somehow wintry
despite the fact that the action proceeds only from the early
spring to the following fall; and the ocean — "sailless, sombre
and cold with the comfortless breath of the east-wind," but brac-
ing and fortifying nevertheless — is felt as a presence throughout the poem. The wind is almost always from the east, and when
John Alden, elated by Priscilla's hope-bringing question, rushes
out into the open air, he apostrophizes it excitedly:

> "Welcome, O wind of the East!" he exclaimed in his wild
>   exultation,
> "Welcome, O wind of the East, from the caves of the misty
>   Atlantic!
> Blowing o'er fields of dulse, and measureless meadows of sea-
>   grass,
> Blowing o'er rocky wastes, and the grottoes and gardens of
>   ocean!
> Lay thy cold, moist hand on my burning forehead, and wrap
>   me
> Close in thy garments of mist, to allay the fever within me!"

The wind is naturally from the west, however, when early in
April the *Mayflower* sets sail again for England — with its master
and seamen but with none of the Pilgrims, though Alden has been
tempted to escape on it — and its departure is evoked with the exuberant seagoing vigor of which Longfellow is such a master:

> Soon were heard on board the shouts and songs of the sailors
> Heaving the windlass round, and hoisting the ponderous anchor.
> Then the yards were braced, and all sails set to the west-wind,
> Blowing steady and strong; and the Mayflower sailed from the
>   harbor,

Rounded the point of the Gurnet, and leaving far to the south-
        ward
Island and cape of sand, and the Field of the First Encounter,
Took the wind on her quarter, and stood for the open Atlantic,
Borne on the send of the sea, and the swelling hearts of the Pil-
        grims.

The Puritan color of the poem is kept up not only by the austere landscape and seascape, but by the constant and always natural recurrence, as in a sacred cantata, of Scriptural language and
imagery, usually in an Old Testament spirit. Alden and Priscilla,
on their way home from the wedding, recall, as we have seen,
Rebecca and Isaac; and earlier, when John has been plunged in
remorse for his "excessive" love of Priscilla, he accuses himself of
"worshipping Astaroth blindly, and impious idols of Baal." When
Priscilla compares the inner lives of many unhappy women with
subterranean rivers, running through caverns of darkness, he protests that, on the contrary, they seem to him like the Euphrates,
flowing through the deserts of Havilah, "filling the land with delight, and memories sweet of the garden!" He is a little inaccurate
in his allusion to Genesis, but that does not keep his simile from
having a delicate appropriateness. And the finest of the similes in
the poem is a reminiscence, Hebraic in its gorgeousness, not of
Genesis but of Exodus or Deuteronomy. There is only one sunset in *The Courtship* — for this is a poem about beginnings, not
endings — but there are two fine sunrises, and the more splendid of these is the sunrise on the morning of the wedding day,
when the sun appears out of the sea like Aaron out of his tent:

Forth from the curtain of clouds, from the tent of purple and
        scarlet,
Issued the sun, the great High-Priest, in his garments resplendent,
Holiness unto the Lord, in letters of light, on his forehead,
Round the hem of his robe the golden bells and pomegranates.
Blessing the world he came, and the bars of vapor beneath him
Gleamed like a grate of brass, and the sea at his feet was a laver!

There is something decidedly Oriental in this, something brilliant, metallic, and ritualistic, as there was in the imagination of Puritanism on one side, though it was mostly overlain by Protestant austerity; and the poem comes to an end in a burst of feeling that is both Israelitish and pastoral. It has that kind of truth to the life of the Plymouth Colony; and *The Courtship of Miles Standish,* modest as it is in the claims it makes, is a minor but honorable achievement in poetic narrative.

X

Birds of Passage

IN LOOKING at the "poems, chiefly lyrical" of Longfellow's middle decades, one has no impression of a surprising or dramatic development in poetic power, of the emergence of wholly new themes or modes, of either splendid advance or dismal decline. In greater poets the middle years, or even old age, have sometimes meant a wonderful renewal, as with Yeats, or a deplorable falling-off, as with Wordsworth. And there are cases such as Whitman's in which all of a poet's best work has been crowded intensely into a period of ten or a dozen years. These conspicuous and even violent seasonal changes are not characteristic of lesser poets, and they are not characteristic of Longfellow. He had reached a kind of upland of his powers as a lyric poet with *The Seaside and the Fireside*, and after that he held his ground with no really startling ascents or descents until perhaps his late sixties, when there is an appreciable, but by no means a miserable, failure of energy. Almost everything he was later to say had been said, or implied, by the time of *The Seaside and the Fireside*, and what remained was, fortunately, not mere self-repetition, but a steady, slight, unsensational, but beautiful refinement and enhancement of what he had already done. The didactic note is struck less and less, and indeed, strictly speaking, it is struck only once, in "The Ladder of St. Augustine," an inferior poem. The note of retrospect, of nostalgic reminiscence, is struck oftener, naturally enough; and the sense of the insubstantial, of the tenuity of the border between the visible and the invisible, the living and the dead, becomes more and more marked. But nothing could be more subtly graduated than these changes, and they cannot be much emphasized.

Technically speaking, Longfellow had never been content to limit himself to a narrow range of inherited metrical and stanzaic forms: he had experimented with hexameters, with free verse, with the *Hiawatha* line, and he continued now, unobtrusively, to explore the expressive possibilities of unhackneyed meters and stanzas. In earlier poems — "Curfew," "Rain in Summer," "Birds of Passage" — he had turned away from the normal syllable-counting of what Hopkins was to call Running Rhythm — iambs, trochees, and the rest — and tried his hand at that mixed measure which is sometimes called, rather pedantically, "logaoedic," and which Hopkins described more simply as Sprung Rhythm. Whatever it is called, this freer rhythm was of course no novelty in English poetry; one meets it repeatedly in Elizabethan songs; Coleridge had, to quite different effect, used it famously in "Christabel," and Poe had followed his example. Longfellow uses it less boldly than most of these other poets, but it would be insensitive not to do justice to the sprung rhythms of such poems as "My Lost Youth" and "Snow-Flakes." This latter poem, thanks not only to its metrical subtlety and the expressive retardation of its pace but to its fine metaphor of snowfall, is one of the most successful pieces in the second "Birds of Passage":

> Out of the bosom of the Air,
>   Out of the cloud-folds of her garments shaken,
> Over the woodlands brown and bare,
>   Over the harvest-fields forsaken,
>   Silent, and soft, and slow
>   Descends the snow.
>
> Even as our cloudy fancies take
>   Suddenly shape in some divine expression,
> Even as the troubled heart doth make

> In the white countenance confession,
> The troubled sky reveals
> The grief it feels.

> This is the poem of the air,
> Slowly in silent syllables recorded;
> This is the secret of despair,
> Long in its cloudy bosom hoarded,
> Now whispered and revealed
> To wood and field.

The hushed and rather sad beauty of beginning snowfall has rarely been made to convey more delicately a state of troubled and half-despairing emotion. The poem trembles on the verge of becoming a minor symbolist piece, like something of Verlaine's, and it may be that, with its snowy imagery and its fastidious feeling, it is one of that "great number of passages in Longfellow" that, as Lafcadio Hearn felt, "very closely resemble, in their best qualities, the compositions of old Japanese poets." Only its length, perhaps, tells against the parallel.

The free verse of "Tegnér's Drapa" or the Prologue to *The Golden Legend* does not recur in these later volumes, but the possibilities of rhymelessness where conventionally one might expect rhymes, interested Longfellow, and in two or three poems he makes use of it to beautiful effect. There is the "incremental" refrain of "My Lost Youth," with its rhymeless first and fourth lines:

> And the voice of that wayward song
> Is singing and saying still:
> "A boy's will is the wind's will,
> And the thoughts of youth are long, long thoughts."

The sound of bells heard at sunset near the seacoast, like a "requiem for the dying day," suggested the fine poem on "The Bells of Lynn," the stanzas of which are couplets of long rhymeless lines that come closer to Tennyson than perhaps any other lines of Longfellow's. The sound of bells, of chimes, even of gongs is audible in much of this poet's work, and when it is associated with the seaside it has a peculiarly personal quality:

> Till from the shuddering sea, with your wild incantations,
> Ye summon up the spectral moon, O Bells of Lynn!

The absence of rhyme is not felt in the poem, or felt only as a beauty, as it is in Tennyson's "Tears, Idle Tears" — a finer lyric, to be sure — and this is equally true of a somewhat earlier poem, "The Golden Mile-Stone," though it is written in a four-line stanza, with a delicate *ritardo* in the third line, such as might seem to cry out for rhymes:

> Leafless are the trees; their purple branches
> Spread themselves abroad, like reefs of coral,
>   Rising silent
> In the Red Sea of the winter sunset.

With its soft "falling" rhythms, its consistently trochaic line-endings, and the quiet of its rhymelessness, the stanza of "The Golden Mile-Stone" is singularly appropriate to the wintry and crepuscular mood it sets out to express.

A quite different stanza, one of six lines in sprung rhythm, is the stanza of a ballad, "The Cumberland," the only "battle-piece" Longfellow wrote during the Civil War; it describes the victory of the ironclad *Merrimac* over the Federal sloop *Cumberland* in Hampton Roads, and is a poem therefore of defeat, not of triumph. It is unexpectedly better than Melville's poem on the same subject. Longfellow could not have written the best poems in *Battle-Pieces* any more than he could have written the best poems in *Drum-Taps*, but "The Cumberland," with its tensely shortened fourth, fifth, and sixth lines, has a martial energy such as Melville and Whitman, in their very different ways, sometimes also achieved:

> Then, like a kraken huge and black,
>   She crushed our ribs in her iron grasp!
> Down went the Cumberland all a wrack,

> With a sudden shudder of death,
> And the cannon's breath
> For her dying gasp.

The stanza of "The Cumberland," with its particular line lengths and rhyme pattern, may well be Longfellow's invention, for like Melville he liked to experiment with unused or little-used arrangements of line and rhyme; and in any case stanzas of six lines had often, as he used them, a special felicity of form. This is true of another poem written during the war, but quite unrelated to it, "Palingenesis," in *Flower-de-Luce*, a meditative poem on the alchemical theme of rebirth; here, in a way not easy to account for, the feminine a-rhymes and the hesitations of the shortened third and sixth lines, seem beautifully expressive of the charmed nostalgic mood the poem conjures up:

> I lay upon the headland-height, and listened
> To the incessant sobbing of the sea
>   In caverns under me,
> And watched the waves, that tossed and fled and glistened,
> Until the rolling meadows of amethyst
>   Melted away in mist.

Like that of "The Cumberland," this stanza has the air of being Longfellow's own; elsewhere he uses, and often with the ease of a practiced craftsman, more conventional six-line stanzas. He does so in "Sandalphon," where the rhymes are of the familiar a, a, b, c, c, b sort, though even here the fact that the c-rhymes, and they only, are feminine gives the stanza an almost imperceptible nuance of particularity:

> The Angels of Wind and of Fire
> Chant only one hymn, and expire
>   With the song's irresistible stress;
> Expire in their rapture and wonder,
> As harp-strings are broken asunder
>   By music they throb to express.

The symbol that gives unity to "Sandalphon" — that of the Angel of Prayer who weaves garlands out of the orisons of men — Longfellow had found in a book of legends from the Talmud; he had always, as we have seen, both in verse and in prose, drawn heavily on literature, on legend, on tradition, not only for the literal subjects of his poems but for their metaphors, and this half-scholarly, half-ingenuous habit grew on him, if anything, with time. When it is a question, as it is in "Sandalphon," of making a whole poem out of a legend or a tale, he seems to have disliked concealing his indebtedness; certainly he loved to begin poems, almost in the manner of a college lecturer, with a bibliographical reference:

> Have you read in the Talmud of old,
> In the Legends the Rabbins have told. . . .

> Saint Augustine! well hast thou said. . . .

> In Mather's Magnalia Christi,
>   Of the old colonial time,
> May be found in prose the legend
>   That is here set down in rhyme. . . .

> I have a vague remembrance
>   Of a story, that is told
> In some ancient Spanish legend
>   Or chronicle of old. . . .

In poems, too, that do not depend, as wholes, upon bookish sources, Longfellow again and again irradiates a thought or an emotion with a literary metaphor that is not, in a bad neoclassical manner, decorative and applied, but imaginatively just. A favorite book, from childhood, had been the *Arabian Nights*, and it is not surprising if images from that work arose in his mind, when he was deeply moved, without his summoning them consciously. The columns of smoke, in "The Golden Mile-Stone," rising from the chimneys of the village, are "like the Afreet in the Arabian story" — and take on thus a legendary, "distanced" character they would not otherwise have had. In the sonnet "To-morrow," not one of his finest, the coming day is an unknown guest who cries to the poet, lest he should be too secure in his happiness and forget the disasters that may overtake the prosperous:

> "Remember Barmecide,
> And tremble to be happy with the rest."*

"Vox Populi," a little poem in a rather uncharacteristically epigrammatic style, about the strict geographical limits that are set to even the most brilliant poetic fame, makes play with the names of two personages, Badoura and Camaralzaman, also in the *Arabian Nights*. But the most beautiful of the metaphors that Longfellow draws from that source appears in the last stanza of the threnody on Hawthorne, who, as was generally known, had left his last book uncompleted:

> Ah! who shall lift that wand of magic power,
> And the lost clue regain?
> The unfinished window in Aladdin's tower
> Unfinished must remain!

Metaphors such as most of these are flares that light up a moment or two in a poem, and then subside, though of course they have affected the light and shade of the whole piece. Sometimes the texture of an entire poem is woven out of traditional or richly associated images — a more deliberate process, reflective, conscious, and curious, and producing an effect that is a kind of blend of emotion and exposition. So it is in such a poem as "The Jewish Cemetery at Newport." This very old burying ground of Rhode Island Jews, adjoining a synagogue that had at that time fallen into disuse, becomes a focusing symbol for the long tragedy of the Jewish people, summoning up a whole cluster of grave, stately, and mournful associations — of ancient greatness, of exile, of persecution — and evoking an emotion of controlled

---

* This sonnet was written five years after Fanny Longfellow's death, and in that biographical sense, rather than intrinsically, has a particular pathos.

and impersonal sadness. In the graves of this tree-shaded cemetery, the dead Jews are keeping, underneath their "leafy tents,"
"the long, mysterious Exodus of Death," and the level grave-
stones themselves

> Seem like the tablets of the Law, thrown down
> And broken by Moses at the mountain's base.

These Jews have been the "Ishmaels and Hagars of mankind,"
slaking the thirst of their hearts with "marah of their tears," hearing from town to town the cry of the curse "Anathema mara-
natha!" and, each man of them a Mordecai, have been "mocked
and jeered, and spurned by Christian feet." Longfellow even in-
dulges in a kind of conceit or "witty" metaphor — the volume of
human history is now spelled backward by the Jews "like a He-
brew book" — which somehow fails to clash with the prevailingly
elegiac soberness of the poem. It ends on a pessimistic note in
which, however mistaken it was to prove, there is at least nothing
of conventional reassurance.

The process of conscious association one finds in "The Jewish
Cemetery at Newport" is a frequent one in Longfellow: he likes
to let his fancy — as Coleridge would certainly say here — hover
about a particular image and allow it to suggest to him a chain of
associated images in, again, a meditative rather than an intensely
lyrical way. This had been true of one of the better poems in
The Seaside, "Sand of the Desert in an Hour-Glass": the red
sand in the glass, brought from Arabian deserts, suggests in a
rather dreamlike manner all the feet that may ever have passed
over it — those of the camels of the Ishmaelites, of Moses, "burnt
and bare," of Armenian anchorites "pacing the Dead Sea beach" —
and at last dilates into "a column high and vast, / A form of fear
and dread." A not uncommonplace object has somehow, under
some unsuspected emotional pressure, been transmuted into an
emblem of mystery and apprehension. A similar thing happens
in "The Ropewalk," a poem in the first "flight" of "Birds of

Passage": here it is a recollection of the mill for rope-weaving, in the Portland of his childhood, that leads the poet's fancy on to thoughts of the cheerful, the useful, or the terrible purposes to which ropes can be put, as the ropes of a swing, as the tightropes on which weary mountebanks must perform, as bell ropes, kite strings, or hangman's nooses. The associative process then returns to the backward-walking spinners in the ropewalk, a reminder, as Howard Nemerov says, that "throws retrospectively a mysterious air, almost of paradox, over the details of the poem, life having been seen simultaneously as remembered, as lived, as spun, or fated, in the spinning of the rope."

There is a paradoxical air, too, or at least a contradictory one, about "The Golden Mile-Stone," the title of which alludes to that *milliarium aureum* in the Forum at Rome from which all distances from the Imperial City were measured. Longfellow identifies it with the domestic fireside from which each man measures, as from a central focus, every distance in the world around him. On the simplest level the poem is a rather sentimental celebration of the ancestral hearth and its "peace and comfort"; after its fine opening — four lovely stanzas — it becomes associative in a rather prosaic manner, and it ends limply. But meanwhile the associations aroused by the flames on the hearth have been, not mainly of peace and comfort, after all, but — in the persons of aged men, of youthful dreamers, and of a couple unhappily wed — of useless regret, of empty aspiration, and of domestic tragedy. The fireside metaphor, which might betoken only cheerful and even cozy emotions, has here, as in "The Fire of Drift-Wood," a curious doubleness of implication.

Certainly the metaphor of a hearth-fire is a recurrent one in Longfellow's verse, but not because fire itself as a symbol was very important to him, as it was to Hawthorne. He could not have written that paragraph on fire as a "destructive element" in Hawthorne's sketch "Fire Worship," which Melville so much admired. The fireside is for him usually an emblem of pleasant associative revery, not of balefulness; and in one poem, "The Wind over the Chimney," the fire itself plays a reassuring role. On a wild night of winter and storm, it inspires in the poet thoughts of high poetic aspiration; but the wind raging over the chimney, playing antagonist to the fire, howls its chilling answer:

> "Hollow
> Are the visions that you follow,
> Into darkness sinks your fire!"

The tongues of flame, lighting up the books on the shelves, remind the poet that in those volumes are recorded the great history-making words of bards and prophets:

> But the night-wind cries: "Despair!
> Those who walk with feet of air
> Leave no long-enduring marks;
> At God's forges incandescent
> Mighty hammers beat incessant,
> These are but the flying sparks!"

The night-wind is quite as eloquent as the tongues of flame; as these sink down, it clamors in his ears that the log on the hearth is a Life Token —

> " 'Tis the brand of Meleager
> Dying on the hearth-stone here!" —

and hints that his inspiration is dying with it. The poem ends on a note of rather banal reassurance, but the dialogue between the wind and the flames has been a singularly equal and, in that sense, an ironic one.

There is an emotional irony, too, in "The Bridge of Cloud," a poem in the same volume, *Flower-de-Luce*. The poet begins by asking the fire on the hearth to awaken pleasant visions for him in this "room of gold" that is so "safe" despite the winds that, again, are shaking the house; but Fancy, as it proves, can no longer build a charming castle for him in the air:

But, instead, she builds me bridges
  Over many a dark ravine,
Where beneath the gusty ridges
  Cataracts dash and roar unseen.

And I cross them, little heeding
  Blast of wind or torrent's roar,
As I follow the receding
  Footsteps that have gone before.

Naught avails the imploring gesture,
  Naught avails the cry of pain!
When I touch the flying vesture,
  'Tis the gray robe of the rain.

He assures himself that, in the mist-wrapped valley on which he is gazing down, there are doors with friendly faces and hearts with loving thoughts of him; but meanwhile these metaphors of dark ravines, dashing cataracts, and roaring torrents — and their freight of unappeasable bereavement — have had an effect of greater emotional authenticity. The tone of reassurance carries less conviction that that of grief, but can it not be said that in these two poems, slight as they are, there is a certain "balance or reconcilement of opposite or discordant qualities"?

Coleridge gave his phrase a very wide application, and so far as it may be applied, on his authority, to the reconcilement of "the sense of novelty and freshness with old and familiar objects," then the principle holds also for that much-mishandled poem "In the Churchyard at Cambridge." The "object" here, if the word may be used, is the perennial theme of Judgment — do human beings dare to sit in judgment upon their fellows? — but there is at the very least a genuine novelty and even oddity in the image that Longfellow finds for the expression of his theme. It is — to go "outside the poem" for a moment — an old monument in the burying ground of Christ Church in Cambridge, the grave of Madame Vassall, the first mistress of the Craigie House, who ordered, according to a local tradition, that a Negro slave be buried at her head and another at her feet. The poet asks very simply what he himself calls the "rude" question whether this was done out of worldly pride or, on the contrary, out of a rare humility? The answer, naturally, is that neither he nor any son of man has a right to say.

Everyone remembers that this was one of the poems I. A. Richards, a generation ago, submitted without hint of their authorship to his students at Cambridge (England) for their unprejudiced commentary, and that it was "by far the most disliked" of all the thirteen poems in question.* One student went so far as to protest that it was certainly written "*by a neurotic or a fanatic with a diseased mind.*" Most of the other critics were less disturbed by it than this one, but "In the Churchyard at Cambridge" evoked a whole series of angry or contemptuous "stock responses." The word "rude" outraged some, and the "by no means uncommon" nature of the thought troubled others. That thought is indeed a commonplace, but the poem is saved from banality by the freshness of the image and the quiet discretion with which an "old and familiar" reflection is stated. It is difficult to see in it that "social, urbane, highly cultivated, self-confident, temperate and easy kind of humor" which Richards himself handsomely attributed to it; one would have said that its tone is one of gravity and a kind of moral tenderness rather than of humor, however urbane or easy. But Richards was surely right in finding in the poem a genuine small distinction.

The thought of death, with the imagery of the churchyard, was never far from Longfellow's mind, not simply because it was a conventional theme, though this fact may have had its effect, but because the thought of death is never far from any poet's mind, and because bereavement — the premature death of his sister Ellen, the death of his first wife, the death of his daughter Fanny as a baby — was an early and recurrent experience for Longfellow.

---

* Their amusingly indignant criticisms may be found in Part II, Poem 13, of *Practical Criticism.*

One of his boyish poems, "Dirge over a Nameless Grave," is "literary" enough, but as time went on, the sense of the precariousness of mortal life was more and more present to him, and there is not one of his volumes from which the expression of it is absent. "The air is full of farewells to the dying," he had written after Fanny's death, in "Resignation," one of the most touching poems in *The Seaside;* and this solemn awareness of the mysterious presence of death in the midst of life, and of life in the midst of death, so that the frontier between them loses any sharpness of definition, is as characteristic of Longfellow as, with all their differences, it is of Whitman. There is no suggestion of an almost erotic relation with death, as there is in Whitman, but one usually finds in Longfellow a somewhat similar acceptance of it as not only an inevitable but even a somehow beneficent fact of experience. He was on intimate terms with what Whitman calls "the knowledge of death," and he did not distinguish very sharply between living men and the spirits of the dead. The latter too were familiars of his.

This comes out in a very uneven but curiously interesting poem, "Haunted Houses," which takes its departure from the not very unusual thought that "All houses wherein men have lived and died / Are haunted houses," and that we encounter their phantoms everywhere, at the doorway, on the stair, along the passages:

> Impalpable impressions on the air,
> A sense of something moving to and fro.

As his mind dwells gravely but not protestingly on this interpenetration of the seen and the unseen, he moves on to the thought that, around the world of sense, the spirit-world "floats like an atmosphere," and that our lives are kept in a kind of mysterious balance by this pervasion of the visible by the invisible; of the merely physical by the ideal. It suggests to him, indeed, an astronomical metaphor of an almost "metaphysical" boldness:

> These perturbations, this perpetual jar
> Of earthly wants and aspirations high,
> Come from the influence of an unseen star,
> An undiscovered planet in our sky.

This is quickly followed by the metaphor, again, of a bridge — a bridge of light connecting the world of spirits and this world,

> O'er whose unsteady floor, that sways and bends,
> Wander our thoughts above the dark abyss.

There is an incongruity in the striking of a moral note in a poem which should have been free from even this slight touch of the didactic. But the poem recovers from this in the last two stanzas, which re-establish the *Stimmung* of ghostliness; and even the moral reflection is expressed, through the metaphor of the unseen star, with a strangeness that redeems it from mere flatness. It is the kind of Longfellow poem that confirms Cesare Pavese's "discovery" that "the message of the Americans is the sense of a mysterious reality underlying the words."

There was a week in the fall of 1853 when the intermingling of life and death was even more present than usual to Longfellow; it was a week in October when his daughter Edith was born and when, a few days later, James Russell Lowell's young and beautiful wife died. The close approach to each other of birth and early death affected Longfellow deeply, and he made it the subject of a rather fine poem, "The Two Angels." The two are of course the Angel of Death, crowned "with amaranth, as with flame," and the Angel of Life, crowned "with asphodels, like flakes of light." They are represented, by a familiar poetic freedom, as arriving at neighboring households at dawn on the same day; it is the Angel crowned with asphodels who knocks at the poet's own door:

> And my soul sank within me, as in wells
> The waters sink before an earthquake shock.

This Angel's errand, however, as he quickly says, is not Death but Life, and it is at the door of the poet's friend that the Angel with the amaranthine wreath, the Angel of Death, arrives. The poem ends, as so often, with two anticlimactic moralizing stanzas which mar its beauty, but the emblematic Angels, with their classical amaranths and asphodels, are finely imaged.

There are two other poems of these years that exemplify Longfellow's gift for the writing of memorial verse. One of these is the quiet threnody on Hawthorne, which contents itself with summoning up the scene of Hawthorne's funeral in Concord on a beautiful day in May:

> Now I look back, and meadow, manse, and stream
>   Dimly my thought defines;
> I only see — a dream within a dream —
>   The hill-top hearsed with pines.
>
> I only hear above his place of rest
>   Their tender undertone,
> The infinite longings of a troubled breast,
>   The voice so like his own.

The single word "hearsed" is of fine effect here, and the hilltop itself is a curious presage of the "wintry hills" in "Monody," Melville's even more affecting poem on Hawthorne's death. The setting of a lovely spring day in the one poem, and of hills draped by "sheeted snow-drifts" in the other, is itself a measure of the contrast between the feelings of the one man and of the other for their friend. Meanwhile, twelve years earlier, Longfellow had written "The Warden of the Cinque Ports," a poem on the death, not of a friend, as almost always with him, but of a public figure, the Duke of Wellington, whom one would not have supposed, warrior and Tory that he was, to have been a particular hero of Longfellow's. And yet, despite the weak last stanza or two, "The Warden" has a fine martial stateliness of lament that rings truer than the rather pompous stateliness of Tennyson's more famous "Ode" on the Duke's death.

Longfellow would not have been so representative an American writer as he was if he had not now and then sounded the note of nostalgia — nostalgia for his own charmed boyhood and aspiring youth. The Things Past that he looked back upon so wistfully did not include, to be sure, as they did for Whitman, a first initiation into the mystery of death, or as for Mark Twain, a boyish innocence that had later been lost. Yet he was not very far from them, after all, in turning back longingly to the emotional freedom, the boyish irresponsibility, the endless ruminations of his *temps perdu* — the boy's will that is as the will of the wind, and the youthful thoughts that are "long, long thoughts." The famous refrain of "My Lost Youth" had come to him from Herder's anthology of folk-poetry, *Die Stimmen der Völker in Liedern*, where he found it in a translation Herder had made of a Lapland folksong:

> Knabenwille ist Windeswille,
> Jünglings Gedanken lange Gedanken.

Longfellow's version of this refrain is about as literal as it could be, and yet, for once, it is an improvement on the German, if only because the "long, long thoughts" are so much more protracted and thus so much more entranced than Herder's rather abrupt *lange Gedanken*. In any case, what he looked back upon, in his Portland boyhood, was not a mystical experience of oneness with Nature, like that of Wordsworth's Boy of Winander, but the much more usual, if hardly less penetrating, charm of a boy's eager sensuous awareness of natural beauty — "the sheen of the far-surrounding seas," "the sea-tides tossing free," "the shadows of Deering's woods"; and of the busy world of human activity, romantic or tragic — "the Spanish sailors with bearded lips," "the beauty and mystery of the ships," "the sunrise gun, with its hollow roar," and "the dead captains as they lay, / In their graves, o'erlooking the tranquil bay." The romance of boyhood, gazed down upon at a distance in time like a countryside from a distant hilltop, has rarely been expressed with so little falsity or mannerism.

Nostalgia, not for boyhood, but for youth, is the emotion behind "Palingenesis," with its metaphor of the rose which the old alchemists believed they could re-create from its ashes, "but without the bloom, / Without the lost perfume." The sense of deprivation the poem expresses is a regret not for the lost enchantments of childhood but for the lost ardors of youth, "the vanished splendors," the eagerness of a swift stream that, bounding over its rocky channel, gives up

> The pond, with all its lilies, for the leap
> Into the unknown deep!

The poem has the dramatic quality that so many good lyrical poems have, for it is partly a dialogue between the backward-glancing poet and the lamenting voice of the sea, which, wailing "like some old prophet," answers his outcry of longing for the past with a kind of tender rebuke and the reminder that his wish is as vain as the hopes of the alchemists. Another poet would have left the matter there, but Longfellow, unwilling to yield to a sentiment of mere self-pity, turns away from the past and forces himself to face forward — he was in his late fifties when he wrote "Palingenesis" — and to look ahead to the autumnal landscape, "and the glow / Of sunsets burning low," which he has still before him. The recoil of will in some of his melancholy poems seems at least a little forced and dutiful, but not here, if only because the poet insists on looking forward not only to "friendly greetings and caresses," but

> To what temptations in lone wildernesses,
> What famine of the heart, what pain and loss,
> The bearing of what cross!

There is, again, a certain emotional complexity in the poem that cannot be disposed of as due to mere perfunctory moralizing.

Longfellow, as we have seen, almost never returned to the openly humanitarian manner of *Poems on Slavery* or the frank politicism of the coda to "The Building of the Ship." As the antislavery movement deepened in intensity, though his emotions were painfully involved, he seemed less and less capable of expressing them in passionate verse, and except for the naval ballad "The Cumberland," he wrote nothing on the eve of the War or during it that might have given to his warmly patriotic feeling the form of a public act. The crisis of Secession, acutely as he felt it, called out from him no such pieces as Whitman's "First O Songs for a Prelude" or Melville's "Conflict of Convictions"; the promulgation of the Emancipation Proclamation was followed by nothing of his that could have vied with Emerson's "Boston Hymn"; and his aversion to any sort of occasional verse effectually kept him from writing anything comparable to Lowell's "Ode Recited at the Harvard Commemoration." In his work as in his life, he had a deep personal distaste for the platform or the rostrum, and it is all the more startling when he momentarily abandons his fireside or his library for Faneuil Hall. He surprised everyone, and outraged some people, by doing this with *Poems on Slavery*, and he did a similar, though less drastic, thing in writing his poems on peace and the last lines of "The Building of the Ship." Twice again, though only twice, during these middle decades, he spoke out in what was essentially a public way. In the late fifties the ardor of his sympathy for the Italian Risorgimento impelled him, in the year of Solferino and Milazzo, to write "Enceladus," a poem on the struggle for Italian liberty; and in 1873, when the depression of that year threw thousands of men out of work, he wrote a quite unpredictably "social democratic" poem, "The Challenge."

"Enceladus," which Longfellow may have thought of as a kind of return gift for Alfieri's odes on American independence, is the better of the two poems, and indeed the best of all his few political pieces. This is partly because he allows the metaphor itself — the giant Enceladus who made war on the tyrannous Olympians and was then punished by Zeus, who chained him under Mount Etna — to carry the whole freight of his meaning, and refrains from making the political bearing of the metaphor painfully explicit. The image of Enceladus, too, though Longfellow endows it with no such metaphysical power of significance as Melville did in a famous passage in *Pierre*, is a fine and fitting symbol in this poem of protest against political oppression:

> The crags are piled on his breast,
> The earth is heaped on his head;
> But the groans of his wild unrest,
> Though smothered and half suppressed,
> Are heard, and he is not dead.

It is a rare case of such imagery in Longfellow, for whom mountains and especially volcanoes had little emotional value; but here, surprisingly, he imparts to the image of a volcanic eruption — the burning cinders, the sinister red light, and the ashes heaped in drifts over vineyards and fields — an extraordinary force of suggestion. "The Challenge" is more commonplace poetically: the haggard faces looking in, out of the cold and darkness, at the banquet going forward in a lighted hall, are the clichés of humanitarian literature; but the poem is saved from being a mere piece of poster-verse by the striking figures with which it opens and closes. The first of these is the figure of Don Diego de Ordoñez, a Spanish knight who, at the seige of Zamora, after King Sanchez had been slain, challenged "with taunting words of scorn" the people of the city as base traitors. We prosperous ones, of course, are the traitors now; the role of King Sanchez is transferred at the end to Christ himself:

> And there in the camp of famine
> In wind and cold and rain,
> Christ, the great Lord of the army,
> Lies dead upon the plain!

It is a startlingly bitter final note, and "The Challenge" has the interest of being a literally unique expression, among New England poets of that generation, of something like socialist protest.

Like so many romantic poets, and like some more recent and more profound poets than he, Longfellow came back again and again to the subject of Poetry itself. On this theme he had little that was audacious or path-breaking to say; he wrote nothing comparable to Emerson's "Merlin" or Whitman's "Song of the Answerer," not to speak of the great English and European poets of romantic poetics. His thoughts on poetry and the role of the bard are mostly the current coin of nineteenth-century aesthetics, and often they hark back to even earlier *artes poeticae*. Yet they are too characteristic of him to be passed over, and in a few poems he gives them a personal turn and a freshness of application that are not negligible. This is especially true of the poems — sonnets mainly — which he wrote about particular poets — Tegnér, Dante, Shakespeare, and others — mostly in his later years. But in all the early and middle volumes there are poems on the Poet and Poetry generally that have some interest or other, however slight.

Like his own Mr. Churchill in *Kavanagh*, Longfellow seems sometimes to have felt, quite mistakenly, that the remote, the romantic, the legendary was a seduction it was his duty to resist: already, in the "Prelude" to *Voices of the Night*, he had told himself to turn his back on "old legends of the monkish age," and heed the admonition of "distant voices": "Look, then, into thine heart, and write!" * It was a quite unreal dilemma for such a poet as he was, but he came back to the point, with a somewhat more Wordsworthian bias, in "Gaspar Becerra," a poem in *The Seaside*, about a Spanish sculptor who tries in vain to carve an

---

* Poe reprimanded Longfellow for plagiarizing Sidney's well-known line, "Fool, said my muse to me, look in thy heart and write"; and indeed it *is* a curiously literal borrowing by one poet from another.

image of the Virgin out of precious wood from the East, but finds instead that a humble oaken brand on his own hearth lends itself to his artist's dream at once; and so learns the lesson that

> That is best which lieth nearest;
> Shape from that thy work of art.

His own experience hardly confirmed this too-dutiful prescription, and as time went on he made less and less of it. Meanwhile, however, he had given expression more than once to what was really a much older view and one that was only in part consistent with his urging of the claims of the near-at-hand — the classical or neoclassical view that the end of poetry is both to delight and to instruct — *aut prodesse volunt aut delectare poetae* — or, as he puts it in an inferior poem, "The Singers," "to charm, to strengthen, and to teach." Perhaps only the word "strengthen" here has postclassical overtones; it recurs in a much better poem, also in *The Seaside*, which was originally a proem to Longfellow's anthology, *The Estray*. This is "Pegasus in Pound," which was certainly suggested by Schiller's "Pegasus im Joche," but which makes charming, and not merely derivative, use of the image of a winged horse which appears one autumn morning in a quiet village and is quickly put into pound. He escapes at midnight, winging his way upward, but leaving behind him a fountain, struck out by his hooves on the greensward:

> From that hour, the fount unfailing
> Gladdens the whole region round,
> Strengthening all who drink its waters,
> While it soothes them with its sound.

The emotionally and perhaps also the morally fortifying and refreshing power of poetry is an aspect that Longfellow loved to dwell on, and it often has, as he expresses it, the authenticity of a recurring personal response.

It is very close in feeling to that other view, more purely romantic in character, that "Our sweetest songs are those that tell of saddest thought," or as Longfellow puts it in "Prometheus, or the Poet's Forethought,"

> Only those are crowned and sainted
> Who with grief have been acquainted,
> Making nations nobler, freer.

"Seaweed," earlier, had come very close to the Heinesque "aus meinen grossen Schmerzen," with its expression of the thought that the poet's songs are always preceded by "storms of wild emotion," and Longfellow in fact wavered between this feeling and his inclination to the moralistic. He brings the two strains together in "Prometheus," where he represents the Titan, in what had become a familiar romantic myth, as "a symbol painted / Of the Poet, Prophet, Seer" — a symbol in his noble theft of fire from the Olympians, in his sharing of it with mortals, but also in his torment:

> Then the vulture, — the despairing
> Cry of pain on crags Caucasian.

The Poet as Prophet had become a convention, in the highest sense, long before Longfellow wrote this poem, but the convention was by no means lifeless even then, and "Prometheus" has an eloquence that shows how much Longfellow had made the conviction his own. Its companion poem, "Epimetheus, or the Poet's Afterthought," which expresses the mood of deflation, disenchantment, lassitude, which so often in his experience followed upon the excitement of creation, is even more striking if only because it is so much more particularly his own: that anticlimactic emotional state can rarely have been described before Longfellow, and he uses a familiar mythical image rather finely in describing it:

> Not with steeper fall nor faster,
> From the sun's serene dominions,
> Not through brighter realms nor vaster,

> In swift ruin and disaster,
> Icarus fell with shattered pinions!

The best of Longfellow's poems about Poetry, indeed, are not those that give expression to romantic or pre-romantic common-places, but those that, like "Epimetheus," spring from his own very full and sensitive experience both as a writer and as a reader of poetry. This is true of "Birds of Passage" itself, which de-pends on the beautiful image of migrating birds winging their way southward on a starlit night. Though he does not see the birds themselves, he hears the cry of their voices "falling dreamily through the sky," and reflects that these are the songs not of birds but of poets, "murmurs of pleasures, and pains, and wrongs":

> This is the cry
> Of souls, that high
> On toiling, beating pinions, fly,
>   Seeking a warmer clime.*

An even more purely personal piece is "Aftermath," the last poem in the volume by that name: it expresses Longfellow's feeling that his poems are now no longer the work of youth or even middle age but of an autumnal season like that in which the rowen, or second crop of hay, is gathered:

> Not the sweet, new grass with flowers
> Is this harvesting of ours;
>   Not the upland clover bloom;
> But the rowen mixed with weeds,
> Tangled tufts from marsh and meads,
> Where the poppy drops its seeds
>   In the silence and the gloom.

The metaphor of the aftermath is entirely his own, like Whitman's "November Boughs," and the poppy of oblivion, though much

---

* The metaphor of birds of passage — *oiseaux de passage* — was not un-familiar in romantic poetry. Lamartine, for example, had used it in an early poem, "Le Poète Mourant." For him, however, the metaphor signified the ephemeral nature of the poet's songs, not, as it did for Longfellow, the long-ing of the poet for "a warmer clime."

less uncommon, delicately enhances the effect of this poem of old age. Longfellow had almost never written better, as a matter of fact, when his harvesting had been that of "sweet, new grass with flowers."

XI

A Wayside Inn

I̶T REMAINED for Longfellow in his middle fifties, and after the crushing blow of his wife's death, to hit upon the most fortunate plan — of an ambitious sort, that is — in his whole career as a poet, the plan of a series of tales in verse contained within a narrative frame. No literary undertaking could have made a happier or more fruitful use of his powers and his equipment than this — of his storytelling genius, his sense of narrative form, his versatility, and the opulence of his literary erudition. He had considered projects of this sort long before, but nothing had come of them — in part, surely, because the right *kind* of frame had not suggested itself to him, as it did now. A trustworthy instinct told Longfellow that the setting for his tales must be as close at hand, as much within easy reach, for an American poet in his day, as the plague-stricken Florence of 1348 and the villa outside the city had been for Boccaccio, or the Tabard Inn and the Canterbury road for Chaucer; it told him too that his cast of characters must be as familiar to him in type as, to Boccaccio, his young noblemen and noblewomen had been, or as his pilgrims had been to Chaucer.* Of these two great predeces-

---

* In his excellent book on Melville, the Italian critic Gabriele Baldini speaks of the *Wayside Inn* as a "dusty forgery" (*un polveroso falso*) of the *Canterbury Tales*. There is a certain concession to critical fashion in this. Longfellow himself was much too modest to suppose that he had done more than follow in Chaucer's footsteps at a great distance; in a late sonnet, "Woodstock Park," he alludes with genuine humility to the inimitableness of the elder poet:

sors, among so many, he was of course particularly conscious: indeed, he had considered calling his collection "The Sudbury Tales" until the last moment, when he wisely withdrew this title as being uncomfortably close to Chaucer's; and as for Boccaccio, Longfellow not only drew upon the *Decameron* for one of the best of his stories, but made a point of alluding to him in his Prelude. The young Sicilian, he remarks, had a passion both for poetry and for novellas in prose — for

> the joyous Tuscan tales
> Of the Decameron, that make
> Fiesole's green hills and vales
> Remembered for Boccaccio's sake.

Longfellow's scene, as everyone knows even now, is an ancient hostelry, the Red Horse Inn, in Sudbury, not far from Boston — as natural a gathering-place for nineteenth-century Americans as the inn at Southwark had been for Chaucer's men and women, with the difference that Longfellow's personages set out on no pilgrimage — whither would they take their steps? — but remain sedentarily in the parlor of the Inn; and that what is thus lost in the sense of ambling movement, of a journey on horseback with a pious goal, is gained in the sense of repose — and, it must be said, of "realism," since a long procession on horseback has its limitations as a setting for group entertainment. However that may be, the parlor of an old inn, formerly a family mansion — not an official one, like Hawthorne's Province House — on a gusty autumn evening, is the curiously appropriate setting for these tales, and the fire blazing on the hearth is, for Longfellow, inescapably indicated as a stimulus to the tale-telling fancy. It is evening, to be sure, only in Part First; in Part Second, one finds the company gathered together again in the parlor on the following morning,

---

Here Geoffrey Chaucer in his ripe old age
Wrote the unrivalled Tales, which soon or late
The venturous hand that strives to imitate
Vanquished must fall on the unfinished page.

a wet, chilly, discouraging autumn forenoon that makes any
sortie abroad uninviting; in Part Third, after a day that has turned
out clearer and pleasanter than it promised to be, the evening has
come round again, and the guests gather about the hearth once
more for a final session of story-telling. They all take their
departure on the second morning, never to come together again,
and the temporal frame of their tales has thus a pleasant roundness.

They are a somewhat varied group, the seven of them, though
they have nothing like the variety, social or moral, of Chaucer's
pilgrims — who of course much outnumber them — and unlike
either Boccaccio's or Chaucer's gathering this one includes no
women; a certain crepitation of sexual interest is missing as a
result, but again, for the American social habits of the time,
this is a gain in verisimilitude. Not that all these personages are
themselves native Americans; they would not have expressed
Longfellow's mind very fully if they had been, and three of them
are Europeans: the tall, blond, blue-eyed Musician from Norway,
the young Sicilian, a political exile after the siege of Palermo,
and the patriarchal Spanish Jew, a silk merchant from Alicante.
The Americans, expectedly enough, are, with one exception, literary or academic characters — a Theologian from Cambridge, a
young Poet, and an equally youthful Student. The only nonintel-
lectual member of the group is the Landlord of the Red Horse
Inn himself, the scion of an ancient local family that has come
down in the world. Yet they are all men of roughly the same
class, a middling one; there are no men of rank or wealth, and
there are no men of really humble condition; no one to compare with the Miller or the Cook; and they pay for the easiness
of the intercourse that results from this homogeneity by a certain
absence of social light and shade.

In the several preludes, interludes, and finales, these seven
personages are lightly and simply characterized — somewhat more
fully than Boccaccio's Filostratos and Filomenas, but far less fully,
less powerfully and broadly, it need not be said, than most of

Chaucer's men and women. There is no portrait here remotely comparable in vigor with that of the Wife of Bath, the Prioress, or the Pardoner; Longfellow's portraits, though they were drawn from actual individuals, are dim and sketchy side by side with these. Yet, in their slighter way, they have a certain vividness, especially the somber and brooding figure of the Spanish Jew, the ardent figure of the young Sicilian, and the romantic figure of the Norwegian Musician, with his air of hailing from a northern world of cataracts, glaciers, and plunging seas. The Americans are more weakly characterized, though the Landlord, with his simple but self-respecting manners, and the Student, with his passion for books and solitude, are not without a fictional vitality: the Student, indeed, with his suggestion of the Clerk of Oxenford, has even a touch of the Chaucerian. Taking Chaucer as his model, too, Longfellow makes an effort to characterize his people in part by the kinds of tales they tell — the Spanish Jew by his dark legends from the Talmud and similar sources, the Musician by his Norse saga and his Danish ballad, the Theologian by his tales with a religious or sectarian setting, and the Landlord by his stirring or humorous stories with a New England origin.*

---

* Longfellow himself said that he had had real individuals in mind in sketching his tale-tellers. The Landlord was a bachelor, Lyman Howe, whose family had maintained the Red Horse Inn since the late seventeenth century; under his management the Inn is said to have declined in prosperity. Henry Ware Wales, the Student, was a youngish Harvard man who had studied medicine but whose health was too delicate to permit him to practice; dying young, he left his large collection of books to the Harvard College Library. The Sicilian was Luigi Monti, who had been exiled after taking part in the Revolution of 1848, and had become, thanks to Longfellow's patronage, an instructor in Italian at Harvard. The Spanish Jew is a rather shadowy figure, but he was probably one Isaac Edrehi, son of Moses Edrehi, a Spanish Jewish scholar, and himself, according to the Boston Directory, a "peddler" in Boston in the late fifties. Daniel Treadwell must have been an amateur Theologian at best, for in fact he was Rumford Professor of Physics at Harvard. The Poet was Thomas William Parsons, author of a much-anthologized "Ode on a Bust of Dante" and translator of the Inferno; he seems to have suggested to Longfellow that he write a poem on Tegnér's death, as of course he did. Ole Bull, the Norwegian violinist, whose musicianship Longfellow much admired, sat for the portrait of the

There is a good deal of mild romantic charm in the setting for all these tales, as there is in Hawthorne's Province House: both writers were looking for such "atmosphere" as was to be found in the rather too sharply lighted American scene, and an old village inn, "now somewhat fallen to decay," "remote among the wooded hills," with no "noisy railway," as Longfellow says, roaring past, comes as close as a human dwelling could do to approximating one of those English manors, old country-houses, or parsonages which James missed so badly in the United States. The sense of the American Past, such as it was, not the pressure of the American Present, was what these tales needed as an accompaniment, traditional and often romantic as they were.

There is a good deal of charm, too, in the small dramatic accessories of the tale-telling, as they emerge in the preludes and interludes — the highly romantic music the Musician plays for his friends on his Stradivarius, the rusty Revolutionary sword the Landlord takes down from its nail (it had been carried by an ancestor in the skirmish at Concord), the striking of the old clock that interrupts the Theologian before he can get on with the story of "Elizabeth." There is a certain amount of give-and-take, too, among the guests, mainly of a literary sort and often suggesting, as Howard Nemerov says, the "discussions" in a college seminar. There is even some friction among them, though it never, as in Chaucer, amounts to real wrangling: the Theologian protests against the Student's tale, "The Falcon of Ser Federigo," chaste as it is, because it is drawn from the "stagnant fen" of the *Decameron,* and the Student, having nursed his resentment over this, objects somewhat later to the Theologian's tale, "Torquemada," as being much too grim. The lighthearted Sicilian, in Part Third, after listening to the Spanish Jew's tale of Azrael, begs him to forbear his "ghostly legends of affright" and let

Musician. In 1855 Longfellow had entertained Bull at dinner with two or three other people, and after dinner, in the twilight, "Ole Bull played and chanted old Norse melodies, which were very striking."

the Talmud "rest in peace." But there is no real acerbity in these interchanges, and the prevailing tone among the friends is one of appreciation and amenity. Only twice does any very passionate feeling break out, and then it is of a generous humanitarian sort. When the Musician has finished "The Saga of King Olaf," the Theologian underlines its moral with unmistakable earnestness; "Thank God," he says,

> "The reign of violence is dead,
> Or dying surely from the world,"

and proceeds to protest not only against the violence of war but against that of theological sectarianism. In Part Second, after the Sicilian has told the story of "The Bell of Atri," the Poet makes a little speech on the horror of cruelty to animals — in the same spirit in which, the evening before, he himself had told the story of "The Birds of Killingworth." It was a subject on which Longfellow felt deeply: in the best possible sense, it is the S.P.C.A. strain in him — the strain he carries on from Cowper and Burns.

In the writing of Part Second and Part Third Longfellow took pains to avoid, by pleasant dramatic devices, an excessive symmetry in the distribution of his tales. He represents the Landlord, on that rainy morning, as unable to overcome his bashfulness in this very literate company, and slipping out from among his guests and taking refuge in the barn, where he spends the day mending harness and the like. Meanwhile, the Student good-naturedly makes up for his absence by telling two stories, "The Cobbler of Hagenau" and "The Baron of St. Castine." On the second evening, the Spanish Jew, aware that some of his audience have found "Azrael" too somber, obligingly tells a second and more stirring tale, that of the Albanian hero Scanderbeg, otherwise known as George Castriota. At the end of the evening the Landlord, who the night before, in spite of his shyness, had led off with "Paul Revere's Ride," yields to the persuasion of his guests and tells a second tale, the amusing "Rhyme of Sir Christopher." There are thus twenty-two tales in all, a modest number compared with Boccaccio's Hundred, to say nothing of the Thousand and One Nights.

They come, as one would expect, from a great variety of sources, though these are not quite so various as Longfellow's other writings would prepare us to foresee. It is surprising, for example, that there is nothing drawn from Greek or Latin literature; nothing from classical myth or history; and equally surprising that, though Longfellow was indebted to some English writers in the *Tales,* he tells no story that has an English setting. Even more unexpectedly, there is rather little that belongs to Germany: the Student's tale of "Emma and Eginhard" comes from a life of Charlemagne and is therefore Frankish; the scene of "The Cobbler of Hagenau" is of course the Alsatian town, but Longfellow found the anecdote in a Swiss history of the Reformation; and though "The Ballad of Carmilhan" certainly suggests some of the Phantom Ships of folklore in which German literature is so rich, it is little more specifically German than the Flying Dutchman. "Torquemada" is the only poem here with a Spanish setting; Longfellow found the subject in a history of Protestantism in Spain. Only in "The Baron of St. Castine," the scene of which is laid in the valley of the Gave in the Pyrenees, does a group of French characters appear, and the story, at one remove, is quite as much a story of New France as of Old; Longfellow came upon it in a history of the state of Maine. The absence of any Englishman or German, any Frenchman or Christian Spaniard from his group of *réciteurs* of course has much to do with these omissions.

These were years, on the other hand, when Longfellow's mind seems to have turned more eagerly than ever to Italy and Italian literature, and five of the twenty-two tales have an Italian setting or at least an Italian source. The Student, as we have seen, retells a story from the *Decameron;* and the young Sicilian, quite naturally, confines himself in his tales to his native literature. The beautiful story of "King Robert of Sicily" Longfellow had found retold by Leigh Hunt, though it went back to the *Gesta Romanorum* of the fourteenth century; and "The Monk of Casal-Maggiore," which the Sicilian also tells, he would certainly have come upon in a collection of Italian novellas by one Michele Colombo. "Kambalu," the Spanish Jew's first tale in Part Second, though it has a Tartar setting, Longfellow had found in Marco Polo. Meanwhile, two of the other stories the Spanish Jew tells, "The Legend of Rabbi Ben Levi" and "Azrael," have a Talmudic or Rabbinical derivation. To the Norwegian Musician, on the other hand, is attributed the longest, the most vigorous, and the most brilliant of the tales, "The Saga of King Olaf," a reworking of part of the *Heimskringla;* and in Part Third the Musician recites "The Mother's Ghost," a straight translation of a Danish ballad from Svend Grundtvig's great collection.

Convinced as he had always been, however, that there was perfectly good "matter" for poetry in American history and tradition, Longfellow quite naturally introduced one or two tales of that sort into each of the three parts of the *Wayside Inn*. On the second evening, indeed, there is a little passage-at-arms between the Student and the Theologian on this head, the Student taking the line that poets are bound to range abroad for much of their inspiration — that they are not "fowls in barnyards born" — and the Theologian maintaining that "what is native still is best." The question has long since ceased to be interesting, and Longfellow raises it here in an only half-serious way. But it is surely not mere chance that Part First begins and ends with American tales — the Landlord's ballad of Paul Revere and the Poet's tale of "The Birds of Killingworth" — or that the final series ends with another tale of the Landlord's, the most "rooted" man of them all, "The Rhyme of Sir Christopher." All these are New England tales of the seventeenth or eighteenth century, and so, too, is "Lady Wentworth," one of the Poet's tales, a story of the days of the colonial governors which Longfellow took from a book about

Portsmouth in New Hampshire. Only one of the five American tales has a scene laid outside of New England: this is the Theologian's last tale, "Elizabeth," which Longfellow based on a story of the New Jersey Quakers that had been told in prose by Lydia Maria Child.* Of all the narratives in the *Wayside Inn*, only one, "The Birds of Killingworth," was not derived from a literary source; it seems to have sprung from a local tradition in the Connecticut town, which had come to Longfellow — perhaps with what James called "the minimum of valid suggestion" — by word of mouth.

There is, in short, an extraordinary variety in the sources on which Longfellow drew for his tales, and there is an even greater variety in the verse forms in which he writes them, as if he wished, with a craftsman's understandable pride, to demonstrate his versatility as a metrist. The meters that bulk largest are those freely rhyming octosyllabics that he had used in so much of *The Golden Legend:* he uses them here, with easy control, in all the preludes and interludes and in one tale, "The Cobbler of Hagenau." In other tales, "Kambalu" and "St. Castine," one comes upon those even freer four-stress verses that, in *The Legend,* had suggested the "doggerel" of many scenes in *Faust,* and that might also be described as a very relaxed and fluent sort of sprung rhythm. More frequent than such rhythms are the pentameter couplets, not "heroic" but romantic, like Byron's or Shelley's, which Longfellow had used so little, before this time: eight of the tales, including some of the best, "King Robert of Sicily" and "Torquemada," are written in this form — how competently, a passage such as this may suggest:

> Now all the leaves had fallen; the branches bare
> Made a perpetual moaning in the air,
> And screaming from their eyries overhead
> The ravens sailed athwart the sky of lead.

* Mrs. Child's story, "The Youthful Emigrant," had been based on a work by a Quaker writer, John Estaugh, *A Call to the Unfaithful Professors of Truth,* which Benjamin Franklin had published in Philadelphia in the 1740's.

With his own hands he lopped the boughs and bound
Fagots, that crackled with foreboding sound,
And on his mules, caparisoned and gay
With bells and tassels, sent them on their way.

This is not one of the heightened passages, but it illustrates very fairly the general tenor of Longfellow's couplets.

He had never used any of the more elaborate stanzaic forms in verse narrative; the life had pretty much gone out of the Spenserian stanza by this time, and Longfellow never wrote in it; but twice in the *Tales* he tried his hand at the old *ottava rima* of Ariosto and Tasso, the eight-line stanza that Keats has used in "Isabella," and Byron, to so different an effect, in *Don Juan*. The stanzas of "The Birds of Killingworth" and "The Monk of Casal-Maggiore" have neither the rhythmical richness of Keats's nor the tireless speed and buoyancy of Byron's, but, since both tales are humorous or at least lighthearted, they are closer to Byron in feeling, and few poets except the greater men have ever written *ottave rime* with so little apparent effort, so little awkwardness. Meanwhile, as we have seen, Longfellow had never been perfectly sure of himself as a writer of blank verse, and he uses it only once in these volumes, in the Poet's very short tale of "Charlemagne," but it has a kind of strictness and strength, as he writes it there, that one could hardly have forecast. So much cannot be said for the hexameters which, for the last time, Longfellow came back to in "Elizabeth"; the tale itself is mild and even rather tame, and perhaps that is why the verse, except for two or three passages, is so invertebrate.

"The Ballad of Carmilhan" and "The Mother's Ghost" are spiritedly written in ballad couplets or stanzas, but far more brilliant than either are the balladlike stanzas and others that Longfellow uses in "The Saga of King Olaf." This poem is indeed the great display-piece, metrically and in other ways, of *A Wayside Inn:* never, before or after, did Longfellow exhibit such virtuosity or such resource in the writing of narrative verse. It looks as if he had written the poem in a playfully competitive spirit: his model, in more senses than one, was Tegnér's *Frithiof's Saga,* and of course he remembered that, in all the twenty-four cantos of his poem, the Swedish poet had never once repeated a stanzaic form. There are only twenty-two cantos in "Olaf," to be sure, but except for the first and the last, there is no repetition among them, nor does Longfellow ever resort, as Tegnér had done, to such really unsuitable measures, in a saga-like poem, as *ottave rime* and hexameters. The two-stress rhymeless lines of the first and last cantos, the couplets-with-refrain of "Sigrid the Haughty," the quatrains-with-refrain of "The Wraith of Odin," the interlocked stanzas of "Iron-Beard," the six-line stanzas of "King Olaf's War-Horns" — these are a few of the forms that variegate this poem metrically with such brilliance, and it would not be easy to say which are the most successful. It is as if Longfellow were emulating the splendid technical ostentation of the Icelandic skalds themselves, different as his patterns are from theirs.

There is almost as great a variety among the tales in tone and in type as in metrical form. Some of them have very much the quality of the American nineteenth-century tale or short story, and indeed one of them, "Elizabeth," as we have seen, was *based* on a short story. It is of the quiet, homespun, domestic sort, in the vein of so many stories in the giftbooks and annuals thirty years earlier and not unlike some of the local color stories of Mrs. Stowe. "The Rhyme of Sir Christopher," on the other hand, with its seventeenth-century Massachusetts Colony setting, is much more in Hawthorne's manner, though it is quite without his somber overtones and moral shadows. It suggests a little "The Maypole of Merrymount," if only because the scapegrace Thomas Morton figures in both tales. Still another scapegrace appears in Longfellow's tale, Sir Christopher Gardiner, an alleged Knight of the Holy Sepulchre, who outrages the Boston magistrates by settling among them with a charming young woman he calls his cousin, and who, as they learn, has "carelessly left behind" two other wives in England. The tale is an anecdotal trifle, as it was meant to be, but it has a real briskness, and like *The Courtship* it demonstrates that Longfellow was refreshingly capable of perceiving the comic aspects of Puritan life. Comic, too, but in a somewhat more astringent vein, is "The Birds of Killingworth," which has something of the satirical edge of "A Little Man in Gosling Green," with its by no means genial sketches of the self-satisfied Squire, the smug Deacon, and the Parson, "the instinct of whose nature was to kill," and who reads "Edwards on the Will" with such fervor. Longfellow had a feeling very like Hiawatha's — or Saint Francis's — for the birds, who sing and sweep through much of his verse; and the slaughter of the birds of Killingworth — the thrushes, the bluebirds, the jays, the orioles — evokes a strain of asperity from him that is quite absent from the tale of the gentlemanly bigamist Sir Christopher.

"Paul Revere's Ride," which might also have been a short story — superficially like "My Kinsman, Major Molineux" — is of course a tale of vigorous action and movement, a patriotic ballad; and its extreme familiarity ought not to blind us to the admirable impetus with which its galloping lines in sprung rhythm tell the tale of this celebrated ride on horseback through the sleeping Massachusetts villages, or to the characteristic touches, not obviously demanded by the tradition, of strangeness and ghostliness that give it another dimension than the strenuous: the "masses and moving shapes of shade" in the belfry chamber of the Old North Church, the "night-encampment" of the dead in the churchyard on the hill, and the belfry tower rising above the graves, "lonely and spectral and sombre and still." Nor should we undervalue the folklore touch at the end, when Longfellow, writing just before the Civil War, predicts that, in every hour of darkness and peril to the Republic, the people will hear "the hurrying hoof-beats" of Paul Revere's horse. "Scanderbeg," too, is a short balladlike poem of vigorous action — more reminiscent of Byron than "Paul Revere" — with its ferocious Albanian hero who treacherously beheads the Turkish Pasha's Scribe by a sudden stroke of his scimitar. It has a certain dash, but it is one of the less interesting of the *Tales*.

All these, including "Scanderbeg," suggest some nineteenth-century fictional form, prose or verse. Two of the other tales, though they are not really mediaeval in origin, have much of the quality of mediaeval *fabliaux*, like the Miller's or the Summoner's Tale, or the quality of Italian novellas that are virtually *fabliaux*, like Boccaccio's tale of Fra Puccio and Dom Felice, without of course the bawdiness. Humor at the expense of monks or clerics is one of the staples of the *fabliaux*, and so it is in "The Cobbler of Hagenau" and "The Monk of Casal-Maggiore." Both tales have a kind of sly sprightliness that nothing in Longfellow's work before the *Tales* would have prepared one for. The Cobbler, a shrewd and skeptical craftsman of the years just before the Reformation, who loves the songs of Hans Sachs and the other Meistersingers better than the Psalter, has a little wife who falls a victim to the wiles of the unscrupulous monk Johann Tetzel, and pays a good golden florin for one of his fraudulent Letters of Indulgence. After her death the Cobbler fails to have a mass sung for the repose of her soul, and when he is dragged before a magistrate for contempt of Church, he protests that the Letter has already provided for his wife's absolution "from all excesses, sins, and crimes." The Magistrate can find no flaw in this reasoning, and the Cobbler is acquitted, with a winking allusion to the end of "Reynard the Fox." It is a harmlessly anticlerical little tale, and the scene in the church at Hagenau, where Tetzel is preaching one of his sermons — "the cawings of that reverend bird," as the Cobbler calls them — is vividly summoned up — the air filled with incense, the organ groaning, Tetzel's red cross standing out against the glare of the altar lights, the indulgences exposed for sale "like ballads at a country fair," while

> A heavy strong-box, iron-bound
> And carved with many a quaint device,
> Received, with a melodious sound,
> The coin that purchased Paradise.

Tetzel's sermon, like the open-air sermon in *The Golden Legend*, is a restrained reproduction, not a parody, of authentic sermons of the sort.

Yet the tone of the whole piece is much too good-natured to justify the charge of bigoted Protestantism against Longfellow, even if there were no other evidence of his liberality; and no sane reader could detect any serious anti-Catholic or even antimonastic bias in "The Monk of Casal-Maggiore," the tale of a lazy, gluttonous, lascivious Franciscan friar, Brother Timothy, who deludes the farmer Gilbert into believing that he, Brother Timothy, had been transformed into an ass for his sins, while the real ass is spirited off to the convent by his accomplice, Brother Anthony. The good Gilbert, conscience-stricken for his harsh treatment of the ass, makes every effort to recompense Brother Timothy for his sufferings in animal guise, but when, at the lavish repast he spreads before the monk, he sees how greedily Brother Timothy stuffs himself and how warm are the glances he casts at Dame Cicely, Gilbert loses his patience and angrily warns him that he is in danger of returning to his animal state, "since monkish flesh and asinine are one." When the real ass is restored to farmer Gilbert, his children, overjoyed to have "Brother Timothy" back among them, proceed to deck his sacred person with garlands, for their childish feelings

> Could not discriminate in any way
> A donkey from a friar of Orders Gray.

There is humor, too, but of a much quieter and less jovial kind, in "Emma and Eginhard," which has little or nothing of the quality of a *fabliau* despite its mediaeval setting, its clerical characters, and its mildly scandalous action. The gifted and handsome young scribe, the Frankish Eginhard (or Einhard), falls in love with Charlemagne's daughter, the Princess Emma, and since she responds to his passion, they spend a night together in her chamber. It is still moonlight when the Emperor, gazing down from his window into the courtyard covered with new-fallen snow, is startled to see the Princess carrying Eginhard on her shoulders back to his own door lest his footprints in the snow should betray them. The Emperor's council the next day recommends that the young scribe be sentenced to death or banishment for this outrage, but Charlemagne is more merciful — for what are all men, as his great schoolmaster Alcuin has said, but "guests of the grave and travellers that pass"? — and he not only pardons Eginhard but gives him Emma's hand in marriage:

> "Thus I repay the royal debt I owe,
> And cover up the footprints in the snow."

This story of the Princess Emma and the young Frankish scribe had been made the subject of a poem, "La Neige," fifty years earlier by Alfred de Vigny. It is a better poem than Longfellow's if only because it is so much more terse and intense in form, so much more purely dramatic in development, and so much more oblique in its handling of the theme — for Vigny "explains" nothing of the circumstances, as Longfellow does. Except for a short lyrical prelude, he begins the piece abruptly with the lovely line, which Sainte-Beuve praised, "Ils sont petits et seuls, ces deux pieds dans la neige," and the poem is made up of but two brief dramatic scenes of a splendid severity and concentration. Longfellow has nothing so fine, but "Emma and Eginhard" has another kind of economy in the telling: mere diffuseness is a fault of which Longfellow is never guilty in these tales, and the Student's tale, relaxed and expository as it begins by being, *wastes* no lines in bringing the scene of the great Frankish court before us, with its scholars, Alcuin and the Abbott Smaragdo, its pupils studying the Trivium and the Quadrivium, the young scribe, "perfect in

Grammar, and in Rhetoric nice," and, in a quite different style, "the armèd knights with spur on heel." The Emperor, touched by the calm of the moonlight night and "the gables capped with snow," and anxiously reflecting that "his own reign was but a troubled dream," is not unworthy to be set beside Vigny's Charlemagne, distressed by the sight of his daughter crossing the courtyard with her revealing burden on her back:

> Le Roi pourtant regarde et voudrait ne pas voir,
> Car il craint sa colère et surtout son pouvoir.

The sense of Charlemagne's struggle between anger and forgiveness is more intense in Vigny's poem, but the scene of pardon and betrothal in Longfellow's has an eloquence of its own.

The satire on monks and friars in "Hagenau" and "Casal-Maggiore," as we have seen, though not without a certain bite, is essentially good-humored; far harsher in its treatment of ecclesiastical bigotry and theological inhumanity is "Torquemada," the only story in the series that could be described as a tale of horror. Nowhere else, not even in *The New England Tragedies*, does Longfellow allow himself to go so far in representing a really insensate spirit of religious persecution as he does in this bitter tale of an old Spanish hidalgo, "proud and taciturn," who, suspecting his two daughters of heresy, betrays them to the Inquisition and, when they are condemned to the stake, begs the Grand Inquisitor to be allowed to light the pyre with his own hands. There is something "Gothic" in the manner in which Longfellow describes the sadistic obsessiveness of the bigoted old hidalgo, whose only diversions are to hunt the boar, to go to bullfights, and to stand in the crowd with a lighted taper "when Jews were burned, or banished from the land":

> Then stirred within him a tumultuous joy;
> The demon whose delight is to destroy
> Shook him, and shouted with a trumpet tone,
> "Kill! kill! and let the Lord find out his own!"

Fire, except for the hearth-fire, as we have seen, is a rare image in Longfellow, but it dominates this poem, and the flames of the Inquisitional pyre are matched by the flames that, on the same night, destroy the tower of the hidalgo's woodland castle and the hidalgo himself along with it. The poem ends with the same fiery metaphor:

> But Torquemada's name, with clouds o'ercast,
> Looms in the distant landscape of the Past,
> Like a burnt tower upon a blackened heath,
> Lit by the fires of burning woods beneath!

Horror of this kind is unique in the *Tales,* but the *frisson* of some sort of fear, ghostly or deathly or simply barbaric, is felt in more than one of the others. It has a fierce Far Eastern quality in "Kambalu," the Spanish Jew's tale of Alau, the Khan's great captain, who punishes the Kalif of Baldecca for resisting the Khan's armies by locking him up in his Tower of Gold — almost in the manner of Ugolino in Dante — and allowing him to die there of hunger in the midst of his golden grains, his bars of silver, and his precious stones. Much more in the supernatural vein of an Oriental apologue is "The Legend of Rabbi Ben Levi," a Talmudic tale of a Jewish rabbi who prays that he may be allowed to look upon God's face "and yet not die": he is permitted to do this, and when, armed with the Death Angel's sword, he finds himself in the Lord's city, he spreads throughout its streets "a sudden breath / Of something there unknown, which men call death." When the Spanish Jew has finished this brief tale, a kind of spell falls upon his listeners:

> The spiritual world seemed near;
> And close above them, full of fear,
> Its awful adumbration passed,
> A luminous shadow, vague and vast.

There is less somberness, but more irony, in "Azrael," another Talmudic apologue, this time the tale of a great Hindostani Ra-

jah who wishes to be saved from the Death Angel by his host,
Solomon, and learns that Azrael has been on his way, at that very
hour, to seek him in his own kingdom.

Saintsbury thought "The Ballad of Carmilhan" "an imitation
of the worst German manner — sham 'silly sooth' "; but it is a
little difficult to see why he should have been so contemptuous
of the poem, unless a certain reminiscence of "The Ancient
Mariner" in its ballad style struck him as inviting a disastrous
comparison:

> The lovely moon climbs up the sky
> As one who walks in dreams;
> A tower of marble in her light,
> A wall of black, a wall of white,
> The stately vessel seems.

Yet the poem hardly deserves so hasty a brush-off; as a Phantom
Ship ballad it has the kind of spectral and foreboding quality that
Longfellow's sea poems so often have, and the movement of the
boastful captain's ship "right through" the ghostly vessel, the
Carmilhan, in the midst of a frightful nocturnal gale, is rendered
with a real enough uncanniness. Though based on traditional
legends, the poem in just this form is Longfellow's own; "The
Mother's Ghost," a ballad about a dead woman who haunts her
children's cruel stepmother, is a direct translation, as we have
seen, of a Danish ballad, but we are told by those who should
know that it is an admirable one.

Poems such as "The Cobbler of Hagenau" and "Torquemada,"
taken in isolation, might be supposed to express a violent anti-
Popery of an almost Puritan kind on Longfellow's part, and it is
true that he found their basis of fact in Protestant sources. How
free he was from any such fanaticism, however, much of *The
Golden Legend* had long since indicated, and the two comic
tales are, in spirit, satires on superstitition *in itself* and on the
familiar vices of monasticism, while "Torquemada," to go no

deeper morally for the moment, is really a parable on the horrors to which theological bigotry in general can lead. Like some other New Englanders of his generation — Emerson, for example, and Hawthorne — Longfellow was as much attracted imaginatively by certain aspects of Catholicism — its liturgy, its aesthetic grandeurs, its spiritual and moral purity on one level — as he was skeptical of Roman Catholic and indeed Protestant dogma, and repelled by many of the abuses, political and otherwise, of which the Church was guilty. How sensitive his feeling was for the loftier aspects of mediaeval faith is evident in such tales as "The Legend Beautiful," which the Theologian tells in Part Second, and "King Robert of Sicily," the Sicilian's tale on the first evening.*

"The Legend Beautiful," which Longfellow owed to an *exemplum* he came upon in Jeremy Taylor, who in his turn may have owed it to a work by a Spanish Jesuit, is a slight but touching story of saintly devotion — the story of a Monk to whom, as he prays in his cell, appears

> the Blessed Vision
> Of our Lord, with light Elysian
> Like a vesture wrapped about Him,
> Like a garment round Him thrown.

The Monk is painfully torn between the feeling that he must not slight his "radiant guest" and the feeling that he must hurry to the convent gate where the poor are waiting for their daily dole of food; a voice in his breast whispers that, in any event, he must do his charitable duty, and he leaves the celestial vision for his

---

* See the very sympathetic account of monasticism in the chapter on "The Devotional Poetry of Spain" in *Outre-Mer*, an abbreviated version of an article Longfellow had published in the *North American*. When, on the other hand, in 1866, he was offered by Victor Emmanuel II the title of Cavaliere in the Order of SS. Maurizio and Lazzaro, he courteously declined the honor, writing to Sumner at the same time that he "did not think it appropriate to a republican and a Protestant to receive a Catholic Order of Knighthood."

hungry poor. In Jeremy Taylor's telling of the story, the Monk leaves his cell only because he hears the bell calling to prayers; the substitution of the charitable motive is Longfellow's own, and there is something of the same compassionate feeling in what follows as there was to be, a year or two later, in "The Challenge":

> At the gate the poor were waiting,
> Looking through the iron grating,
> With that terror in the eye
> That is only seen in those
> Who amid their wants and woes
> Hear the sound of doors that close,
> And of feet that pass them by;
> Grown familiar with disfavor,
> Grown familiar with the savor
> Of the bread by which men die!

When the Monk returns to his cell, the Visitant is waiting for him with the reassuring words, "Hadst thou stayed, I must have fled!" The tale is told with a beautiful simplicity and the tenderest unction.

It is a parable not only of charity but of humility; "King Robert of Sicily," a considerably longer and more richly amplified tale, in a similarly "exemplary" vein, is a parable on the sin of worldly pride. It is one of the two or three tales fullest of feeling in these volumes. King Robert, attending vespers on St. John's Eve and listening to the priests chanting the Magnificat, catches the words, "Deposuit potentes de sede, et exaltavit humiles." When he is told that these words mean "He has put down the mighty from their seat, / And has exalted them of low degree," he mutters scornfully, "There is no power can push me from my throne!" He is punished for this sin of pride by being not only pushed from his throne, which is occupied by an Angel in his guise, but transformed into the king's jester and made the butt of the coarse mockery of courtiers and pages. Only after years of humiliation, and a visit to the Papal court at Rome, where his brothers, the Pope and the Emperor, fail to recognize him in his motley, is King Robert at length overcome by contrition and forgiven for his sin. When his courtiers enter his throne room, they find him, appareled again in ermine and cloth of gold, "kneeling upon the floor, absorbed in silent prayer."

The emotion in the poem has an unmistakable personal vibration, though worldly pride, or indeed any other, would not seem to have been peculiarly a vice of Longfellow's. It is a vice, nevertheless, of which all men are said to be, and doubtless are, at least *in potentia* guilty; and just as the painful sense of this gave a moral tinge to the character of Prince Henry, so it does, but more penetratingly, to the character of King Robert. The story is told with admirable slowness of pace, but quite without diffuseness, and the sense of the scene — the church at vespers and during the strange night that follows, the banquet room of the Court at Palermo, the pomp and circumstance of the meeting in St. Peter's square in Rome — is richly conveyed. So, too, is the splendor of the cavalcade that proceeds from the Sicilian court to Rome, with its plumes and cloaks and housings — and the contrast of Robert's wretched role:

> And lo! among the menials, in mock state,
> Upon a piebald steed, with shambling gait,
> His coat of fox-tails flapping in the wind,
> The solemn ape demurely perched behind,
> King Robert rode, making huge merriment
> In all the country towns through which they went.

The humbling of Robert is rendered, in this and other passages, with surprising stringency, and the depth of his repentance at the end is suggested rather than labored, but its emotional quality is acute.

A comparable fall from power to humiliation, or at least from wealth to penury, is the setting for "The Falcon of Ser Federigo," but nothing is made of this fall morally, and "The Falcon" is not in any strict sense an *exemplum*. It is told in the pure novella manner, as its source in one of Fiammetta's tales in Boccaccio would lead one to expect, and it is really only the Italian mediaeval stage set that associates it particularly with "King Robert." The scene, more specifically, is a small farm in the hills above Florence, and the fallen protagonist here is a Florentine gentleman who has been ruined by his extravagance and forced to retire to his tiny property in the country with very little of his former state but his faithful and magnificent falcon. The falcon has to be sacrificed when, unexpectedly one morning, Monna Giovanna, the beautiful widow with whom Ser Federigo had been hopelessly in love, visits him, and for want of suitable viands to set before her, he wrings the bird's neck in secret and serves it up to her as a dish. Monna Giovanna, alas, had come to beg the falcon from him as a gift for her little boy, who is dying and has cried out for it. The child does die, but his mother and Ser Federigo are united in marriage at last, and on the back of the chair in which Monna Giovanna is now enthroned at table is "the image of a falcon carved in wood."

This touch is Longfellow's own; he had not found it in the *Decameron*, and in general he retells Fiammetta's story with a fullness of poetic feeling that is absent from Boccaccio's characteristically atmosphereless telling of it. The falcon, in Boccaccio, is simply a bird, "one of the best in the world"; we hear no more of it for its own sake, and it is clearly a mere narrative peg. To Longfellow, no bird, especially not a sacrificial bird, could remain so neutral as this, and the falcon takes on under his hand a half-human, half-heraldic character, inspiring love as well as pride in his master and stirring the imagination of the small boy as if it were a bird beyond nature. In its dream, as it drowses motionless beside Ser Federigo, it hears

The sudden, scythe-like sweep of wings, that dare
The headlong plunge through eddying gulfs of air,

and when the troubled host is anxiously casting about for the materials of a proper breakfast, the bird, in a manner for which Longfellow had no warrant in Boccaccio, offers *itself* as a sacrifice to hospitality. There is no undercurrent of symbolism in all this: Ser Federigo's falcon is no Coleridgean or Baudelairean albatross, no Mallarméan or Yeatsian swan. But he is treated with a warmth of fancy and dramatic feeling that goes beyond anything in Fiammetta's tale. The story is told, too, with a restraint and even an elegance that lifts it appreciably above the level of the padded-out and rather airless play, *The Falcon*, which Tennyson later wrote on the same subject.

There was something genuinely Latin or Mediterranean in Longfellow's temperament — something warm, expansive, impulsive, and lighthearted — and these Italian tales, like *The Spanish Student*, are the expression of it. But there was another strain in his make-up, less predictable, less close to the surface, less reconcilable with the state of feeling that produced "The Village Blacksmith" or "The Children's Hour." This was the Northern strain, and it was the stronger of the two, though it was no more expressed externally in his personal life than a similar strain was expressed in Thomas Gray's or Leconte de Lisle's. Longfellow was not the first writer of quiet personal habits in whose grain there was a contradictory streak of imaginative violence, and we need not smile when we are told that he often reminded people of a Viking or that he enjoyed being described as a skald. From the time of his first acquaintance with them, he had been powerfully affected by the fierce lays of the Elder Edda, by the Viking arrogance of the skaldic poems, by the austere unsentimental prose of the sagas, and by the more romantic Danish ballads. Sooner or later this sense of deep kinship with the Scandinavian was bound to come out in his work — on a more ambitious scale than in "The Skeleton in Armor" or "Tegnér's Drapa" — and it did so at last in "The Saga of King Olaf."

The subject of the Musician's Tale, as we have seen, is the career of Olaf Tryggvason as Longfellow had found it recounted by Snorri Sturlason in a long section of the *Heimskringla*. This Olaf was a tenth-century Viking who had been converted, while in exile, to Christianity, and who then, proceeding to Norway with his freebooter followers, had avenged himself for the death of his father, Trygve Olafsson, by bringing about the murder of the usurping Earl Hakon, and making himself king.* He had then gone on to "Christianize" the country not by persuasion but by force, and for the most part in a decidedly strong-armed manner. There is an ironic incongruity, as a result, between the action of the poem and its ostensible theme. What "King Olaf" allegedly does is to dramatize the triumph of the mild and gentle religion of the White Christ over the savage old worship of the Norse Æsir, Odin and Thor and Tiw. The first canto, "The Challenge of Thor," is a defiant monologue put into the mouth of the heathen god of thunder, whom Longfellow thought of also as the god of war, ruling the nations from his seat amid the icebergs, his red beard streaming through the heavens in the form of the northern lights:

> Force rules the world still,
> Has ruled it, shall rule it;
> Meekness is weakness,
> Strength is triumphant,
> Over the whole earth
> Still it is Thor's-Day!

Olaf takes up the challenge, of course, and in the last canto, an epilogue, "The Nun of Nidaros," we see the Abbess Astrid, kneeling in her chamber in the convent of Drontheim, praying

---

* Longfellow may have known Oehlenschläger's poem on "Hakon Jarl's Death" (which Robert Hillyer translated many years later), but in any case he would have found in the *Heimskringla* (Chapter LV) the story of the murder of Hakon by the thrall Kark (whom Longfellow, for the sake of the rhyme, calls Karker). He himself, indeed, twenty years before he wrote "Olaf," had considered writing "The Saga of Hakon Jarl: a poem."

to the Virgin, and hearing, in "gusts of the night-wind" outside, the meek voice of St. John accepting — he too — the challenge of Thor — "but not with the weapons / Of war that thou yieldest":

> "Stronger than steel
> Is the sword of the Spirit;
> Swifter than arrows
> The light of the truth is,
> Greater than anger
> Is love, and subdueth." *

The Theologian draws the pacifist moral in the Interlude that follows, but the poem itself has little to do with the sword of the Spirit or the light of the truth. Olaf Tryggvason, as Snorri's account had made clear, was motivated quite as much by the spirit of revenge, by ambition and the love of power, by the zest of heroic action, as by devotion to the principles of Christianity; and Longfellow's imagination is at work on behalf of Olaf, not of Astrid the Abbess. Olaf is a splendidly heroic figure from first to last — from the time when we see him, "beautiful of mien" and "royal in attire," sailing northward toward Drontheim fiord —

> There he stood as one who dreamed;
> And the red light glanced and gleamed
>   On the armor that he wore;
> And he shouted, as the rifted
> Streamers o'er him shook and shifted,
>   "I accept thy challenge, Thor!" —

from that time to the last great sea fight with his enemies "under the Isle of Svald," when he leaps into the sea, his shield high in the air, and disappears for good. He has perhaps Christianized

---

* The first and last cantos of "Olaf," which serve as prologue and epilogue, are the only parts of the poem that are not based on the *Heimskringla;* they are Longfellow's own inventions. "The Challenge of Thor," indeed, was written many years earlier and intended as a prologue to *The Golden Legend;* its place here is obviously a much more suitable one.

Norway meanwhile, but in a manner that Longfellow does nothing to idealize or sentimentalize.

In his essay on "Worship" Emerson had observed that "the religion cannot rise above the state of the votary," and that the first pagans to be converted to Christianity often remained essentially pagan still. "Among our Norse forefathers," he went on, "King Olaf's mode of converting Eyvind to Christianity was to put a pan of glowing coals on his belly, which burst asunder. 'Wilt thou now, Eyvind, believe in Christ?' asks Olaf, in excellent faith. Another argument was an adder put into the mouth of the reluctant disciple Raud, who refused to believe." Longfellow passes over the torture of Eyvind Kinnriff, but he retells the tale of Olaf's torturing and killing Raud the Strong, who resists him, with no attempt to mitigate its savagery:

> Then between his jaws distended,
> When his frantic struggles ended,
> Through King Olaf's horn an adder,
> Touched by fire, they forced to glide.
>
> Sharp his tooth was as an arrow,
> As he gnawed through bone and marrow;
> But without a groan or shudder,
> Raud the Strong blaspheming died.

Earlier than this, Olaf has summoned a Hus-Ting at Mere, gathering the farmers together from near and far, and announcing to them that he commands the land to be Christian and will now proceed to have them all baptized. The surly Old Iron-Beard refuses to yield, and is slain "midway between the assailed and the assailing." Meanwhile, Olaf has entered the pagan temple at Mere, smitten with his war axe the wooden images of the ancient gods, "and downward shattered to the pavement flung them."

He strides through the poem with the fine arrogance and the barbaric heroism of a rude Viking Achilles or Roland, overbearing not only the great earls and thanes but women like Queen Sigrid the Haughty who stand in his way — forcing Gudrun, the daughter of Old Iron-Beard himself, to marry him; sending the quarrelsome Thangbrand the Priest to Iceland to Christianize it, and taking to wife, when Gudrun deserts him, the bride of King Burislaf the Wend, when she escapes to his court. In one way or another he succeeds in antagonizing the most powerful men in the North — the Danish King, Svend of the Forked Beard, now Queen Sigrid's spouse; the King of Sweden; King Burislaf of Wendland, and Earl Eric, the son of that Hakon whom Olaf had had done to death — and they form a league to destroy him. His cause is hopeless, but he faces his collected foes, at the sea fight in the Baltic, on board his great ship the Long Serpent, with the high-spirited and undaunted bravery of a typical Heroic Age warrior. The battle itself is related, in five episodic cantos, with an energy — balladlike, to be sure, rather than sagalike — that has few parallels in modern English verse.

Virtually all the characters in the poem are as passionate and as headstrong as Olaf himself. They are quite without Christian feeling of any kind, except perhaps Bishop Sigurd, who performs the miracle of Salten Fiord; the other priest, Thangbrand, is a swaggering bully whom the Icelanders drive out of their island in disgust. These men and women are the men and women of the sagas themselves; they are the brothers and sisters, in spirit, of all those Grettirs and Gislis, Hallgerds and Hildigunnas, who carry on their implacable feuds in the sagas — proud, quick-tempered, wrangling, vengeful, and unforgiving. The language of the poem abounds in this feeling:

> "Here I defy thee!"
>
> Queen Sigrid the Haughty sat proud and aloft.
>
> Then forth from the chamber in anger he fled.
>
> Bitter as home-brewed ale were his foaming passions.
>
> Smarting with the insult,
> Through the streets of Drontheim

> Strode he red and wrathful,
> With his stately air.

Queen Sigrid never forgets the insult Olaf has done her; Gudrun attempts to stab him to death in his sleep; Earl Eric pledges to Olaf "a death-drink salt as the sea" for the murder of his father. Violent emotions and violent deeds are the rule in the poem: it is difficult to understand how it could be described, as Andrew Hilen has described it, as "a softened version of Snorri's catalogue of intemperance and bloodshed" — except on the ground that Longfellow is *expected* to emasculate all his sources. His poem, to be sure, is composed of a selection from Snorri's narrative, but it is not a selection based on any principle of emasculation.

Snorri's saga, if one may judge from the translation Longfellow used, is a masterpiece of historical narrative — swift, direct, terse, and often dramatic — but it is a masterpiece of prose, and it is quite without the particular heightening of poetry — the enhancement of sensuous detail, the drawing out of emotion, the excitement of meter and rhyme. These are the qualities that Longfellow imparts to his transmutation of Snorri's prose, as William Morris had done in *Sigurd the Volsung* with the prose of the *Volsunga Saga;* and though Longfellow's rehandling of the *Heimskringla* sacrifices something of Snorri's powerful concentration, it gains something in romantic resonance. The whole of the twentieth canto, "Einar Tamberskelver," seven eight-line stanzas, is a rewriting of a chapter in the *Heimskringla* that occupies half a page. A detail or two may be enough to suggest what Longfellow does generally with his source. Earl Eric, on board his ship, orders a man named Fin to shoot the tall man by the mast of Olaf's ship, who is Einar:

> Fin shot; and the arrow hit the middle of Einar's bow just at the moment that Einar was drawing it, and the bow was split in two parts.

"What is that," cried King Olaf, "that broke with such a noise?"

"Norway, king, from thy hands," cried Einar.

In Longfellow's poem this becomes:

> Sooner than the word was spoken
> Flew the yeoman's shaft;
> Einar's bow in twain was broken,
> Einar only laughed.

> "What was that?" said Olaf, standing
> On the quarter-deck.
> "Something heard I like the stranding
> Of a shattered wreck."
> Einar then, the arrow taking
> From the loosened string,
> Answered, "That was Norway breaking
> From thy hand, O King!"

This is, in fact, closer to Snorri than Longfellow usually gets, but even here how can one mistake the gain in frank expressiveness? There is nothing like Einar's laugh in Snorri; it has the effect of a bright color added to a strong but rather dry line-drawing.

In general, as is well known, the sagas are "linear," not painterly; they make everything of action and dialogue and almost nothing of color, of light and shade, of the tone and temper of landscape. One would hardly gather from them that the physical scene in Norway and Iceland has any particular grandeur or ruggedness, boldness or violence; that scene is mostly taken for granted, and we must evoke it as best we can for ourselves. Longfellow's poem abounds in the sense of landscape, or rather — for there is comparatively little of the land — of seascape. "The Saga of King Olaf" is an oceanic poem if ever there was one: the sense of the ocean is in it from first to last, and the turbulence of the northern seas becomes the poetic equivalent of the emotional turbulence amid which these men and women live and act. Olaf and his men are essentially sea kings and seafarers: in that sense, the imaginative heart of the poem is the fourteenth canto, in which Longfellow calls the roll of the crew of Olaf's great war vessel, the Long Serpent:

> These, and many more like these,
> With King Olaf sailed the seas,
>   Till the waters vast
> Filled them with a vague devotion,
> With the freedom and the motion,
> With the roll and roar of ocean
>   And the sounding blast.

The most constructive act in the poem is the building not of a hall or a church but of the Long Serpent itself — that vessel which Olaf commands the master-builder, Thorberg Skafting, to build on such a scale that it shall be "twice as large and long" as Raud the Strong's Dragon. There is a reminiscence of "The Building of the Ship" in this canto, which pleased Hawthorne more than anything else in the poem: "I was especially charmed," he wrote, "with the description of an old Scandinavian ship-of-war, with her officers and crew; in which, by some inscrutable magic, you contrive to suggest a parallel picture of a modern frigate."

The poem begins and ends at sea, and the awareness of the sea — of its agitations and heavings, its wild tempests, its foaming billows, the sullen roar of its tides upon the rocky coast — is all but constant. The *sound* of the sea and the sea winds dominates the poem like the cannonading of a natural artillery — roaring, wailing, shrieking, dashing, tossing — and indeed the poem is filled with violent sound, both natural and human. There are *pianissimo* passages for the sake of relief, but what one mostly hears, humanly speaking, is the sound of men shouting angrily, laughing boisterously, or singing in chorus, like the waves or the winds. The songs of Halfred, King Olaf's skald, are pitched in a high, warlike key:

> Then the Scald took his harp and sang,
> And loud through the music rang
> The sound of that shining word;
> And the harp-strings a clangor made,
> As if they were struck with the blade
> Of a sword.

Only less striking than this accompaniment of oceanic and human sonority are the effects of brilliant luminosity — of flashing, gleaming, flaming, glaring light. In the prelude, as we have seen, the light streaming through the heavens "in flashes of crimson" is the red beard of the god Thor, "affrighting the nations," and this image is taken up again immediately in the next canto, "King Olaf's Return":

> All these thoughts of love and strife
> Glimmered through his lurid life,
> As the stars' intenser light
> Through the red flames o'er him trailing,
> As his ships went sailing, sailing
> Northward in the summer night.

When Olaf insults Queen Sigrid, "the lightning flashed o'er her forehead and cheek"; when the Easter sun rises, it "streamed with one broad track of splendor"; in Olaf's banquet hall the gleams of the firelight dance "upon helmet and hauberk and lance"; and when Olaf and Kolbiorn the marshal, in the final battle, leap into the sea, what we see is

> Two shields raised high in the air,
> Two flashes of golden hair,
> Two scarlet meteors' glare.

All this, to compare very great things with modest ones, has something of the sensuous quality of the *Iliad* — something of its Heroic Age brilliance of lighting and clangor of sound — and indeed "King Olaf" is unique in Longfellow's work, among poems of any length, in its sustained celebration of the virtues, and even the vices, of an age of warlike action. Olaf meets his death, it is true, as the penalty of his high-handedness and a kind of *húbris*, but he meets it magnificently, and in fact it is only through the treachery of his enemies that he is overcome. Meanwhile, Longfellow, however "intentionally" or unintentionally, has done nothing but aggrandize him throughout the poem: he is a rare example of genuine masculine power in Longfellow's work, and it is striking that he should be a tenth-century Viking, not a mediaeval prince or an Acadian blacksmith's son. The "censor" gave way when Longfellow was composing the poem, and all his deeply buried love of physical force and moral energy came to the surface. As a result, "King Olaf" has something of the quality of a skaldic *drapa* and much of the quality of a nineteenth-century romantic ballad; it is as if Egil Skallagrímsson had collaborated with the Tennyson of "The Revenge." The poem is incomparably the most successful of all the tales in the *Wayside Inn,* and the book as a whole is Longfellow's major achievement as a poet.

XII

Longfellow as Translator

IF, AS Dryden said, translation is a disease, then it is a disease
with which Longfellow was afflicted during most of his life.
We know of at least one translation he made, an ode of
Horace's, while he was still an undergraduate; among the last of
his poems that can be dated is a rather fine sonnet from the
French of Xavier Marmier ("A Quiet Life"), which he wrote at
the age of seventy-two. There was only one decade, that of the
fifties, when he enjoyed at times some remission of the "disease,"
but the periods when it was most active were the thirties and early
forties and the three or four years in the sixties when he was at
work rounding out his translation of Dante. Very soon after
coming home from his first stay abroad, when he had established
himself at Bowdoin, he began, no doubt for the benefit of his
students, his series of translations from Spanish poets; the very
first of these, surprisingly enough, may have been a poem by
Góngora ("Let Me Go Warm"), whose revival was at that time
far in the future. The painful pleasures of translation soon proved
to be habit-forming. As we have seen, Longfellow's rendering of
the "Coplas" of Jorge Manrique ("Verses on the Death of His
Father") gave its title to the first volume published under his
name, and the articles on European languages and literatures
which he contributed to the *North American* gave him the excuse, if he needed one, for publishing a few more poems in trans-

lation. *The Poets and Poetry of Europe* called for still others, now mostly from the German.

Longfellow was a born translator, if there be such a creature, though not a great one; not a translator in the class of Dryden himself or, say, in German, of Goethe or Schlegel; his translations, as with any writer, are approximately as good as his own work, occasionally rising a shade above it, sometimes falling perceptibly below it. But the zest with which he performed the act is not to be mistaken. "There is evidently a great and strange fascination in translating," he wrote. "It seizes people with irresistible power, and whirls them away till they are beside themselves. It is like a ghost beckoning one to follow." The notoriously challenging and, in one sense, insoluble problem of carrying over a poem from one language to another, obviously teased Longfellow's literary sense like some problem of transformation by magic, and he could not for very long leave it alone. He felt, too, as doubtless other poets have done, that the act of translation had the effect of a stimulant to his own productive power. "It is like running a ploughshare through the soil of one's mind," he wrote to Freiligrath; "a thousand germs of thought start up (excuse this agricultural figure), which otherwise might have lain and rotted in the ground." It was, in fact, his early translations that kept the soil of his mind stirred up during that long "silent" period between his boyhood poems and *Voices of the Night:* they were a kind of poetic calisthenics, to change the metaphor rather violently, which in the end proved to have wrought a real advance in strength and agility.

If sheer linguistic range were a test of greatness, Longfellow would be one of the greatest of all translators. At one time or another, if Old French and Old English are to be counted, he made versions of poems or parts of poems from eleven languages — from Greek, Latin, Italian, Spanish, Portuguese, Old French, French, German, Danish, Swedish, and Old English. He published no translations from the Greek, but he made a handful of

versions from the Anthology and elsewhere which were published after his death. Nor did he do very much with Latin poetry; so far as one knows, he translated nothing from Horace during his adult life — oddly, since Horace was his favorite Latin
poet — perhaps through the feeling that that writer had already
been treated fully enough and successfully enough by English
poets. He seems to have considered translating all of Vergil's
Eclogues, but he actually made a version only of the first, and
the one other Latin poet he carried over was Ovid, who is represented by two elegies from the *Tristia*. The languages that bulk
largest in Longfellow's work as a translator are Italian (thanks
largely to the Dante), Spanish, French, German, and (thanks to
the versions of Tegnér) Swedish. Except for the "Coplas," "The
Children of the Lord's Supper," and the *Divine Comedy*, these
are all versions of short poems.*

Fortunate would it be if we could add "and all of very good
poems." But this is not possible. The fact cannot be suppressed
that, both as an anthologist and as a translator, Longfellow's taste
was of the most uncertain. There are as many deplorable poems
as good ones in both *The Waif* and *The Estray*, and the list of
his translations is a crazy-quilt of qualities that range from the
highest to the trashiest; like some other writers of genuine gifts,
Longfellow was hospitable to the point of extreme indiscriminate-
ness. And he often disappoints us as much by what he avoids as
by what he tackles. We look in vain for any versions of the
French poets of the Pléiade except for a trifle of Ronsard's ("To
the Forest of Gastine"), but we come upon a painfully sugary
piece ("The Child Asleep") by that allegedly fifteenth-century
lady, "Clotilde de Surville," who existed only on paper. Longfel-

---

* Included under the rubric of Translations in Longfellow's collected
works are four poems described as being "From Eastern Sources." Two of
these are of Tartar origin, two of them Armenian. Strictly speaking, they
are not translations by Longfellow but versifyings of prose translations by
others — by Alexander Chodzko (*Specimens of the Popular Poetry of
Persia*) and by the Rev. L. M. Alishan (*Armenian Popular Songs*).

low shrank, too, from the attempt, surely not an impossible one, to make versions of André Chénier, of Lamartine (so much his own kind of poet), of Hugo, of Vigny; but he devoted a day or two to translating an appalling piece of sentimental hokum ("The Blind Girl of Castèl Cuillè") by the "barber-poet" of Agen, Jacques Jasmin. It should be added that he translated three pleasant small poems of Charles d'Orléans.

The record of Longfellow's translation from Spanish and German is a less disappointing one. From the former language he made versions, as we have seen, of such poets as Jorge Manrique and Góngora, and the names of Gonzalo de Berceo, Francisco de Aldana, Lope de Vega, and Saint Teresa de Avila, though not of Garcilaso de la Vega, could be added to theirs. As for German, we should probably not expect to find Longfellow Englishing any of the great baroque poets of the seventeenth century — Paul Fleming, Andreas Gryphius, Angelus Silesius — who seem to have been little known even in Germany in his time; and it is not surprising to find him making versions of more familiar writers of that age — Martin Opitz, Friedrich von Logau, Simon Dach: these were poets who were esteemed in Germany itself in the nineteenth century.* Yet it is disappointing to encounter, among Longfellow's versions of later poets, the names of so many crickets and grasshoppers of the caliber of Julius Mosen, Gustav Pfizer, and Ernst Stockmann, and not the names of Hölderlin, Novalis, or Eichendorff. Schiller, too, he almost completely avoided, and of Goethe he published only translations of the two "Wanderer's Night-Songs," though it is but fair to remark that he rendered several passages from *Faust* for his Harvard classes, which he never published. Heine, who made Longfellow un-

---

* Longfellow's version of one of Logau's epigrams has achieved the currency that almost confers on a poem the distinction of anonymity:

Though the mills of God grind slowly, yet they grind exceeding small;
Though with patience he stands waiting, with exactness grinds he all.

easy, is represented by one tiny lyric.* Except for these, the most authentic names are those of Platen and Uhland. Esaias Tegnér was the only Swedish poet Longfellow attempted to turn into English, and no doubt he was the best poet of his generation in Sweden, but Longfellow's enthusiasm for that prosy idyl of village pietism, "The Children of the Lord's Supper" — over which he wept "more than once" as he worked on it — we can account for only on the most indulgent grounds. We should probably regret that he translated none of Tegnér's shorter poems, some of which are said to be admirable.

Every serious translator is bound to have a theory of translation, whether he formulates it consciously or not, and Longfellow had his. It was a theory that had the advantage, but also the disadvantage, of extreme simplicity. He outlined it very lucidly in his preface to the "Coplas" in 1833. "The great art of translating well," he said, "lies in the power of rendering literally the words of a foreign author while at the same time we preserve the spirit of the original." It is of course the qualifier that makes the essential difference, as Longfellow perfectly realized; mere literalness is difficult enough, but to "preserve the spirit of the original" — *hoc opus, hic labor est.* A sculptor, as he went on to say, cannot preserve "the rigid truth of nature" without, often, violating its spirit, and so with the translator, who is a kind of sculptor. "As there are certain beauties of thought and expression in a good original, which cannot be fully represented in the less flexible material of another language, he, too, at times, may be permitted to transgress the rigid truth of language, and remedy the defect, as far as such a defect can be remedied, by slight and judicious embellishments." Longfellow, in short, was a partisan of the view that a good translation is in no sense a free and au-

* In an article on Heine for *Graham's* (March, 1842) Longfellow included his own translations of certain passages in Heine's *Reisebilder;* these are of course in prose.

tonomous poem, but a version that aims at the closest possible fidelity to the original consistent with the truth of poetry in the second language. His ideal was not paraphrase, and decidedly not "imitation," but what Dryden called "metaphrase."

This sounds discouraging. Yet in practice Longfellow was too genuine a poet to fall, more than rarely, into the kind of dull literalness that this suggests; he knew instinctively that, as Dudley Fitts has said, "The translation of a poem should be a poem, viable as a poem, and, as a poem, weighable"; and though most of his translations are very minor poems, they are viable in their modest way. He might use the word "literally," but what he always had in mind was fidelity not only to the letter but to the spirit of the original. A former student of his at Bowdoin remembered, years later, that, whenever he got back from Professor Longfellow a translation from Latin that he had struggled to make faultless, it would be "defaced by his corrections." " 'Is not my translation correct?' I inquired. 'O yes, severely correct,' " Longfellow would answer, " 'but that is not the only quality of a good translation.' " If he had made a fetish of severe correctness himself, he would never have translated from eleven languages, some of which he had not mastered in any ultimate way; there are said to be not only wrong shades of meaning but outright mistakes in "The Children of the Lord's Supper," for Longfellow's Swedish was less than perfect. Tegnér himself, nevertheless, had said that, of all the translations he had seen of *Frithiof's Saga*, Longfellow's fragments were the only ones that had "*fully* satisfied him," and he had wished that Longfellow would render the whole poem in English. At his best, what strikes us is, as Andrew Hilen says, Longfellow's "uncanny ability for preserving intact the meaning and form of the original lines, without burdening them with the uneasiness which so often characterizes literal translations." He could do this with poets for whom he felt a temperamental sympathy; he could do it because he was a poet himself, because his feeling for languages was so intuitive, and because, for some sorts of poetry, his resources in his own language were so adequate.

A few lines will of course give only an inkling of these powers, but they can at least do that. August von Platen was a poet to whom Longfellow was sufficiently close in temper to enable him to render a poem of Platen's about as faithfully as is humanly possible. One could wish that he had translated either or both of those two very familiar but, in their romantic balladlike manner, beautiful poems, "Der Pilgrim vor St. Just" and "Das Grab im Busento," but one can rejoice that he did translate "Wie rafft' ich mich auf," which he calls "Remorse" — a poem that with its nighttime setting, its mood of dejection, its restless agitated rhythms, and its imagery of brook, bridge, and stars, he might almost have written himself. This is the second stanza of the German:

> Der Mühlbach rauschte durch felsigen Schacht,
> Ich lehnte mich über die Brücke,
> Tief unter mir nahm ich der Wogen in acht,
> Die wallten so sacht
> In der Nacht, in der Nacht,
> Doch wallte nicht eine zurücke.

Longfellow renders it thus:

> The mill-brook rushed from the rocky height,
> I leaned o'er the bridge in my yearning;
> Deep under me watched I the waves in their flight,
> As they glided so light
> In the night, in the night,
> Yet backward not one was returning.

It would surely not be possible to get closer than this to the feeling, the rhythms, and even the diction of the original — though Longfellow, as always, resorts without hesitation to such "slight and judicious embellishments" as "in my yearning" and "in their flight," and "height" is justified by the rhyme, not by the literal meaning of "Schacht" (gorge). There is no violation here of the spirit of Platen's poem, and one has to agree with J. T. Hatfield that Longfellow's version "almost captures the haunting music of the original."

The six or eight translations from Greek epigrams that Samuel Longfellow published have no great interest from any point of view, though a mild interest is attached to one of them. This is a translation of the lovely epitaph attributed to Plato, which Shelley also translated:

> Thou wert the morning star among the living,
>   Ere thy fair light had fled;
> Now, having died, thou art as Hesperus, giving
>   New splendour to the dead.

This is Longfellow's version:

> Thou as the morning star among the living resplendent,
>   Dead among the dead, shinest as Hesperus now.

Of the two, Shelley's is the finer English poem, free as it is, and romantic as it is, but Longfellow's elegiac distich is of course closer metrically to Plato, and in its grave and restrained terseness has its own kind of fidelity to the Greek. Neither version brings out as explicitly as prose could do the poignancy of the contrast between the two stars. Mackail's prose version does this: "Morning Star that once didst shine among the living, now deceased thou shinest the Evening Star among the dead."

What Longfellow made of Vergil's First Eclogue keeps one from regretting that he did not carry out his purpose to translate them all; though the poem was published late, the hexameters into which it is rendered are so halting and awkward that one imagines it must have been written much earlier; the Vergilian music is simply absent. One, and only one, good line might be quoted: "Chestnuts soft to the touch, and clouted cream in abundance" ("castaneae molles et pressi copia lactis"). C. S. Calverley, in his Victorian blank verse, did more delicate justice to the

Eclogues, and Longfellow himself proved to be much more at his ease with Ovid than with Vergil. Ovid, of course, presents no such excruciating problems to the translator as the greater poet does, and the pathetic notes of the *Tristia*, the lamentations of exile and homesickness, were much more within Longfellow's range. He had, moreover, experimented with elegiacs in English with some success, and achieved a certain facility in writing them; his renderings of two of the elegies from the *Tristia* make one wish that he had translated more of them. These two are the tenth and twelfth elegies of Book III — those in which Ovid evokes the brutal winter of the Black Sea coast, evidently so like the winters of New England, and the coming of spring in that same bleak clime. His nostalgia for Rome is particularly acute in the latter:

> otia nunc istic, iunctisque ex ordine ludis
>   cedunt verbosi garrula bella fori.
> lusus equi nunc est, levibus nunc luditur armis,
>   nunc pila, nunc celeri volvitur orbe trochus;
> nunc ubi perfusa est oleo labente iuventus,
>   defessos artus Virgine tinguit aqua.

This is Longfellow's version of these lines:

> Now it is holiday there in Rome, and to games in due order
>   Give place the windy wars of the vociferous bar.
>
> Now they are riding the horses; with light arms now they are
>   playing,
>   Now with the ball, and now round rolls the swift-flying hoop:
>
> Now, when the young athlete with flowing oil is anointed,
>   He in the Virgin's fount bathes, over-wearied, his limbs.

Surely not much of Ovid's minor music is lost in this rendering, and there are small felicities of paraphrase — "windy wars" for "garrula bella" — that are not negligible.

Much more surprising than to find Longfellow translating Ovid well is to find him translating seven sonnets of Michelangelo's (in the unreliable form given to the world by his nephew) without merely diluting their impassioned Platonism — and with a praiseworthy fidelity at least to the more paraphrasable aspects of their language and imagery. It is true that the air these sonnets have of having been painfully and even tormentedly hewn out of language, as some of the artist's statues seem to have been hewn out of stone — their ruggedness, their distortions, their bold incompletion — are not really carried over in Longfellow's too-lucid and too-finished lines. These suggest Houdon rather than Michelangelo, perhaps, but the difficulty involved is all but insuperable, and these versions of Longfellow's are rather better than the two Wordsworth made — of other sonnets. They are at any rate quite free from the Pre-Raphaelite mannerisms of John Addington Symonds ("perchance," "howbeit," "holpen," "impiteous"); their diction is pure and unaffected, and the rhyme-patterns of the original are preserved with extraordinary resource. The first quatrain of "Non ha l'ottimo artista alcun concetto" appears thus in Symonds:

> The best of artists hath no thought to show
> Which the rough stone in its superfluous shell
> Doth not include: to break the marble spell
> Is all the hand that serves the brain can do.*

Emerson, who rendered the same sonnet in lines of irregular length and a quite unsonnetlike rhyme-pattern, does this with the quatrain:

> Never did sculptor's dream unfold
> A form which marble doth not hold
> In its white block; yet it therein shall find
> Only the hand secure and bold
> Which still obeys the mind.

* The Italian of this quatrain reads thus:

> Non ha l'ottimo artista alcun concetto
> c' un marmo solo in sè non circonscriva
> col suo soverchio; e solo a quello arriva
> la man che ubbidisce all' intelletto.

This is the frankest "imitation," rather than translation, but the poem that results has a genuine independent interest. This is less true of Longfellow's poem, which is closer to metaphrase than Emerson's and a shade more faithful than Symonds to the original:

> Nothing the greatest artist can conceive
> That every marble block doth not confine
> Within itself; and only its design
> The hand that follows intellect can achieve.

This is superior to Symonds, surely, if only because the word "intellect" (intelletto) is truer to Michelangelo's philosophical meaning than "brain" — or even than Emerson's "mind."*

Easily first among Longfellow's translations, in quality as in time, are probably his renderings of Spanish poetry. Such a judgment, at any rate, is strongly suggested by some remarks of the Spanish scholar Miguel Romera-Navarro. "Longfellow possessed a talent by no means common," this writer has said, "for rendering foreign poetry in his native idiom, even to the point of making his versions appear to have been written originally in English: so great are his freshness and flexibility. This is so, in spite of the fact that he observes strictly, almost literally, the feeling and the meter of the original." It is true that the same scholar has also said, of Longfellow's translation of the "Coplas," that "The English version has the pure and worthy simplicity of the Biblical psalms, but it lacks the grave majesty, the solemn and profound tone of the original, its sobriety and precision." This is doubtless true, and it probably means that Longfellow could not enter wholly into the emotions of a Spanish Catholic poet of the fifteenth century or render them perfectly in nineteenth-century English. Jorge Manrique's poem itself has been called

---

* It is the same word that, in the Inferno, Vergil uses in describing the damned souls to Dante, "le genti dolorose, / C' hanno perduto il ben de l' intelletto" (the miserable folk who have lost the good of the intellect).

— by an English writer, to be sure* — "a string of common-places"; but they are at any rate noble and austere common-places, and Longfellow preserves their sententious gravity with extraordinary success. He follows the Spanish closely but without servility, and misses perhaps mainly an indefinable "precision" ("justeza") of diction, which is like the rather harsh strains of some archaic stringed instrument:

> Our lives are rivers, gliding free
> To that unfathomed, boundless sea,
> The silent grave!
> Thither all earthly pomp and boast
> Roll, to be swallowed up and lost
> In one dark wave.
>
> Thither the mighty torrents stray,
> Thither the brook pursues its way,
> And tinkling rill.
> There all are equal; side by side
> The poor man and the son of pride
> Lie calm and still.

"The poor man and the son of pride" — the line is loose and vague compared with the dry exactness of the original ("los que viven por sus manos / y los ricos" †); but something is always lost, and one ends by feeling the justice of Whitman's impressionistic tribute: "There is no undue element of pensiveness in Longfellow's strains. Even in the early translation, the Manrique, the movement is as of strong and steady wind or tide, holding up and buoying."

On a very small scale, and without the exigencies of rhyme, something like perfection in rendering is possible, and Iris Lilian Whitman has said that Longfellow's version of "Saint Teresa's Book-Mark" is "as nearly perfect as a translation can be":

* Gerald Brenan in *The Literature of the Spanish People.*
† "Those who live by their hands / and the rich."

> Let nothing disturb thee,
> Nothing affright thee;
> All things are passing;
> God never changeth;
> Patient endurance
> Attaineth to all things;
> Who God possesseth
> In nothing is wanting;
> Alone God sufficeth.

Longfellow's translations from French poets are competent but unexciting, owing partly to the mediocrity, or worse, of most of the poems he rendered; and the version of a passage from the *Chanson de Roland* in heroic couplets is perhaps as untrue to the spirit of its original as anything Longfellow did in this connection. His four or five renderings of Danish poems, on the other hand, are said by Andrew Hilen to be among the most successful in the language. The version he made, while staying in Copenhagen, of the Danish national ballad "King Christian" ("King Christian stood by the lofty mast") is, we are told, "generally considered the best," but an intrinsically more interesting poem is "The Elected Knight," a mediaeval ballad full of a fairy-tale and chivalric strangeness which Longfellow rendered in English, it appears, with extraordinary fidelity to the irregularities of the original:

> He saw under the hillside
> A Knight full well equipped;
> His steed was black, his helm was barred;
> He was riding at full speed.

This poem is the most attractive of Longfellow's translations from the Danish; the least attractive — for he could never hold out against the sentimentality of infancy — is his version of Jens Immanuel Baggesen's immensely popular "Childhood" "(There was a time when I was very small"); the poem itself would seem to be bad enough, and Longfellow's version is justly described by Daniel Kilham Dodge as "wooden."

"A translation," said Pasternak, "must be produced by an author who has undergone the influence of the original long before his task begins." Pasternak had undergone the influence of Shakespeare for many years before he began to translate him, and a similar thing could be said of Longfellow and Dante. The *Divine Comedy*, to be sure, had by no means been required reading in the generation before Longfellow's in this country, and even in England it was only with the romantic generation — Coleridge, Byron, Shelley, Leigh Hunt — that Dante's poem had begun to impose itself as Tasso's poem had imposed itself on the Elizabethan mind. The first English translation of the *Comedy*, the Reverend Henry F. Cary's, had not appeared as a whole until 1814, but Longfellow might conceivably have read this version while he was still an undergraduate at Bowdoin. Certainly it was not long before he had turned to the original itself; in Rome, in 1828, he was "poring over the gloomy pages of Dante," and protracting his nightly vigil over those pages "till the morning star was in the sky." The Inferno he was always to find distressingly gloomy, but even that *cantica* he found to be "full of wonderful pathos, horror, and surprise," and his feeling for the rest of the poem, especially the Purgatorio, grew deeper with every year that brought him back to it. A course in Dante was one of his earliest undertakings at Harvard; his lectures on the Italian poet were perhaps matched in fervor only by his lectures on Goethe, and if we can judge from some of his lecture notes, they were in the imaginative and metaphorical style that was characteristic of his appreciation generally. The *Divine Comedy*, he says in one of them,

> reminds me of the Roman aqueducts, built solidly with those stanzas, like blocks of granite, piled one upon the other, and not cemented together, but held in their places by their own weight and the clamps of the rhyme. Magnificent and beautiful structure! As you stand beneath it, you can hear the living waters of song flowing on from century to century.

Very soon he was visited by the impulse to try his hand at the formidable task of translation, and four passages from the Purgatorio had appeared, as we have seen, in *Voices of the Night*. These were the first versions of the poem that any American writer had yet made.

No doubt the ideal translator of any great poem would be a poet whose depth of spirit and power of art were comparable with those of the original maker. But such translators are rare in any language, and there are no such renderings of Dante in English. Longfellow was no closer to Dante in depth or power than some of the French translators, say, have been to Shakespeare; and he had at any rate a profound reverence for the *Comedy*, a deep and strong feeling for its grandeur, an intuition of its moral and spiritual greatness, a poet's love of its "magnificent structure" and its perfection of detail. Along with that, he had an erudite understanding of Dante's mediaeval context, an intimate familiarity with Italian, and the stylistic resources of an accomplished minor poet in his own right. It is doubtful whether any other English translator has been better equipped than he.

Everyone who has ever attempted to render Dante in English has had to confront at once the question of the form in which he can properly be carried over. The possibility of a prose rendering, such as John Carlyle undertook a little later, did not of course exist for Longfellow; the principal question for him was whether the rhyme-pattern of Dante's *terza rima*, so much more difficult to sustain in English than in Italian, must be preserved at the cost of constantly sacrificing the literal meaning of the original. Given Longfellow's theory of translation, there can have been no real hesitation for him. "In translating Dante," he said in his journal many years after his first versions were made, "something must be relinquished. Shall it be the beautiful rhyme that blossoms all along the lines like a honeysuckle on a hedge? It must be, in order to retain something more precious than rhyme; namely, fidelity, truth, — the life of the hedge itself." The only serious possibility, for him, was blank verse, not the quasi-Miltonic blank verse of Cary, with its run-on lines and its indifference to Dante's tercets, but a blank verse that, adhering line by line to Dante, would make for the utmost possible closeness and at the same time, rhymeless as it might be, would preserve — somewhat as Eliot did in "Little Gidding" — the feeling of the tercet structure.

The result is perhaps the most literal rendering of Dante in verse that has ever been attempted. It has its limitations in consequence, as we shall see, but there are few great poets with whose work such a process is so suitable as with Dante. "With a writer whose vocabulary," said Pater, "is so significant and searched through as that of Dante, whose words withal are so sensitive and picturesque, there can be no fidelity which does not include a certain literal exactness." And he seems to have had a respect for Longfellow's rendering. The blank verse of this rendering has none of the fine freedom, the fullness of rhythm, the swell and heave of English blank verse at its best; it is slow, constrained, rather stiff, and often monotonous, but often, too, it suggests, thanks to just this character, something of the wonderful terseness, the intense concision, the severe and yet delicate rhythm of the original. And the language itself, sacrificing everything to fidelity, does often convey something of the apparently effortless choiceness of Dante.

Much is lost on the way, including a sustained fidelity to the spirit of English itself as a language. Even without the shackles of a difficult rhyme-pattern, Longfellow is occasionally forced, by the necessities of his plan, into awkward and sometimes unclear inversions:

> As grades he wishes it should be thrust down.

> Than had the mind preoccupied imagined.

The syntax of his sentences is sometimes, though rarely, quite unEnglish:

> The here descending down into this centre.

In his zeal for closeness, Longfellow is capable of violating English idiom:

> The vigor of my legs was put in truce.

He cannot always avoid the prosaic:

> I fear the coming may be ill-advised.
>
> But said: "Speak, and be brief, and to the point."

He is sometimes so close to Dante that he seems to be writing neither English nor Italian:

> Our dexter shoulders it behoves us turn.

And in this translation Longfellow manifests from time to time a penchant for archaisms, for verbal oddities, for quaint Latinisms ("maledict," "withouten," "serotine," "antelucan," "lubrical") which is wholly uncharacteristic of his own verse; it led Howells to remark that Longfellow translated Dante "into the English dictionary rather than the English language."

Yet a certain unfairness is involved in speaking of such infelicities in just this way; they are not constant, and there are sustained passages where they are quite absent — passages in which Longfellow succeeds both in achieving fidelity to his original and in writing English verse that is quite free from eccentricity, awkwardness, and dullness; verse that has as much intrinsic poetic character as perhaps can be looked for in a very faithful translation. A comparison of Longfellow with one of his predecessors and one of his successors, though of course too brief to be decisive, may suggest something of the strength, rather than the weakness, of his rendering. He is not, in general, at his best in the Inferno, but he is sometimes, even there, surprisingly skillful. A few lines from Canto III, those which conjure up the first dreadful assault of sound upon the senses of Dante and Vergil as they pass through the Gate of Hell, are not unrepresentative. This is the passage in Dante:

> Quivi sospiri, pianti e alti guai
>> Risonavan per l' aere sanza stelle,
>> Per ch' io al cominciar ne lagrimai.
> Diverse lingue, orribili favelle,
>> Parole di dolore, accenti d' ira,
>> Voci alte e fioche, e suon di man con elle,
> Facevano un tumulto, il qual s' aggira
>> Sempre in quell' aura sanza tempo tinta,
>> Come la rena quando turbo spira.

Cary, who must be honored as a pathfinder, translated these lines thus:

> Here sighs, with lamentations and loud moans,
> Resounded through the air pierced by no star,
> That e'en I wept at entering. Various tongues,
> Horrible languages, outcries of woe,
> Accents of anger, voices deep and hoarse,
> With hands together smote that swelled the sounds,
> Made up a tumult, that forever whirls
> Round through that air with solid darkness stained,
> Like to the sand that in the whirlwind flies.

This is itself, literally speaking, close enough to the original, and it is not without felicities of a quiet sort — "the air pierced by no star," which is an "embellishment" — but the verse is limited rhythmically, and the language and rhetoric have rather little intensity or resource.

A relatively recent translator, Laurence Binyon, was a better poet than Cary; Ezra Pound said of his version that it "sheds more light on Dante than any translation I have ever seen." Whether this is an overstatement or not, Binyon's rendering of the *Comedy* has a marked and sometimes a powerful character of its own, all the more noteworthy since he undertook the *tour de force* of preserving Dante's triple rhymes in tercets — "the frightful tercets," as Heine called them. Binyon's version of the passage in question reads thus:

> Here lamentations, groans, and wailings deep
> Reverberated through the starless air,
> So that it made me at the beginning weep.
> Uncouth tongues, horrible shriekings of despair,
> Shrill and faint voices, cries of pain and rage,
> And, with it all, smiting of hands, were there,
> Making a tumult, nothing could assuage,
> To swirl in the air that knows not day or night,
> Like sand within the whirlwind's eddying cage.

This is remarkable, considering the difficulties overcome, but the necessities of rhyme have forced Binyon to render "alti guai" (loud lamentations) as "wailings deep," and "the whirlwind's eddying cage" is a doubtfully happy embellishment of Dante's simple "turbo spira." Nevertheless, there can be no mistaking Binyon's superiority to Cary in verbal energy and precision.

Longfellow's version of the passage is as follows:

> There sighs, complaints, and ululations loud
> Resounded through the air without a star,
> Whence I, at the beginning, wept thereat.
> Languages diverse, horrible dialects,
> Accents of anger, words of agony,
> And voices high and hoarse, with sound of hands,
> Made up a tumult that goes whirling on
> Forever in that air forever black,
> Even as the sand doth, when the whirlwind breathes.

Rhythmically speaking, this is at least as satisfactory as Binyon's version, which has its own kind of constriction, and it preserves the tercet form in every respect except for the rhyme-words. The gain in felicity and exactness is not negligible, and neither Cary nor Binyon has lines so fine rhetorically as Longfellow's sixth and eighth. "Horrible dialects," too, is more expressive than Cary's "horrible languages" and closer to Dante than Binyon's "horrible shriekings of despair." "Shrill and faint voices," in Binyon, comes close to being a mistranslation of Dante's "voci alte e fioche"; Longfellow's "voices high and hoarse" is almost certainly more faithful to the letter, in addition to being poetically truer: the voices of the lost are probably neither "shrill" nor "faint." "Voices *deep* and hoarse," in Cary, is also a shade less true to Dante.

Cary's superiority to Longfellow arises partly from the greater ease of movement of his blank verse, its relative freedom from tightness, and partly from the absence of some of the mannerisms we have spoken of. Binyon has the superiority of the triple rhyme, which he often uses with extraordinary skill, and of a certain strength and sharpness of verbal expression ("Beneath the rain that scorched them with its sting") that is less characteristic of Longfellow. Longfellow is superior to them both in closeness, in accuracy, and sometimes in feeling. As a whole, his rendering of the *Comedy* has doubtless been superseded by later translations, more contemporary in tone and no less faithful to Dante; but there are *passages* in all three of the canticles which, both for fidelity and for intrinsic poetic grace, he renders so effectively that he has not yet been outdone. He was most at home neither among the horrors of Hell nor among the transcendent splendors of Paradise but among the more human tendernesses of Purgatory. But there are passages in the Inferno — the meeting with Brunetto Latini and his "herd" ("Which goes lamenting its eternal doom") — and passages in the Paradiso — the encounter with Cacciaguida in the Heaven of Mars ("And came from martyrdom unto this peace") — which, no doubt because they express such warmth and reverence of personal feeling, are not likely to be wholly superseded. In the Purgatorio there is more on this level — the meeting with Casella on the shore of the Mount, the speeches of Buonconte and La Pia among the Unshriven, the encounter with Arnaut Daniel on the Seventh Terrace. The whole of Canto XXVII, which recounts the last night Dante spends be-

fore he enters the Earthly Paradise and then the leave-taking of
Vergil at dawn, has, as Longfellow renders it, a sustained nobility
of tone. The canto comes to a conclusion, of course, with Vergil's
final words to his erring but repentant disciple:

> When underneath us was the stairway all
>   Run o'er, and we were on the highest step,
>   Virgilius fastened upon me his eyes,
> And said: "The temporal fire and the eternal,
>   Son, thou hast seen, and to a place art come
>   Where of myself no further I discern.
> By intellect and art I here have brought thee;
>   Take thine own pleasure for thy guide henceforth;
>   Beyond the steep ways and the narrow art thou.
> Behold the sun, that shines upon thy forehead;
>   Behold the grass, the flowerets, and the shrubs
>   Which of itself alone this land produces.
> Until rejoicing come the beauteous eyes
>   Which weeping caused me to come unto thee,
>   Thou canst sit down, and thou canst walk among them.
> Expect no more or word or sign from me;
>   Free and upright and sound is thy free-will,
>   And error were it not to do its bidding;
> Thee o'er thyself I therefore crown and mitre!"

The success with which this renders Dante's unstraining gravity, his severe sweetness, has not been excelled by that of one or
two recent translations; it is not without flaws, but no version
yet made is free from them, and the virtues of Longfellow's version outweigh, in this passage and others, its defects. He must be
judged by his best as well as by his worst, and his best is admirable. There are parts of the *Divine Comedy*, sometimes single
lines, sometimes whole cantos, which will always have an interest
for the reader of Dante in English. And in general, if he is compared with any other American writer of his time, there is something almost Elizabethan in the range and freshness of Longfellow's work as a translator.

XIII

Dramatic Poems (II)

As WE READ the *Tales of a Wayside Inn*, we feel ourselves in the presence of a poet who is at work in his most natural and spontaneous vein, a poet whose matter and form are at one with each other, and who has found his happiest means of expression. As we read Longfellow's dramatic poems, we feel ourselves, a good deal of the time, baffled and, sometimes, bored by writing that clearly expresses an aspiration, an ambition, but that is somehow not quite naturally directed; writing that is willed, even determined, but only intermittently borne up and carried along by a true afflatus. Much of this writing remains impressive, nevertheless, and the chances are that, so far as these dramatic poems fail, it is not essentially due to any innate want of dramatic talent in Longfellow's make-up; there are scenes in them that are dramatic enough, at least in a free sense of the word, to belie such a view. What kept Longfellow from writing more perfectly successful dramatic poems was much more the complete absence of any real and practical relation, in his time, between the serious writer and the American stage — an absence more complete than in nineteenth-century England itself, and even there none of the best poets ever wrote with full success for the theater, though almost all of them aspired to do so. In England, nevertheless, *Remorse* and *Strafford* and *Queen Mary* could be, and were, produced; there was never any serious question of producing *The*

Spanish Student or *The Golden Legend* or "Giles Corey of the Salem Farms."

These were "closet dramas" in the most thoroughgoing sense, and Longfellow thought of them as such from the beginning. They were purely literary performances, and though remarkable pieces of dramatic writing not intended for the stage do exist — *Samson Agonistes*, *Atalanta in Calydon*, and others — they are the work of greater poets than Longfellow. He needed, far more than Milton or Swinburne did, the support of an actual theater if any latent talent for dramatic writing he might have had was to be drawn out and made effectual. He wrote dramatic poems because he loved the drama of the past, because he thought of the drama as one of the great literary modes, and because he aspired to a more major expression than his capacities warranted. Its youthful freshness gives *The Spanish Student* a small but genuine authenticity; *The Golden Legend* owes its relative success to the wholly congenial theme and to the sensitiveness of Longfellow's feeling for the Middle Ages. A certain youthfulness remained with him to the end, and he had a certain sensitiveness, as *Miles Standish* had suggested, to some aspects of seventeenth-century New England. But these were not enough to invigorate *The New England Tragedies* with full dramatic life, and Longfellow was simply not on congenial ground in dealing with the Judaea of Judas Maccabæus or of Jesus. Only with the Renaissance Italy of Michelangelo — and the themes it suggested to him — was he, as *Michael Angelo: A Fragment* demonstrates, almost as much in his own imaginative *pays* as in the Middle Ages. The story of his later dramatic writing is a story of complete or partial failure and of one very close approach to success.

Never did he undertake a task more mistakenly than when he set himself to compose a first panel for his sacred trilogy, *Christus: A Mystery*, and attempted, as he did in *The Divine Tragedy*, to dramatize poetically the life of Christ. It is a subject beyond the powers of any poet, certainly of any poet since the Middle Ages, as even *Paradise Regained,* even Klopstock's *Messias,* should have demonstrated, and it was wholly beyond the powers of a poet whose Christian faith, sincere as it certainly was, was New England Unitarianism in its coolest, most reasonable, and most optimistic form. Most of what was left of dogma even in Unitarianism was distasteful to Longfellow; what remained for him was a genuine religious sentiment, serious and deeply felt, but Christian only in the most tenuous and etherealized sense. In spite of "Torquemada," Longfellow's awareness of human evil, of sin, was almost nonexistent, or so intermittent as to be largely ineffectual in his work, and the redemption of mankind from its burden of guilt by a transcendent Saviour was a theme of which he was utterly unable to make dramatic poetry of any but the most unconvincing sort. A kind of reverence for the figure of Jesus, which indeed hardly rises above a tender respect, is the most intense feeling he can command: it is very far from being enough to animate a tragedy on the sacrifice of a Son of God. The mystery plays were written by men whose faith was passionate and complete; *The Divine Tragedy,* as a whole, is a weak nineteenth-century "Passion Play" without even the seventeenth-century intensities of Oberammergau.

Formally speaking, it consists of three acts which Longfellow calls "Passovers" (First, Second, Third), and which represent the life of "Christus" from the Temptation on the Mount to the Crucifixion, the Resurrection, and the appearance of the risen Saviour to the disciples at the Sea of Galilee. These Passovers, in whose number the symbolism of the Trinity is easily visible, are divided into a series of short scenes — too short, for the most part, to be dramatically telling — representing such events as the Marriage in Cana, the healing of Blind Bartimeus, the Transfiguration, the Entry into Jerusalem, and the Agony in the Garden of Gethsemane. The gospel narratives only occasionally lend themselves to the dialogue form, and in any case they can scarcely be improved upon, though they can be translated into the naïve

manner of the mystery plays without one kind of loss. Longfellow
hardly even attempts to improve upon the gospel narratives; on
the whole, he is content to paraphrase them — with what certainly seemed to him reverence — in language which adheres to
the Authorized Version with exaggerated and tedious closeness.
Passages such as this are characteristic:

> Ah, whosoever drinketh of this water
> Shall thirst again; but whosoever drinketh
> The water I shall give him shall not thirst
> Forevermore, for it shall be within him
> A well of living water, springing up
> Into life everlasting.

Was it worthwhile to write a modern mystery play so close in
language to the gospels themselves that their exquisite prose, in its
English form, is merely denatured in uninteresting blank verse?

It is true that, even in the scenes based literally on the gospels,
Longfellow sometimes goes beyond the narrative itself, amplify-
ing it with speeches which have no warrant in the text, and that
sometimes these speeches have a certain charm as verse. This is
true, for example, of some lines from the scene "In the Cornfields," in the First Passover — the scene of the calling of Nathanael in Galilee, which derives from the first chapter of St.
John:

> The summer sun grows hot: I am anhungered.
> How cheerily the Sabbath-breaking quail
> Pipes in the corn, and bids us to his Feast
> Of Wheat Sheaves! How the bearded, ripening ears
> Toss in the roofless temple of the air;
> As if the unseen hand of some High-Priest
> Waved them before Mount Tabor as an altar!

The "Sabbath-breaking quail" has a pleasant appropriateness here
since the calling of Nathanael is immediately followed — too
quickly, it is true, and arbitrarily — by the appearance of the
Pharisees and their reproach to Christus for allowing his disciples

to pluck the ears of corn on the Sabbath. The scene of the Entry into Jerusalem, in the Third Passover, is preceded by a lyric, sung by the daughter of the Syro-Phœnician Woman, about the healing of Bartimeus, which has taken place in an earlier scene. This lyric had appeared many years before, in *Ballads and Other Poems,* as "Blind Bartimeus," and Long-fellow simply transferred it now to *The Divine Tragedy.* It is a fine poem in itself — with its association of literal and spirit-ual blindness, and its bold use of the actual Greek phrases from St. Mark — and it gains something from its transference to this dramatic setting.

In a few cases, too, Longfellow has added whole scenes, some of them in soliloquy form, which have no literal basis in the gospels. There is a certain gentle pathos in the soliloquy of Mary Magdalene, as she sits on the Tower of Magdala, gazing down at the Sea of Galilee below her, and seeing as in a vision the whole of her sinful past unrolling before her:

> The princes and the merchants come to me,
> Merchants of Tyre and Princes of Damascus,
> And pass, and disappear, and are no more;
> But leave behind their merchandise and jewels,
> Their perfumes, and their gold, and their disgust.

Between the scene of Christus's denunciation by Caiaphas and the scene of his appearance before Pilate, Longfellow introduces two scenes in a wholly different emotional tone, which provide an effect of sharp irony — or, rather, would do so if the two en-closing scenes were themselves more intense in tragic feeling. One of these invented passages is a soliloquy by Pontius Pilate, pre-sumably in a private chamber, which strikes with some skill the note of cultivated Roman skepticism and detachment, of revulsion from Jewish fanaticism and contempt for a religion in which there are no goddesses. This scene is followed by one in which Barabbas addresses his fellow prisoners in the rhymed stanzas and humorous manner of some speeches in the mystery plays:

> I was once, to say it in brief,
> A highwayman, a robber-chief,
>   In the open light of day.
> So much I am free to confess;
> But all men, more or less,
>   Are robbers in their way.

The haling of Christus before Pilate and the ordering of the Crucifixion are followed by a scene in which, departing from the letter of St. Matthew's account, Longfellow represents Judas Iscariot soliloquizing in Aceldama, the "field of blood," before he flings himself to his death over a cliff. There are faint echoes of Byron's *Cain* in this passage, but it quite fails to convey the terrible anguish of a traitor's, a great sinner's, remorse.

In a few other scenes Longfellow departs even more widely from the gospel narratives, and introduces two characters from the Acts of the Apostles. One of these is the Manaen who is described in Acts as having been brought up with Herod the Tetrarch and whom Longfellow, following another source, calls Manahem the Essenian. He is a representative of the purest, the most unworldly, the most ascetic elements in Judaic life in the generation of Jesus, and unlike some of the other Essenes he recognizes Christus as the promised Leader. At the Marriage in Cana, beholding the youthful Christus for the first time, he hails him, in an aside, as the true Anointed, and has a prophetic intuition of the Crucifixion. At the Crucifixion itself, Manahem apostrophizes the Cross as a symbol

> that shall forever
> Shine through the darkness, and shall conquer pain
> By the triumphant memory of this hour!

In an earlier scene, in Herod's banquet hall, when the Tetrarch reminds him that in their childhood Manahem had prophesied his kingship, Manahem for his part reminds Herod that he had also prophesied that, in the end, the Lord would punish him for his injustice and inclemency. Rushing out from the banquet hall as John the Baptist's head is about to be brought in at the behest of Salome, Manahem breaks out, under the walls of the prison, into a prophetic denunciation of vengeance upon Herod for his sins. This soliloquy, in three-stress lines and in sprung rhythm, has a certain Biblical grandeur of language and imagery; in quite a different tone, the speech Manahem delivers, again aside, at the Marriage in Cana ("The things that have been and shall be no more"), expresses, with curious eloquence, a melancholy vision of human life as

> A dream within a dream, a wind at night
> Howling across the desert in despair,
> Seeking for something lost it cannot find.

Nowhere else does Longfellow give voice to quite so mournful a view of human destiny; and though the speech has a dramatic appropriateness here, as the utterance of a deeply spiritual mind caught between the end of one dispensation and the beginning of another, the vibrations of a more lyrical and subjective feeling in it are unmistakable. There is no such identification of the poet with the other character taken from Acts — and other writings — Simon Magus, the sorcerer who was converted by St. Philip and later denounced by St. Peter for his venality. Simon had given his name, as Longfellow well knew from his reading of Dante, to the Simoniacs who are punished in the Eighth Circle of Hell; it is not, however, as a Simoniac that he appears in *The Divine Tragedy*, but as a false Messiah, a heretical prophet, who laid claim to being himself an incarnation of the Godhead and who was recognized by the people of Samaria as "the great power of God." Simon appears in a scene at night, on a housetop at Endor, accompanied by the woman known to legend as Helen of Tyre — the woman, formerly a prostitute, whom Simon claimed to be a female emanation of the Deity. Helen is the subject of a later short poem of Longfellow's ("What phantom is this that appears"), and clearly the sadness of her fate — dragged

by a superior and ruthless will into a role that fatigues and fright-
ens her — made a particular appeal to his feelings. She is a figure
of touching pathos here, but the scene is mainly taken up by Simon's inflated and megalomaniac speeches, and of course he
serves the dramatic purpose of furnishing a foil to the purity of
the suffering Christus. He too, like Manahem, appears at the
Crucifixion, but only to mock at the dying Christus and the "ruin"
of his hopes, and to cry with ironic exultation: "This is my hour
of triumph, Nazarene!"

The scenes in which these three figures appear, or at least the
passages in which they speak, have both a poetic and a dramatic
force that very little else in *The Divine Tragedy* has. They add
something appreciable to its intellectual interest, but they do not
suffice to save the poem from its fundamental ineffectualness and
tepidity. The central figure, Christus, as Longfellow conceives
him, cannot be characterized as Godhead Incarnate, since Longfellow's conception of Jesus Christ was a vaguely Socinian or
anti-Trinitarian one; he cannot, on the other hand, be fully and
powerfully characterized as a tragic hero, since Longfellow's conception is, after all, too reverent for that. He can be "characterized" only by a selection from his words in the gospels, very
literally paraphrased, as we have seen, and by a certain choice
among his acts. The total effect is one of mildness, benevolence,
and melancholy, but not of supernatural power and certainly not
of divinity. And the sin from which, according to Christian doctrine, Christ came into the world to redeem mankind — this
deep and deadly guilt is hardly felt at all. Satan, or rather Lucifer, appears only once — in the scene of the Temptation at the
very beginning — and though his speeches there, in stanzaic form,
have a certain lyrical beauty, the sense of his malignancy as the
Father of Lies is hardly present in the slightest. Milton's Satan
was at least a Titan; this Lucifer is a minor romantic poet.

The Divine Tragedy, or rather the whole trilogy, is preceded
by an Introitus in which we see an Angel bearing the prophet

Habakkuk aloft through the air toward Babylon, the City of Gold, to carry food to Daniel, who has been lying for five days in the lions' den. Longfellow is drawing here on the Apocryphal story of Bel and the Dragon, and Habakkuk figures so conspicuously at the outset partly because he is an image of meekness and charity — he had been about to go into the field and bring pottage to the reapers — and partly because he represents the prophetic power generally. He represents it in his sufferings as well as in his foresight:

> Alas! how full of fear
> Is the fate of Prophet and Seer!
> Forevermore, forevermore,
> It shall be as it hath been heretofore;
> The age in which they live
> Will not forgive
> The splendor of the everlasting light,
> That makes their foreheads bright,
> Nor the sublime
> Fore-running of their time!

In its irregular line-lengths and rhyming, this Introitus echoes — or anticipates — the Epilogue of *The Golden Legend*, to which it is also bound thematically; they are both, in part, descants on the virtue of meekness.

The Epilogue of *The Divine Tragedy* itself consists simply of the Apostles' Creed recited by the Apostles one by one in a series of twelve clauses. It has little more than a decorative effect, for the theology expressed in it is neither prepared for by what precedes nor illustrated by what follows. Between *The Divine Tragedy* and *The Golden Legend*, in the finished trilogy, appears a First Interlude: it is in the form of a soliloquy by the Abbot Joachim — the twelfth-century Joachim of Flora — in a room in the convent of Flora in Calabria. It is a stormy night, as it is in the Prologue of the play that follows, and Joachim sets forth in his soliloquy the doctrine of the Three Ages of Humanity —

the Age of the Father, or of Fear; the Age of the Son, or of Wisdom; and the Age of the Holy Ghost, or of Love.* As he concludes, Joachim gives utterance to his hatred of Hate and his love of Love in lines that Longfellow doubtless meant to serve as a moral and even religious nucleus of the whole trilogy.

In a Second Interlude, which intervenes between *The Golden Legend* and *The New England Tragedies*, the Catholic Joachim is superseded by the Protestant Martin Luther, whom we see writing — in the morning, now, not at night — in a chamber of the Wartburg. What he is writing is his great hymn, "Ein' feste Burg," which Longfellow of course translates, though not in his best manner; Luther interrupts the successive stanzas of his hymn with a kind of discontinuous soliloquy. There is something of the rugged power and spiritual independence of early Protestantism in Luther's reflections, but there is even more of its harshness and intolerance, for the two plays that follow are to deal with the theme of persecution. Even so, it is puzzling that, after putting his deepest feelings about the cardinal virtue of Charity into the mouth of the Abbot Joachim, Longfellow should underline so insistently the more repellent aspects of Protestant intolerance in what he represents Luther as feeling — his hatred of the Pope of Rome, "with all his diabolic crew," of "that odious monk John Tetzel," of "all the busy, multifarious / Heretics, and disciples of Arius," and particularly, and most bitterly, of the tolerant humanist Erasmus:

> He is the vilest miscreant
> That ever walked this world below! . . .
> Whenever I pray, I pray for a curse
> On Erasmus, the Insincere!

It is one of the principal defects of the trilogy as a whole that its third part, instead of actually dramatizing the virtue of Charity,

---

* Longfellow found this doctrine summarized, in a French work on "The Eternal Gospel," from Joachim's *Exposition of the Apocalypse*, but he seems to have adapted it rather freely to his own purpose.

as Longfellow's early design required, should do little more than dramatize the vice of theological hatred — and fear. If this had expressed a settled and philosophic conception of the inferiority of Protestantism to Catholicism, it would have been at least understandable, and the result might have been impressive in its own manner. But it is unimaginable that Longfellow could have intended any such effect: the result has an air of inadvertence and almost of casualness, and the trilogy ends on a note of moral anticlimax. This effect is already anticipated in the soliloquy of the heresy-hunting Luther.

The two *New England Tragedies*, "John Endicott" and "Giles Corey of the Salem Farms," have a kind of vitality that is missing from *The Divine Tragedy*: in writing them, Longfellow was not oppressed by the constraint and self-consciousness that evidently weighed on him in writing the first part of the trilogy. The subjects themselves were fresher, closer at hand, and more purely human than the Gospel subject, and Longfellow could, and did, handle his historical authorities with much greater freedom. Neither play succeeds in arousing the emotions of tragedy in any profound way, but of the two "John Endicott" comes closer to doing so, no doubt because the heroism of the Quakers in resisting persecution had a reality for Longfellow that the suffering of the "witches" at Salem did not quite evoke. The play is preceded by a Prologue in which the theme of Charity — and tolerance — is rather prosaically set forth; and "John Endicott" itself dramatizes the persecution of a group of Quaker men and women — particularly Wenlock Christison and his daughter Edith — by the Massachusetts magistrates and ministers — particularly John Endicott, the Governor, and the minister, John Norton — in the year, by a slight poetic liberty, 1665, when Endicott died. The imprisonment of the Quakers, the condemning of Christison to death, the sentencing of Edith to be "scourged in three towns with forty stripes save one," the reluctant freeing of the Quakers when a Mandamus to that effect comes from the King in London — these incidents furnish the main action of the play.

Some sense of the ferocious bigotry of the Puritan colonial leaders is genuinely conveyed by the language and the action of "John Endicott." The insane rage of heresy-hunting is almost as forcibly depicted in the characterization of John Norton as in that of the old hidalgo in "Torquemada" — John Norton, for whom toleration is "the first-born child / Of all abominations and deceits," and who, in the first scene of Act I, preaches a sermon that quivers and even "quakes" with a mingling of superstitious terror and sectarian hatred. John Endicott is less simply and less unsympathetically characterized than Norton: Longfellow, indeed, is probably dealing very freely with the biographical "facts" in representing Endicott as a man — to use the words of another character — "both loving and severe; / A tender heart; a will inflexible." This rather softened Endicott, torn between his loathing of heresy and his love of justice, is historically, in all probability, less credible than the grim protagonist of Hawthorne's "Endicott and the Red Cross" or the "haughty Endicott," with his "lion glare of bitter hate and scorn," of Whittier's poem, "Cassandra Southwick." Imaginatively speaking, however, Longfellow's Endicott is a little more interesting than either Hawthorne's or Whittier's one-dimensional character, and it is expressive of his rather ambiguous humanity that he should express his horror of heresy in a metaphor of singular beauty:

> The sin of heresy is a deadly sin.
> 'Tis like the falling of the snow, whose crystals
> The traveller plays with, thoughtless of his danger,
> Until he sees the air so full of light
> That it is dark; and blindly staggering onward,
> Lost and bewildered, he sits down to rest;
> There falls a pleasant drowsiness upon him,
> And what he thinks is sleep, alas! is death.

Unlike John Norton, Endicott is a figure of mingled repellency and pathos: Longfellow invents for him a son, a second John Endicott, who hates intolerance as much as his father hates heresy, and who, falling in love with Edith Christison, throws himself upon the side of the Quakers. His father's grief, at war with his indignation, is humanly convincing, and the emotional tension between the father and the son has something of the archetypal quality of that between David and Absalom. When, indeed, the younger man is arrested and thrown into prison on his father's orders, the Governor himself breaks out with the anguished cry, "O Absalom, my son!" A kind of Puritan intensity is characteristic of both the elder and the younger Endicott: the latter is given to dreams and visions, like his dream of the elm tree on the Common on which the Quakers had been hanged; he hears accusatory voices, and even in the most innocent aspects of nature he sees the stains of guilt. Wandering through the "wilderness" in search of the fugitive Edith, he breaks out in a passionate soliloquy:

> Blood! blood! The leaves above me and around me
> Are red with blood! The pathways of the forest,
> The clouds that canopy the setting sun,
> And even the little river in the meadows
> Are stained with it! Where'er I look, I see it!
> Away, thou horrible vision! Leave me! leave me!

Young Endicott is a minor Macbeth, without Macbeth's good reasons for seeing blood everywhere; he might also be described as a more haunted and obsessed John Alden. He is not a figure of great masculine force in characterization, any more than most of Longfellow's young men are; but one feels in him a quality of sensitive truth to one side of the Puritan temper.

The Quakers themselves are seen in a wholly sympathetic light: their own fanaticisms and extravagances, in this early phase, are almost entirely passed over, and they have perhaps, again, a less authentic historical character than the Quakers in Hawthorne's

tale "The Gentle Boy." They embody the virtues of Protestantism on its purest and most spiritual side, in their entire rejection of outward conformities and their entire surrender to the
admonitions of the Inner Light; their willingness to labor, as one
of them puts it in this play, "for an inward stillness, — / An inward stillness and an inward healing." They face their persecutors
and judges calmly but undauntedly, and they meet their punish-
ments, as Edith Christison does, in a kind of ecstasy of zeal. They
are conscious of no conflicts in their commitment to the Truth
they see; even Cassandra Southwick, in Whittier's poem, had
yielded for a moment to the weakness of the flesh and listened to
the low voice of the Tempter, but Edith Christison is absolutely
unswerving, as her father is. She does not yield even to the
younger Endicott's declarations of love or his appeals to her to
let him help her to escape; she simply turns a deaf ear to these,
and quotes Revelation to him, rather finely though very literally:

> Put this temptation underneath thy feet.
> To him that overcometh shall be given
> The white stone with the new name written on it,
> That no man knows save him that does receive it,
> And I will give thee a new name, and call thee
> Paul of Damascus and not Saul of Tarsus.

Edith and the other Quakers are somewhat idealized, in short,
but not to the point of real distortion, and only in a spirit that is
appropriate to Longfellow's purpose.

Around these principal characters are grouped a few others
who combine to build up some feeling for the whole life of the
little Boston community in Endicott's and Norton's later days,
the declining days of the first heroic generation. By no means all
the citizens of the town are in sympathy with the harshness of the
magistrates, and the dissenters are represented by a kindly old
man, Nicholas Upsall, who gives shelter, at considerable risk to
himself, to Wenlock Christison and his daughter, and who be-
friends the younger Endicott when his father casts him out. There

is a hearty sea captain, too, Simon Kempthorn of the *Swallow*, who is arrested and fined for having brought the Quakers from Barbados to Boston; he is also clapped into the pillory for "profane swearing." Kempthorn introduces an agreeable note of comedy into this otherwise somber play, making a joke of his uncomfortable position in the pillory and jeering at the respectable citizens of Boston as they pass along the street:

> I'm getting tired
> Of being perched aloft here in this cro' nest
> Like the first mate of a whaler, or a Middy
> Mast-headed, looking out for land! Sail ho!
> Here comes a heavy-laden merchantman
> With the lee clews eased off, and running free
> Before the wind. A solid man of Boston.
> A comfortable man, with dividends,
> And the first salmon, and the first green peas.

On the other hand, there is a bluenosed tithingman, Walter Merry, who rejoices that he has succeeded in bringing the "contumacious" town to a strict observance of the Sabbath day by suppressing every expression of cheerful activity; only the doves on his roof disturb him by billing and cooing on that day; he denounces them as Quakers, and throws stones at them in an effort to disperse them.

In the original prose version of "John Endicott," the unpublished "New England Tragedy," there were still other characters, including the Governor's wife, Mistress Endicott; by eliminating them in the revised play, Longfellow no doubt concentrates and unifies its interest, but he rather impoverishes it too, and one regrets that he cut them out. The action also is pared down and somewhat attenuated in the revision: we see nothing of the younger Endicott after his release from prison, and nothing of Edith Christison after she returns to old Upsall's protection; the play comes to an end with John Endicott's sudden death by a kind of stroke as he sits in his private room talking mournfully with Richard Bellingham. In the original version, we learn that Wenlock Christison and his daughter, here called Theophila, are to be deported to hard labor in Barbados for not paying their fines, and the play ends with a scene in the streets near the wharves: Wenlock Christison and his daughter are led in between files of soldiers, while young Endicott rushes in distractedly and tries to persuade Theophila to let him accompany her into exile. Richard Bellingham, who stands nearby, has him arrested and dragged off to prison again, and as the two Quakers are led off-stage we hear the prophetic voice of Wenlock Christison denouncing woe to the "bloody city" of Boston. This is perhaps a less touching conclusion than the later one but, given the theme of the play, it is surely somewhat stronger. And on the whole, in spite of a few fine passages, the verse into which, for the sake of bringing the play into line with the rest of the trilogy, Longfellow translated his original prose is curiously less vigorous and dramatic than the prose had been. In spite of these changes, "John Endicott" in its final form is the most interesting part of the trilogy after *The Golden Legend*, and one can understand, if one cannot quite share, Howells's feeling for its "high solemnity," its "solemn and serious beauty."

"Giles Corey of the Salem Farms" is less impressive in every way. "John Endicott" communicates something of the emotional tension of a community in the grip of heresy-hunters; "Giles Corey" fails, in the end, to communicate with any real power the emotional tension of a community pathologically attacked by a peculiarly virulent hysteria. There was a morbid horror in the subject of Salem witchcraft, unlike that of theological persecution, which Longfellow's kindly spirit shrank, perhaps half-consciously, from rendering with any real sternness or rigor; the poisons of panic terror, of malignant hostility, of superstitious cruelty were so alien to his own nature that, in this connection at least, he could not master them imaginatively, and though they are present in "Giles Corey," they are never represented with full dramatic conviction. Correspondingly, Longfellow fails to evoke any deep tragic sense of the heroism, the moral grandeur, of those who held out against the hysteria and, in some cases, went to their deaths in unavailing innocence.

The failure of the play is partly due to the simple fact of its mistakenly small scale. It consists of five very short acts, broken up into scenes that, for the most part, could be prolonged for only a few minutes each on the stage; and the inevitable result is an almost constant dissipation of dramatic energy. There is something comic in the brevity of some of these scenes — of the very last one, for example, in which John Hathorne and Cotton Mather appear in a field near the graveyard where Giles Corey lies dead, "with a great stone on his breast," and, in two speeches of no more than fourteen lines altogether, draw their several morals from what has happened. Such abbreviation of scene makes any real dramatic development impossible, and, consistently with this, the cast of characters is itself too small to enact the tragedy of a whole community's moral disaster. Only two of the alleged witches, Giles Corey and his wife Martha, appear, though one or two others are alluded to. Of the hysterical adolescent girls who precipitated the horror, only one, Mary Walcot, is brought on the stage, and the evil-disposed minister, the Reverend Samuel Parris, in whose household the hysteria began, is not included in the cast. The only representative of the clergy is Cotton Mather, whose role in what actually took place in Salem is, legitimately enough, much exaggerated. John Hathorne alone, among the three examining magistrates, appears as a character; neither Jonathan Corwin nor Samuel Sewall enters the scene, and the absence of the latter is particularly deplorable from the point of view of a rich historical treatment. The scene itself is confined to the Salem Farms and Salem Village, and though this simplification can be defended on the ground of dramatic unity, there is little or nothing in the dialogue to suggest the epidemic spread of the hysteria to the neighboring villages — Beverly, Andover, Glouces-

ter — and even to Boston. Nothing in the play effectively hints
at the appalling number of persons who were arrested and jailed
before the hysteria had spent itself, or even at the much more
limited number who were hanged. The whole terrible episode is
made to seem smaller, more narrowly localized, and less feverish
than it really was.

The language and the verse of the dialogue itself are expressive
of the low vitality out of which "Giles Corey" seems to spring.
Some of the speeches in "John Endicott," even in its blank verse
form, have, as we have seen, a certain poetic energy; there is
next to nothing of this in "Giles Corey," the language and the
verse of which are mostly so nerveless, so gray and prosaic, that
one feels the play could only have gained by being written, like
the first version of "Endicott," in prose. Metaphor, in any strict
sense, is almost wholly absent, and even rhetorical eloquence, such
as one feels in John Norton's sermon, has virtually disappeared.
Cotton Mather alone among the characters expresses himself more
or less sustainedly with some picturesqueness; a fair example of
this is one of his speeches in a dialogue with Justice Hathorne:

> The spiritual world
> Lies all about us, and its avenues
> Are open to the unseen feet of phantoms
> That come and go, and we perceive them not,
> Save by their influence, or when at times
> A most mysterious Providence permits them
> To manifest themselves to mortal eyes.

With all these deductions, however, "Giles Corey" is not lacking in a certain fragile interest and a modicum of dramatic truth.
There is a genuine pathos, if no real tragic force, in the characterization of Giles Corey — in the firmness and fortitude with which,
a simple and superstitious man himself, he refuses unflinchingly to
confess to a crime of which he knows himself innocent. There is
some force, too, in what Longfellow makes of Corey's wife, Martha, who is courageously willing to declare openly the skepti-

cism that she feels about the whole ugly subject of witchcraft.
John Hathorne the Magistrate has something of John Endicott's
superstitious severity — "For one," he says to Mather, "I do not
fear excess of zeal" — and Cotton Mather himself, victim as he is
of the most puerile superstitious terrors, speaks out, as he did in
fact, against the uncritical use of "spectral evidence," and openly
expresses his fear lest the authorities, in their undiscriminating
zeal, should punish some who are not guilty of what they are
charged with: something of the historical Cotton Mather's complexity of mind and spirit comes through in his characterization.
And the malice of John Gloyd, Corey's hired man, who spitefully
accuses him of witchcraft and precipitates his destruction, is
rendered with a genuine veracity: there were dozens of John
Gloyds in Essex County in 1692, and this one stands more or
less adequately for them all. Two or three of the scenes themselves might well have a disturbing theatrical impact if well
performed on the stage, especially the scene in the Meeting-
house in Act IV in which both Giles and Martha Corey are haled
before the examining Magistrates and accused of witchcraft by
the malignant little Mary Walcot. The last scene, however, is a
lamentable anticlimax, as we have seen, and it is quite incredible that Cotton Mather could ever have used the words with
which Longfellow represents him, in the interest of the theme, as
concluding the play:

> Those who lie buried in the Potter's Field
> Will rise again, as surely as ourselves
> That sleep in honored graves with epitaphs;
> And this poor man, whom we have made a victim,
> Hereafter will be counted as a martyr!

Samuel Sewall might just conceivably have made such a speech,
but not the author of *The Wonders of the Invisible World*. And
the ambitious structure of the whole trilogy — *considered* as a
whole — leans insecurely upon an abrupt and inconclusive ending.

It is true that "Giles Corey," or rather the trilogy itself, is rounded off with a Finale in which St. John is seen "wandering over the face of the Earth" and soliloquizing in mild and melancholy tones on the sorrowfulness of man's destiny. St. John, the apostle of Love, is a pendant to the beneficent Habbakuk of the Introitus at the very beginning, and he suggests, though in plaintive interrogations rather than strong affirmations, that Faith and Hope and Charity have not failed and will not fail. But he does this in a context so mournful and so close to despair that one is forced to wonder what Longfellow is really saying at the end of it all. Protestantism has hardly been revealed, in *The New England Tragedies,* as a great and secure gain for the human spirit, and what is to follow upon Protestant orthodoxy — unless Quakerism is the last word — is never opened up with any force or fervor or prophetic vision. We can only conclude that, in his later years, Longfellow was reduced to a kind of spiritual last stand — to a kind of Tennysonian trust that "somehow" all is well. There is something admirable in the restraint with which he refrains from saying more than he can say with any fullness of conviction, but the last word of *Christus: A Mystery* is a curiously muted one:

> Poor, sad Humanity
> Through all the dust and heat
> Turns back with bleeding feet,
> By the weary road it came,
> Unto the simple thought
> By the great Master taught,
> And that remaineth still:
> Not he that repeateth the name,
> But he that doeth the will!

The subject of *Judas Maccabæus* was almost as unsuitable a subject for Longfellow's gifts as *The Divine Tragedy* had been, and the poem has even fewer elements of interest than the other has. It is on an almost perversely small scale — five tiny acts, divided into even tinier scenes and amounting to hardly a thousand lines in all. As a result, the poem produces somewhat the effect of an epic drama in a puppet theater or an oratorio reduced to a few brief and rather thin recitatives. Naturally, the theme that had struck Longfellow as so fruitful for a play — the collision of Judaism and Hellenism — could not be, and is not, developed in this space with any real richness or complexity: it is broached, but it is not worked out; grazed lightly, but not seriously *treated*. And even if the theme had been amplified on the scale it deserved, it is doubtful whether the result would have been at all impressive; few characters in history, except the great sinners, could have lent themselves less happily to treatment by a poet like Longfellow than the heroic, the leonine Judas Maccabæus: "In his acts he was like a lion, and like a lion's whelp roaring for his prey." The romantic Northern figure of Olaf Tryggvason, Longfellow had been able to summon up with extraordinary — though, for him, exceptional — boldness; but the martial Hebraic zeal of Judas, his passionate and dedicated nationalism, were beyond him, and the three or four scenes in which Judas appears are quite without dramatic energy or spirit. He declares in one of them that he hears the trumpets sounding from Bethhoron, but the blare of those trumpets never reaches our ears.

There is somewhat more reality in the character of Antiochus Epiphanes, the Hellenistic King of Syria, who attempts so misguidedly to turn the City of David into an Hellenic *polis* and the Jews themselves into aesthetes and athletes who will speak exquisite Greek and exercise themselves, no doubt naked, in his Gymnasium. Antiochus is rather more within Longfellow's range than Judas, and the scene in Act I in which he discusses his purposes with the renegade Jewish priest Jason, has a pleasant humor and, in the light of what of course follows, a mild irony. There is a touching melancholy, too, in the very last scene, in which the death of the defeated and disappointed Antiochus among the mountains of Ecbatana is represented; but the strains of true tragedy are inaudible. These two scenes have more life, tenuous as it is, than any other in the play, with the possible exception of the scene in Act II, "The Dungeon of the Citadel," in which Longfellow dramatizes the terrible story, from II Maccabees, of the torture and death of the seven recalcitrant brothers in the presence of their mother. Something of the unyielding Jewish piety, its exulting fortitude in the face of persecution, comes through in this scene, especially in the speeches of the Mother. But the frightfulness of the original is largely emasculated, and the language and the verse are not up to the requirements of the tragic action. It is understandable that *Judas Maccabæus* has been, perhaps, more completely forgotten than any other of Longfellow's ambitious poems.

The character and career of a great artist made less unnatural demands on Longfellow's power than the character and career of a great patriot-warrior, and the "Fragment" of *Michael Angelo,* which he never regarded as finished, has too much vitality, autumnal as that vitality mostly is, to be disposed of as a mere failure. The full Titanism of Michelangelo, his demiurgic or demonic character, hardly emerges in any towering way from the fragment, but what is perhaps surprising, and unexpected, is that so much of his force of mind and spirit, so much too of his purely human idiosyncrasy, does emerge. The poem, to be sure, is still less a drama, even in a free sense, than those which preceded it: it consists, rather, of a series of scenes, some of them monologues, illustrating the lives of Michelangelo and his friends — and enemies — over a period of perhaps thirty years, from the beginning of his labors on the "Last Judgment" to the eve of his death. It is not so much a play as a versified and mildly dramatized biography, looser in form even than an Elizabethan chronicle-history play; it suggests such later genres as the biographical novel or the fictionalized biography, though it is composed with much more sobriety and fidelity to the facts than most examples of these forms have been.

The cast of characters, and the scenes which they enact, are clearly intended not only to furnish a dramatic setting for Michelangelo's life and work but to bring before us, at least in characteristic glimpses, the Italian Renaissance itself in its exuberance, its creative prodigality, its violence, its worldliness, its ideality. The great Pope Julius III, Michelangelo's patron and defender, appears in one scene, along with two of Michelangelo's detractors, the Cardinals Salviati and Marcello. Another cardinal, an admirer, Ippolito de' Medici, with his unecclesiastical Spanish cloak and slouched hat, his luxurious surroundings, his Numidian slaves, and his loving allusions to Ovid and Livy, figures interestingly in some of the early scenes, and at second hand we hear a good deal about the very literary ducal court of the Estes at Ferrara. Two and only two great ladies appear — the worldly and discontented Julia Gonzaga, Duchess of Trajetto, and, more importantly, her friend, and of course Michelangelo's friend, the celebrated Vittoria Colonna, beautiful, learned, philosophical, lofty-minded, devoted to her husband's memory, and profoundly, though perhaps heretically, religious. In the great artist's idealizing love for her, and still more in his grief over her death, there may be a poetic echo of Longfellow's sorrowing memory of his dead wife.

More numerous than these great lords and ladies are the artists of one sort or another, some of them obviously introduced as foils for Michelangelo; we either actually see them or hear about them at second hand. There is much rather majestic namedropping, in fact, and we hear a good deal about such artists as Raphael, to whom Michelangelo pays a generous tribute, or the young Veronese, "still a mere stripling," who promises so brilliantly. Benvenuto Cellini — on whose memoirs Longfellow was partly drawing — appears in person, describing exuberantly to the greater man his labors over the casting of his Perseus, his prowess during the siege of Rome, his vision in the prison of St. Angelo. Michelangelo rebukes Benvenuto for wasting his great talent on such unworthy trifles as gold rings and saltcellars, but his admiration and affection for the younger artist are evident enough. So are they, too, for another contemporary, the painter Sebastiano del Piombo, but Fra Sebastiano's worldliness, his sensuality, his contentedness with less than his best, he cannot forgive; and when the prosperous, indolent painter invites him to a supper at which a French friar named Rabelais will be present, the unsociable old man rejects the invitation.* The greatest artist to appear is Titian, during his Roman sojourn, whose studio Michelangelo visits and whose new painting, the "Danaë," he praises, when it is exhibited to him, with unfeigned enthusiasm. The young nobleman, Tomaso de' Cavalieri, to whom some of Michelangelo's most ardent sonnets are addressed, appears in only one scene.†

There is a good deal of quiet truth and reality in the portrait of the great protagonist himself. His wilder traits, to be sure — his truculence, his morose suspiciousness, his pathological fears, his *sauvagerie* — are touched upon lightly, if at all. But as an embodiment of the Hero as Artist, Michelangelo is credibly and humanly characterized. His lofty and ideal consecration to his art, his just pride in his own work (imperfect as he feels it to be), his haughty independence of control, his passionate love of freedom, his determination to labor on diligently to the end — all these veracious traits are accounted for in his characterization. So, too, however, are his deep melancholy, his unsociable habits, his

---

* Among the scenes which Longfellow dropped as not to be incorporated in *Michael Angelo*, but which were published by his editors in an appendix, is a scene representing this supper party in Fra Sebastiano's garden. Rabelais here is interestingly allowed to defend the bawdiness of his great book on the ground that he had a serious purpose behind it, but Longfellow seems to have omitted the scene as "jarring with the tone of the poem."

† This is the fine scene in the Coliseum with Michelangelo, whom Tomaso praises as a far nobler architect than Gaudentius, the builder of that famous, or infamous, structure. Tomaso also appears, it is true, in a rejected scene — the scene of Michelangelo's actual death — comforting and soothing his last moments.

impatience with fools, his contempt for titles of ceremony, and his inconsistent pride in his own lineage. He is capable even of a rather harmless vengefulness, as when he retaliates upon the papal master of ceremonies, Ser Biagio, who has censured the nudities of the "Last Judgment" — Longfellow is drawing on Vasari here — by painting him as Minos, "master of ceremonies / In the Infernal Regions." The sadness and the loneliness of Michelangelo's old age are touchingly rendered, and indeed there is more of his tenderness here than of his *terribilità* — more of the sculptor of the "Pietà" than the painter of the "Last Judgment"; but the distortion, if it is that, is not extreme, and so few poets have ever attempted to dramatize the lives of great artists at all — Browning still remains an exception — that we can hardly grudge Longfellow our respect for what he made of *this* life.

The poem has no intense or profound intellectual interest, any more than, by this time, one would expect it to have, but two or three thematic strains run through it and give it a certain weight and coherence of thought or of feeling. One of these is the philosophical-aesthetic theme, the theme of Art and its spiritual, its ideal, its even religious mission — the theme that Emerson had voiced, forty years earlier, in his lecture on Michelangelo. It was the transcendental view of Art, of course, held in one form or another by all the romantics, and when Longfellow wrote, it had become a commonplace. It has a relevance, however, in a poem about so good a Platonist as Michelangelo, though it is expressed most tangibly not by him, but by Vittoria Colonna:

> Art is the gift of God, and must be used
> Unto His Glory. That in art is highest
> Which aims at this. . . .
>
>   So that art
> Which bears the consecration and the seal
> Of holiness upon it will prevail
> Over all others.

Michelangelo holds this view, of course, and Longfellow represents him also as expressing the belief, which in fact he held, that the supreme art is the art of architecture, and that, after that, sculpture is superior to painting. "Truly, as you say," he observes to Cellini,

> Sculpture is more than painting. It is greater
> To raise the dead to life than to create
> Phantoms that seem to live. The most majestic
> Of the three sister arts is that which builds;
> The eldest of them all, to whom the others
> Are but the handmaids and the servitors,
> Being but imitation, not creation.
> Henceforth I dedicate myself to her.

He is at work, when he says this, on the great task of designing the dome of St. Peter's, on which he is expending the last wonderful powers of his old age; he cannot, and will not, rest from his high labors. He is convinced that the golden age of art is over, and that the field is now occupied only by mediocrities and charlatans: Longfellow may have felt, writing in *his* old age, that something of the same sort had happened to the arts in his time. "Not events," says the aged eagle,

> Not events
> Exasperate me, but the funest conclusions
> I draw from these events; the sure decline
> Of art, and all the meaning of that word;
> All that embellishes and sweetens life,
> And lifts it from the level of low cares
> Into the purer atmosphere of beauty;
> The faith in the Ideal . . .

Michelangelo is already an old man when the action begins — a man of perhaps sixty when he converses with Vittoria in the church of San Silvestro — and the poem is an old man's poem in two senses, full of the reflections on old age and death which occupied Longfellow's mind during these years. Sunset, twilight, or

night is the setting of most of these scenes, youthful and vital as
some of the characters are; and the bitterness of old age, its sense
of declining power, its loneliness, run like a sorrowful undersong
through much of the poem. "Old men work slowly," says the
aged master to Vittoria:

> Brain and hand alike
> Are dull and torpid. To die young is best,
> And not to be remembered as old men
> Tottering about in their decrepitude.

When Cellini tries to persuade him to return to Florence and re-
sume his work on the Sacristy, Michelangelo protests that it is
impossible; he is too old now ever to make such a move:

> I will stay here in Rome,
> Where all is old and crumbling, like myself,
> To hopeless ruin.

The death of Fra Sebastiano and, far more important, the death
of Vittoria leave him in what he feels to be a solitude like the
solitude at the end:

> Death's lightnings strike to right and left of me,
> And, like a ruined wall, the world around me
> Crumbles away, and I am left alone.

The last note struck in the poem, like the Finale of *Christus*, is a
cry of pain and distress such as Longfellow never uttered lyrically,
but which, in its dramatic form, has a singular intensity of personal feeling. Michelangelo is working at midnight in his studio,
with a lamp, on his statue of the Dead Christ, when Giorgio
Vasari enters; after a little talk, he asks what the marble group
represents. "My own tomb," answers the old man, and then, let-
ting the lamp fall, breaks out:

> Life hath become to me
> An empty theatre, — its lights extinguished,
> The music silent, and the actors gone;
> And I alone sit musing on the scenes

> That once have been. I am so old that Death
> Oft plucks me by the cloak, to come with him;
> And some day, like this lamp, shall I fall down,
> And my last spark of life will be extinguished.
> Ah me! ah me! what darkness of despair!
> So near to death, and yet so far from God.

It is curious how little of Michelangelo's fervid Christian piety is represented in the poem; the strongest convictions he expresses are not those, but his convictions on the subject of Art—and of political liberty. The loss of Florentine freedom under Alessandro de' Medici and his successors is part of the background of the poem. In an early scene Jacopo Nardi, the Florentine historian and patriot, a political exile — like Longfellow's friend, Luigi Monti, and for that matter like Gaetano Salvemini many years later — appears as an old man at Cardinal Ippolito's palace in Rome, mourning for "the imperilled liberties of Florence," and bringing to Ippolito an account of the tyranny now exercised by his cousin. When, much later, Cellini brings to Michelangelo the message that, if he will return to Florence, Duke Cosimo will load him with honors — will make him one of his Senators — the old man declares passionately that he no longer wishes to be a Florentine; now that Cosimo reigns supreme, he says, all liberty in Florence is dead:

> Ah, woe is me!
> I hoped to see my country rise to heights
> Of happiness and freedom yet unreached
> By other nations, but the climbing wave
> Pauses, lets go its hold, and slides again
> Back to the common level, with a hoarse
> Death-rattle in its throat. I am too old
> To hope for better days.

Longfellow, in the 1870's, like so many elderly men of his generation, no doubt had the sense, after the Civil War, of being a kind of stranded survivor of an earlier and more innocent age, a survivor for whom the great promise of the young republic was, to all appearances, being corrupted and undone by the iniquities of the new era; is it fanciful to hear, in these lines of Michelangelo's, some echo of this sharp disappointment?

At any rate, it is very striking, though in a sense "accidental," that the most exalted passage in the whole poem should be a speech of the aged artist's in which he summons up, with almost Biblical sublimity, an apocalyptic vision of the world going down to its annihilation. The passage seems in fact to have been written twenty years and more before Longfellow incorporated it in *Michael Angelo;* perhaps he had meant it to be an independent poem; perhaps he had intended to use it in *The Golden Legend.* At any rate he now introduced it, a little awkwardly, into the fine scene in the Coliseum between Michelangelo and Tomaso de' Cavalieri, and it is worth quoting in full:

> All things must have an end; the world itself
> Must have an end, as in a dream I saw it.
> There came a great hand out of heaven, and touched
> The earth, and stopped it in its course. The seas
> Leaped, a vast cataract, into the abyss;
> The forests and the fields slid off, and floated
> Like wooded islands in the air. The dead
> Were hurled forth from their sepulchres; the living
> Were mingled with them, and themselves were dead, —
> All being dead; and the fair, shining cities
> Dropped out like jewels from a broken crown.
> Naught but the core of the great globe remained,
> A skeleton of stone. And over it
> The wrack of matter drifted like a cloud,
> And then recoiled upon itself, and fell
> Back on the empty world, that with the weight
> Reeled, staggered, righted, and then headlong plunged
> Into the darkness, as a ship, when struck
> By a great sea, throws off the waves at first
> On either side, then settles and goes down
> Into the dark abyss, with her dead crew.

It is hard to believe that this appalling passage was not written with *Michael Angelo* in mind, at any rate when we attend to such Michelangelesque images as that of a great hand being reached out of heaven, the dead being hurled from their sepulchres, the living mingled with them, and the denuded core of the earth itself surviving only as a skeleton of stone. In any case, the passage has a peculiar fittingness in a poem about the painter of the "Last Judgment," and, however accidentally, it seems powerfully to express an awareness of Final Things which, during many hours, must have been present to the elderly Longfellow. As a whole, *Michael Angelo*, whatever its shortcomings, is by no means unimpressive as a poetic and even as a "dramatic" treatment of its difficult and complex subject; fragmentary as it is, along with *The Golden Legend* it is the most interesting of all Longfellow's dramatic experiments.

XIV

In the Harbor

SOME THINGS in *Christus* and *Michael Angelo* are enough to tell us that, now that Longfellow had reached what he called "the western side of life," the deeper inward currents by no means flowed so smoothly and even blandly as the conventional image of the aged poet would imply. His purely private world had never been perfectly tranquil, as we have seen, and during the years of this last decade Longfellow doubtless underwent his due allotment of grief, of dread, and even, at moments, of bitterness. But his old age can certainly not be described as embittered, as fury-haunted, in the way Mark Twain's old age was to be, or as bleak and inconsolable as Henry Adams's. Whatever his spiritual uncertainties may have been, and whatever his disappointments in the direction things were taking, Longfellow had too long ago come to terms, in his own way, with the frustrations of existence, to be merely resentful of them now, or soured by them: we may think what we will of his "way," but like Emerson's and Whitman's it insured that Longfellow's old age would be, if not tranquil, then at least outwardly serene and inwardly self-possessed. What Norton called "the sweet mellowing of his old age" was not a mere mask: it was, in part, the moral and psychological ripeness it was in his nature to manifest at the end, and in part the product of deliberate preference.

He had never, it is true, been coolly indifferent to the disturbing tendencies in the public world around him, and he was by no

means untroubled by the political abominations, the social dis-
order, the moral squalor of what Mark Twain was calling, about
this time, the Gilded Age. "The low tone of everything," he wrote
to Greene in the middle seventies, "disturbs and discourages me";
and two or three years earlier, while Norton was in Europe,
Longfellow had found a letter from his younger friend "rather
gloomy with the gigantic scoundrelism of your native country.
And no wonder," he went on. "At times it seems to me that we
have the millstone round our neck, and that the rest is coming."
Emerson and Whitman had seen the same millstone, but they belonged, as he did, to the older and more habitually hopeful America, and they had refused to throw in the sponge. Nor would
Longfellow throw it in. "Still," he continued to Norton, "I have
faith that the good will conquer, and do not fall upon my sword."
This may be the complacency of optimism, and it may be a quiet
refusal to succumb to sentimental pessimism.

In any case, his later years were saddened also, but now in the
natural and universally human way, by the gradual removal in
death of his oldest and closest friends. Goethe said in his old age
that, when he looked back at his early and middle years, his life
took on for him the semblance of a stay at a watering-place.
When you arrive, he said, you form friendships with those who
have already been there for some time, and who leave after a few
weeks: "the loss is painful." You then become intimate with a
second contingent, but these contemporaries of yours depart also
at last, and leave you alone with a third generation, which arrives
just as you are going away, "and with which you have really
nothing to do." For Longfellow, Irving and Bryant had been the
older guests, and Irving had left even before the war, though
Bryant, the apparently indestructible, survived almost as long as
his junior did. Longfellow's own contemporaries and intimates had
begun to take their departure not much later than Irving had done.
Felton and Hawthorne had both died, somewhat prematurely, during the war, and Agassiz had died in the year of *Aftermath*. The

greatest loss of all, the death of Sumner, occurred a year later, and when Lowell left the country, in 1875, to be Minister to Spain, Longfellow was not to see him again. These were irreparable losses, but they were not in fact quite uncompensated for: however mellow he may have become, Longfellow retained, as Goethe did also, a genuine youthfulness to the very end, and it would not be true to say that, with the new arrivals at the end of his stay, he felt that he "really had nothing to do."

On the personal level, he proved able, in his very last years, to form friendships with newcomers a whole generation younger than he, friendships that could never, of course, have had the closeness and warmth of his relation with Sumner, but that were more than merely casual. This was true of his friendship with Howells when the younger man, immediately after the war, came to Cambridge to live — and to edit, in Boston, the *Atlantic Monthly*. The young Westerner, with his literary and linguistic enthusiasms, his freshness and simplicity, his humor and his charm, very evidently proved attractive to Longfellow, as he did to Lowell and Holmes, and something like an intimacy sprang up between them. This did not happen to be true of other new arrivals, but even when they came from worlds that might have seemed utterly remote from his, he never failed in his courteous accessibility, and usually not in his spontaneous interest in *them*. When Oscar Wilde, on his flashing progress through the country, came to call in the obligatory way at the Craigie House, he is said to have patronized the elder poet most kindly; if so, Longfellow was unaware of any intention on his guest's part to condescend, and could only report that Wilde was "a very agreeable young man" whose eccentricities could easily be pardoned for the sake of his talents. He was equally undisturbed by the more virile, the more open-shirted flamboyance of Joaquin Miller, the Byron of Oregon, whom Fields brought to dine with him, and whom Longfellow, in his inexhaustibly indulgent way, found "a rather wild, but to me very interesting, personality."

However thrown off he may have been — to go back half a generation — by the audacities of *Leaves of Grass*, both in matter and in style, he did not allow any such feeling to distort his attitude to Whitman as a person. On a visit to the Centennial Exposition in Philadelphia in 1876, Longfellow was taken by his host, the wealthy George W. Childs, over the river to Camden to call on Whitman, as he could easily have declined to do. Their colloquy, it appears, had to be brief, owing to delays in transportation, but it must have been friendly enough; four years later, during his last visit to Boston, Whitman felt free and even obliged to go out to Cambridge and call on Longfellow. He said later that he would not soon forget "his lit-up face and glowing warmth and courtesy, in the modes of what is called the old school." Certainly that courtesy had manifested itself, a little earlier, to Mark Twain, whose rather unsuitable humor at the famous birthday dinner to Whittier, might understandably have given him some pain. "I am a little troubled," he wrote to the anguished offender, "that you should be so much troubled about a matter of such slight importance. . . . I do not believe that anybody was much hurt. Certainly I was not. . . ." The chances are that he was, but his instinct was to reassure the younger man at any cost.

Meanwhile, there was no falling off in Longfellow's youthful susceptibility to literary enthusiasms; no diminution, until the very end, in his appetite for literature, old and new, or his openness to novelty and strangeness. Mrs. Fields describes an evening in the early seventies when Longfellow, going home with them after a reception for the Grand Duke Alexis of Russia, talked about Russian literature to them, speaking of its "modernness," and saying that he had sent them "a delightful novel by Tourgénief, *Liza*, in which we should find charming and vivid glimpses of landscape and life like those seen from a carriage-window." At the end of that decade, Longfellow himself speaks in his journal of listening, with evident excitement, to a reading of "parts of a wild Russian story of Cossacks" — which sounds like Tolstoy's novel. If he had been forty years younger, he would certainly have thrown himself eagerly into the study of Russian, and mastered it in a few weeks. The refrain of a very late poem, "The White Czar" — "Batyushka! Gosudar!" — shows that he had picked up somewhere at least two words of that rich language. Meanwhile, he did not allow his other languages to collect rust. In 1872 he is reading Taine's new *History of English Literature*, "a prodigiously clever book." A little later he has turned to Oehlenschläger's *Helge* in Danish, and still later, in the same language, to Henrik Hertz's drama, *Svend Dyrings Hus*. In 1874 he is delighted when the great Salvini, spending an evening at the Craigie House, reads to him and Greene some scenes from Alfieri's tragedy *Saul*. The names of Ovid and Tasso, of Corneille and Hugo, of Voss and Schiller and Goethe continue to echo through his journals quite as they had done forty years earlier. It was only during the last weeks of his life that he ceased to be able to take pleasure in his books. In one of his last poems, a sonnet called "My Books," written the day after Christmas, 1881, he compares himself in his library to an aged knight gazing sadly at the sword and shield that hang in his hall but that he can no longer wield:

> While secret longings for the lost delight
> Of tourney or adventure in the field
> Came over him, and tears but half concealed
> Trembled and fell upon his beard of white.

Meanwhile, even after *Christus* and the *Wayside Inn* were finished, and Longfellow moved into his late sixties, there had been no real ebb in his productivity as a poet, nor was he to fall entirely silent even in his very last days. The two or three years that followed *Aftermath* (1873) were as fruitful of work as any similar period in his career had ever been. He had already begun to write *Michael Angelo,* and in 1875 he published a sizable small volume, *The Masque of Pandora and Other Poems,* which indicated that, if the rowen *was* "mixed with weeds," there was no want yet of "sweet new grass with flowers." The title poem was in fact a little dramatic piece in the form of a masque, which, unlike any of Longfellow's more ambitious dramatic poems, was adapted for the stage and produced, with very little success, at the Boston Theatre in 1881. In the fall of 1874 Longfellow had been asked by one of his classmates at Bowdoin to write a poem for the fiftieth anniversary of their graduation, and though he had a settled dislike of composing occasional poems, he yielded in this instance, and wrote "Morituri Salutamus," which he delivered at the Commencement exercises at Brunswick the following July. It was of course a great occasion, and to Longfellow a deeply moving one, and the poem was a little later included in *The Masque of Pandora*. Included, too, was a longish fireside poem on marriage and domestic life, "The Hanging of the Crane," which had been suggested to Longfellow a few years earlier when he had called, one spring morning, on Thomas Bailey Aldrich and his wife, immediately after their marriage, in their small house on Pinckney Street. Far more interesting, in *The Masque of Pandora*, is the group of fourteen sonnets in a section entitled "A Book of Sonnets." The volume was rounded out with a handful of short poems under the rubric "Birds of Passage, Flight the Fourth."

It was true now, as it had been in the forties, that in addition to his own writing Longfellow was conscious of having energy of a literary sort left over for anthologizing, and two or three years after finishing the revised edition of *The Poets and Poetry of Europe*, he conceived the scheme of preparing "a kind of poetic guidebook" — an anthology of poems of a descriptive or local or evocative sort. Once he had set to work on it, the idea took hold of him pleasantly and even absorbingly, and in the end the enterprise proved to be, at least in scale, an extraordinarily ambitious one. Longfellow made a few new translations expressly for this anthology — Xavier Marmier's "At La Chaudeau," for example — and even wrote some new poems of his own for the purpose — a proem, "Travels by the Fireside," "To the River Rhone," and

"Venice," for example — and between 1876 and 1879 there appeared the thirty-one small volumes, bound in rather ugly brown or green cloth, of *Poems of Places*. There is the usual mingling, in these volumes, of good, mediocre, and bad poems, but whatever else may be said of *Poems of Places*, its comprehensiveness can hardly be called into question: it ranges from England, Scotland, and Wales through all the countries of Europe and Asia, the United States (five volumes), Central and South America, Australasia, Polynesia, and "Miscellaneous." The sense of place has, at least, never been anthologized more thoroughly.

In the years that remained to him, Longfellow was to publish two more collections of short poems. In 1877, his mind turning back to the old pottery in the Portland of his childhood, he had written a "poem on the Potter's wheel," which he called by the Greek word for pottery, "Kéramos," and this became the title poem in a volume, *Kéramos and Other Poems,* which he published in 1878, and which included a final group of "Birds of Passage." Two years later, in the spring of 1880, he published what he doubtless regarded as a final volume, for he called it by the rather terminal-sounding title *Ultima Thule*. But he had still almost two years to live, and even during the last weeks of his life, though he could no longer read or study with pleasure, he continued to feel impelled to write; a few days before his death, inspired by a travel essay on Mexico in *Harper's,* he wrote his last, and not one of his least worthy, short poems, "The Bells of San Blas." This poem, along with more than a score of others, was included by his editors, later that year, in a posthumous volume, *In the Harbor.*

In the fall of 1881 he had had a violent attack of vertigo, followed by "nervous prostration," and for some weeks was confined to his bedroom. He gradually recovered from this prostration, but it must have been clear to him that his hold on life was weakening. In January, nevertheless, he wrote two short poems, "Mad River" and a sonnet about poetry, "Possibilities," and in

February, by a touching anticipation of the date, a poem on Decoration Day. On a Saturday afternoon late in March, he took a turn on his veranda for a little exercise, but though he was warmly wrapped he caught a chill, and Luigi Monti, who came to dine with him as usual on Saturdays, noticed that Longfellow seemed unwell. That night he came down with an attack of peritonitis, and not quite a week later, on the afternoon of the twenty-fourth of March, he "sank quietly in death." Two days later a funeral service was held at the Craigie House, which was attended only by the family and a few close friends, and the body was then carried, "under the gently falling snow," to Mount Auburn Cemetery, where it was buried. One of the few friends present was Emerson, who had himself only a few weeks more to live, and whose hold on the factual had almost entirely failed him. Howells, who was also present, tells us that, after the services were over, Emerson turned to his daughter Ellen and said: "The gentleman we have just been burying was a sweet and beautiful soul; but I forget his name." The name, indeed, in a sense, had ceased to matter.

XV

Utmost Isle

OLD AGE and the approach of death are, as we have seen, one of the conspicuous motives of *Michael Angelo,* and there is even a note of emotional protest in the tones with which it is expressed. Yet if that Fragment did not exist, we should hardly suspect, from the rest of Longfellow's latest work — except, indeed, for obvious reasons, "Morituri Salutamus" — that we had to do with the utterance of an aged man, "a tattered coat upon a stick," a poet in the December of his powers. Neither for better nor for worse is Longfellow's "last manner" generally that of senectitude, either powerful or feeble — either that of Goethe and Yeats or that of Wordsworth and Whitman. It might be more impressive, in some sense, if it were, but in fact what strikes one about his aftermath, on the whole, is its youthfulness — its naïveté, its freshness of spirit, its almost boyish romanticism, the absence from it of the note of disenchantment, of elderly sagacity, of ironic wisdom. This "beautiful youthfulness of spirit" was what led Lafcadio Hearn to maintain that, especially among nineteenth-century poets, Longfellow remains "the poet of young men." He himself recognized that something like this was true. When an admiring correspondent asked him, in 1875, how he could write so many things that sounded as if he were as happy as a boy, he replied by citing the case of Governor Endicott's pear tree, planted two hundred years earlier, which "still bears fruit not to be distinguished from that of a young tree in flavor." He added that he supposed the tree made new wood every year, "so that some parts of it are always young." Certainly many of his latest poems have the flavor of Governor Endicott's pears.

It is not that he did not now write a good many weak and uninteresting poems, or that their proportion to the whole is not somewhat larger than it had once been. Yet their faults are mainly the old faults — banality of thought, laxity of feeling, facility of utterance — and not such as can be set down to mere senility. "The Hanging of the Crane" is a kind of *summa* of the sentimentalities to which Longfellow had always been subject. With its symbols of the crane or iron arm hung in the fireplace to celebrate a wedding, and the extensible dining-table that expands and contracts with the growth and diminishment of the wedded couple's family, the poem is almost a parody on Longfellow's fireside manner; and Tennyson himself was never more saccharine than Longfellow is in his conjuring up of the "little angel," the baby boy, whom the happy parents, improbably, entertain "unaware," and of the sister who succeeds to his place, "the very pattern girl of girls." Gulfs of sensibility seem to divide us, at such moments, from both Longfellow and his readers — for the tough-minded Sam Ward said that the poem "made music [for him] all night in the car" — but we remind ourselves that it was the age of Hugo's and Swinburne's poems about babies as well as Longfellow's, and pass on. Or rather, pass on after observing that the bridge-passages from section to section of the poem, with their delicate imagery of emerging and dissolving views, have an illusionistic charm that almost redeems the feebleness of the rest.

"The Masque of Pandora" has no great density of substance, but it is quite free from the cloying dulcitude of "The Crane," and it has a modest formal interest as a relatively rare experiment, in the nineteenth century, in the genre of the masque — for Shelley's "Mask of Anarchy" is a masque in name only. Longfellow's poem represents an attempt to reproduce the manner of the Elizabethan masque, with its mythological personages, its allegorical flavor, its Renaissance-classical imagery, its choruses (with the music they imply), and its general "artificiality" and decorativeness. Only the absence of any provision for dances keeps "Pandora" from being, stylistically speaking, an almost complete Victorian pastiche of Ben Jonson or Fletcher. The subject is of course the familiar myth from the *Works and Days* — the gift of the lovely maiden created by Hephaestus and bestowed on Epimetheus, to his and all men's sorrow — but the misogyny that comes out so openly in Hesiod is naturally quite suppressed in Longfellow's version. His Pandora is not so much "the bane of men that live by bread" as she is a Christianized myth, a kind of lesser Eve in Greek costume. She opens the forbidden chest, she alleges, not out of mere feminine inquisitiveness, but because the Gods who created her

> filled me with desire
> Of knowing good and evil like themselves.

The results of this are both Hesiodic and Biblical, as the Chorus of Dreams from the Gate of Horn — true dreams, of course — describes them:

> Fever of the heart and brain,
> Sorrow, pestilence, and pain,
> Moans of anguish, maniac laughter,
> All the evils that hereafter
> Shall afflict and vex mankind,
> All into the air have risen
> From the chambers of their prison;
> Only Hope remains behind.

The Eumenides, in the final Chorus, are rather unexpectedly stern — for Longfellow — announcing as they do that "souls like these" shall never escape their torches and scourges — since every guilty act "holds in itself the seed / Of retribution and undying pain" — until Pandora and Epimetheus have been purified by the heavenly fire of Helios, by suffering, and have begun a new and nobler life. Pandora herself puts the case in familiar Aeschylean, and also Christian, terms:

> Only through punishment of our evil deeds,
> Only through suffering, are we reconciled
> To the immortal Gods and to ourselves.

Commonplace as this ethical truth is, it strikes a rather more solemn note than one expects in a masque, and in fact "Pandora" is only outwardly Jonsonian; the bottle may be Elizabethan, but the wine is romantic — a little German, remotely Goethean, and not without a hint of Tennyson and Browning. Epimetheus, Prometheus, and Pandora belong, not to Elizabethan pastoral or idyl, but to nineteenth-century romantic allegory. Prometheus is the "self-centered, self-reliant" Titan, "wrapped in visions and illusions," like a smaller Faust, who robs himself, according to the Chorus of the Fates, "of life's best gifts," but who will ultimately attain to the highest things "by toil and self-denial." Epimetheus, on the other hand, is a kind of Tennysonian dreamer and aesthete, who inherits, not like Prometheus their father's strength, but their mother's weakness, "the yielding nature that cannot resist"; he, too, however, is disciplined by pain, and assures the stricken Pandora that, after all, "youth, hope, and love" remain to them:

> To build a new life on a ruined life,
> To make the future fairer than the past,
> And make the past appear a troubled dream.

There may be nothing very remarkable intellectually in all this, but the genuineness of the emotion behind it is unmistakable, and it is expressed with so much of Longfellow's characteristic limpidity and unpretentiousness that one feels no inclination to scoff. There is a lyrical grace, moreover, and even something firmer and closer-knit than that, in some of the choruses — the Chorus of the Graces, of the Eumenides, and especially, in the sixth scene ("In the Garden") the Choruses of Birds, of Reeds, of Dryades, and of Oreades. This last, the chorus of the mountain-spirits, interrupted as it is by the Voices of the Waters, of the Winds, and of the Forests, has a kind of energy in its use of dynamic imagery from nature — driving snows, tempests of wind, hurrying streams, flying clouds — that is not wholly unworthy of the great parallel that suggests itself. The "moral," at any rate, that these Voices enforce is as strenuous, as expressive of "endless endeavor," as the Chorus of Elves and the speeches of Ariel in the first scene of Part II of *Faust*. No one would seriously compare the two choruses for lyrical splendor, but it is of Goethe that Longfellow manages, without utter absurdity, to remind us.

In "Kéramos" he reminds us not of Goethe but once more, as in "The Building of the Ship," of Schiller. Again the central symbol is a handicraft, not now bell-casting or shipbuilding, but pottery, and the central figure is the Potter, shaping the plastic clay on his turning wheel and singing to himself as he does so. The symbol is of course by no means an original one with Longfellow; it is less fresh, indeed, than the symbol of the shipwright was; we are bound to be reminded of the Epistle to the Romans ("Hath not the potter power over the clay?"), as well as of Fitzgerald's Omar and "Rabbi Ben Ezra." But Longfellow's Potter is no mere archetypal Potter out of literature; he is an old-fashioned craftsman who had been genuinely observed and is now particularized:

> Thus sang the Potter at his task
> Beneath the blossoming hawthorn-tree,
> While o'er his features, like a mask,
> The quilted sunshine and leaf-shade
> Moved, as the boughs above him swayed,
> And clothed him, till he seemed to be
> A figure woven in tapestry,
> So sumptuously was he arrayed
> In that magnificent attire
> Of sable tissue flaked with fire.

The "magnificent attire / Of sable tissue" might seem a little grandiose for the Potter's black apron, but the intention is to suggest

that he is a kind of magician as well as a plain handicraftsman, and
in this spirit the language is not excessive. As for the "tenor" of
the symbolism, it too is traditional, on one level; Longfellow's
Potter, like St. Paul's, is the Creator himself, and his pot is the
creature:

> *Turn, turn, my wheel! This earthen jar*
> *A touch can make, a touch can mar;*
> *And shall it to the Potter say,*
> *What makest thou? Thou hast no hand?*
> *As men who think to understand*
> *A world by their Creator planned,*
> *Who wiser is than they?*

This Potter, in short, is an inscrutable but not a merely arbitrary
craftsman like Fitzgerald's, and Longfellow is expressing not a
Victorian pessimism but, along with a sense of mystery, a Job-like
or Pauline submissiveness to the will of the Creator.

The symbolism of the poem, however, is more complex than
this, and in a prose sense could be said to be "confused." The Potter is not only the Creator of mankind — and of all things — but
the Artist, too, not simply the Divine Artist, but the creative
human Artist; and the beautiful objects he creates — jars, cups,
porcelains, tiles, terra cotta reliefs — are, so to say, synecdoches
of all works of human art. The poem, formally speaking, has two
elements, the songs of the Potter and the narrative which is interspersed by them; and after the Potter has been introduced,
"Kéramos" turns into a kind of guidebook poem, not unlike others of Longfellow's, in which we are carried "on wings of song"
from land to land, wherever great potters have been, or are, at
work. There is a great deal of charm in this poetic aviation and in
the glimpses we are given of the great potteries of Europe and
Asia — the "pretty town" of Delft, "the crown / And centre
of the Potter's trade," the town of Saintes in France where the
great Bernard Palissy toiled so obsessively over his enamels, the
old centers of Italian manufacture, Gubbio and Urbino and

Faenza, then Cairo, then the "burning town" of King-te-Chin in China, and last the villages of Imari in Japan with their "thronged and flaming workshops." The aesthetic moral that is drawn from all this, near the end of the poem — that "Art is the child of Nature" — is banal enough, and the passage in which it is made explicit is the weakest in the poem. Apart from this, however, "Kéramos" is an extraordinarily animated performance on the part of a man of seventy: the love of fine workmanship has fused with a tenacious memory of childhood to produce a small masterwork in its own right.

Memory is at work, too, in "Morituri Salutamus" — memory, not of childhood, of course, but of college days — and the piece, which (except for the early Phi Beta Kappa poem) is the only "occasional" poem Longfellow ever wrote, is surely the best piece that has ever been written for a class reunion, characteristically American as that institution is. The feeling in it is peculiarly penetrating and, without being exactly complex, is yet fluctuating and various, and the language and the verse have a noble adequacy, for the most part, to the occasion. The emotion at the center is naturally the nostalgia of an elderly man, shared with his contemporaries, for his happy, ardent, aspiring youth as an undergraduate; but this emotion is colored also by the melancholy of approaching death, by affectionate remembrance of his old teachers, dead or still living, by a feeling of mingled envy and tenderness for the young men who are now graduating, and by grief for the classmates who have already died — of whom Hawthorne, though he is not named, was of course one. These emotions are expressed gravely and without false emphasis, and Longfellow, after an apostrophe to the high calling of the scholar, comes back to the subject of old age — its stern limitations, its waning powers, but still, its possibilities of final achievement:

> The night hath not yet come; we are not quite
> Cut off from labor by the failing light. . . .

Age, too, like youth, means opportunity, though of another sort,

> And as the evening twilight fades away
> The sky is filled with stars, invisible by day.

The metaphor that furnishes the title and the substance of the first few lines — that of the gladiators in the Roman arena, "who are about to die," saluting Caesar as they stand "face to face / With death and with the Roman populace" — a metaphor that was suggested to Longfellow by a once-famous painting by Gérôme — is not insisted on beyond the first lines. It is followed, however, by a touching invocation to the familiar scenes of the poet's undergraduate life — the "groves of pine / That once were mine and are no longer mine" — which, himself on the eve of death, he salutes in a spirit not unlike that of the gladiators. Much of the imagery of the poem, suitably enough, is learned or at least literary, and the tribute to the poet's old teachers is beautifully enhanced by a reminiscence of Dante's meeting with *his* old teacher, Brunetto Latini, in the Seventh Circle of Hell, and Dante's passionate address of gratitude to him. As he turns to the graduating youths, Longfellow compares himself to Priam sitting on the walls of Troy, gazing at the young warriors in the field and wondering who is the tallest and strongest among them. His advice to these boys keeps up the Homeric reference, with a glance at Spenser:

> Write on your doors the saying wise and bold,
> "Be bold! be bold!" and everywhere, "Be bold;
> Be not too bold!" Yet better the excess
> Than the defect; better the more than less;
> Better like Hector in the field to die,
> Than like a perfumed Paris turn and fly.

The tale Longfellow tells to illustrate the vices that may divert and corrupt the scholar — the tale of the avaricious clerk from the *Gesta Romanorum* — is of doubtful relevance and of somewhat disproportionate length; and the passage in which he cites the cases of aged poets who have produced great masterpieces, is a little prosaic in its exemplary quality. But the metaphor of the falling barometer that follows — a curiously "Augustan" image for Longfellow — lifts the poem again away from the prose level; and "Morituri Salutamus" ends with the metaphor of the failing light and the star-filled sky which brings the poem as a whole back to the emotional gravity and elevation of its opening.

The sonnet was not a form that Longfellow had much cultivated in his earlier career, any more than he had cultivated the romantic ode as Wordsworth, Coleridge, and Keats had practiced it. Yet as early as *The Belfry of Bruges* he had shown that he was capable of writing beautifully in the form: four sonnets had appeared there, two of which, "Mezzo Cammin" and "Dante," were as fine as any poems in the volume. Years went by, however, when, except for a mediocre piece on a reading by Fanny Kemble, in *The Seaside and the Fireside,* he wrote no sonnets at all; it was not until he was ready to publish his translation of the *Divine Comedy* in the sixties that, remembering perhaps again Michelangelo's sonnet on Dante, he wrote the six fine sonnets, "Divina Commedia," which he used as proems, two each, to the Inferno, the Purgatorio, and the Paradiso. Still later, in the seventies, a late-flowering love of the form took hold of him, and, both in "A Book of Sonnets" and elsewhere, he published between thirty and forty poems of the sort. In some of these Longfellow revealed himself to be the most accomplished writer of sonnets in the American nineteenth century.

He does not belong among those great sonneteers who, ever since Dante himself, have used the sonnet as a medium in which to express the emotion of love. He wrote, indeed, virtually no "love poems" of any sort, and oddly enough the only piece in all his mature work that could be so described *is* a sonnet, "The Evening Star," in *The Belfry of Bruges,* addressed to his wife.* It is a

---

* It is not surprising that one of the very weakest of his boyish poems, "To Ianthe," is a love poem, in a derivative Byronic vein.

curious poem; it evokes the image of Mrs. Longfellow retiring for
the night, and its awkwardness is a clue, if one were needed, to
the constraint which fell upon Longfellow when he even contemplated the literary expression of sexual love. Friendship, the love
of children, the bitterness of personal bereavement — such feelings
he could objectify in language without self-consciousness or undue
restraint; but to give utterance to the passionate personal attach-
ment he certainly felt for Mary Potter and then for Fanny Appleton — this was beyond his poetic powers. It is one of his limitations as a poet. Yet he could make the sonnet a vehicle for the
expression of feelings no less private, one would have said, than
passionate love — of the self-reproach, for example, of a man
who has arrived at Dante's "middle of the journey" ("Mezzo
Cammin") and who feels that he has failed, hitherto, to achieve
the goal he has set for himself. (It is characteristic that his remorse
is of this kind, not, like Dante's, remorse for having gone astray in
the dark wood of sin.) It is sorrow, says Longfellow in this sonnet, "and a care that almost killed" that have kept him from this
— and then, turning in the sestet to the metaphor of climbing he
had used so conventionally in "Excelsior," he makes use of it with
a quite unconventional force; he may yet, he says, reach his goal,

> Though, half-way up the hill, I see the Past
>   Lying beneath me with its sounds and sights, —
>   A city in the twilight dim and vast,
> With smoking roofs, soft bells, and gleaming lights, —
> And hear above me on the autumnal blast
>   The cataract of Death far thundering from the heights.

It was sorrow for the death of his first wife that Longfellow
expressed in "Mezzo Cammin"; nearly forty years later, the even
more excruciating pain he suffered in the death of Fanny Longfellow came out in the more familiar sonnet, "The Cross of
Snow." In this, again, the metaphor is postponed to the sestet — a
fresher image this time, or rather one that unites a conventional
symbol for suffering, that of a cross, with the unhackneyed sym-

bol of a "natural" cross, a snow-filled cross concealed, as it were, in a remote ravine among the Rocky Mountains. The only real defect in this admirable poem is the use of the rather affected word "benedight," for the sake of the rhyme; it is almost redeemed, however, by the fine coinage "sun-defying," in the sestet, with what it suggests of Longfellow's unappeasable grief. An equally fresh and unhackneyed metaphor, not now for grief but for the happy fatigue that follows on intense creative work, is the metaphor in "The Broken Oar." An oar cast up on the coast of Iceland, Longfellow had read, was found to have inscribed on it the sentence, "Oft was I weary when I tugged at thee"; he makes these words — though he changes "tugged" to the more conventional "toiled" — serve as the "sweet Amen," the final line, that a weary poet inscribes at the end of his volume. The image of a seashore, with billows rolling and plunging on the sand, is as fine as such imagery usually is in Longfellow, and in its perfection of shape — the fastidious proportioning of its few elements — the sonnet is among the most successful that he wrote.

It was to be expected that the sea and the seashore would figure in Longfellow's sonneteering, and of course they do. They figure least impressively in "A Summer Day by the Sea," which is defaced by a rather tasteless metaphor for lighthouses — "the streetlamps of the ocean" — but two or three other sonnets of this sort are genuinely memorable. In "The Tides," it is the distressing sense of ebbing forces, which are then mysteriously succeeded by new influxes of power, that Longfellow expresses through the metaphor of ebbing and flooding tides; the metaphor itself is by no means novel, but he uses it here with a fresh and personal turn. After fearing that all thought, feeling, and desire have ebbed from him forever —

> Suddenly o'er me
> They swept again from their deep ocean bed,
> And in a tumult of delight, and strong
> As youth, and beautiful as youth, upbore me.

It is the turning tide again that sets off the emotion in "The Sound of the Sea" — the tide, however, heard now at midnight as the sea rouses itself from its slumbers with a voice, almost Whitmanesque, "out of the silence of the deep," bringing with it intimations "from the unknown / And inaccessible solitudes of being." The sonnet communicates with real subtlety the strangeness of this supernormal state of mysterious closeness to the transcendent. A similar state is still more subtly communicated in "Chimes," where three of Longfellow's talismanic symbols — chimes, stars, and the sea — come together to produce an even more complex and beautiful effect of mystery and transcendence. The chimes are heard at night by the unsleeping poet, marking as he listens to them "the movements of the myriad orbs of light." With his eyelids closed, he can see

> the constellations in the arc
> Of their great circles moving on, and hark!
> I almost hear them singing in their flight.

With such majestic images before his inner vision, it is better to lie awake even than to sleep —

> to feel
> The slumbering world sink under us, and make
> Hardly an eddy, — a mere rush of foam
> On the great sea beneath a sinking keel.

No less characteristic than these sonnets of the sea are the sonnets devoted to poets and poetry, in the manner of Keats's sonnet to Homer or Swinburne's "Sonnets on English Dramatic Poets." The earliest of them is of course the sonnet on Dante, which makes such touching use of Fra Ilario's story about Dante at his monastery, and this was followed, at a wide interval, by the six sonnets on the *Divine Comedy*. The metaphor, for the *Comedy*, of a great cathedral, which gives form and richness to these sonnets, is one that Longfellow might have remembered from the lecture in *Heroes and Hero-Worship* in which Carlyle compares the poem to "a great supernatural world-cathedral, piled up there, stern, solemn, awful." But the metaphor is one that might easily have occurred to many minds, and Longfellow develops it with a fullness and weight of his own. The architectural image, bringing together the vastly structural and the delicately decorative — the cruciform whole, with all its adornments, like "a cross of flowers"; the towers, the statues, the gargoyles; the interior aisles and tombs and blazing windows — is worked out with a kind of grandeur; and it comes to a noble climax in the fifth sonnet, which echoes not unworthily the vision of the Mystic Rose at the end of the Paradiso.

None of the other literary sonnets are so fine as these, but they all — the sonnets on Chaucer, Shakespeare, Milton, and Keats — have a pleasingly evocative and associative quality, conceived as they are in the mode of picture — Chaucer as an old man writing in a chamber at Woodstock and listening to the song of a lark, Shakespeare as himself a tangle of city streets filled with tumultuous human life, Milton or rather Milton's verse as a succession of billows beating upon a sea beach, Keats as the young shepherd Endymion sleeping in the moonlight that falls upon a solemn grove. This last is the best of the four, perhaps because the personal tragedy of early death drew out from Longfellow a strain of feeling that is absent in the others; in any case he makes fine use, in the sestet, of the words Keats himself suggested for his epitaph, along with a familiar image from Isaiah:

> Lo! in the moonlight gleams a marble white,
>   On which I read: "Here lieth one whose name
>   Was writ in water." And was this the meed
> Of his sweet singing? Rather let me write:
>   "The smoking flax before it burst to flame
>   Was quenched by death, and broken the bruised reed."

The death not only of Keats, but of some of Longfellow's friends and acquaintances, is naturally the subject of several sonnets. Some of them are disappointing; except in the case of Hawthorne — and of Fanny Longfellow — the closer the friendship, the less successful did Longfellow seem to be in expressing his grief, and the five sonnets on "Three Friends of Mine" — Felton, Agassiz, and Sumner — are somehow wanting in intensity, though there is a kind of poignancy, in the sonnet on Sumner, in the image of a friend and guest who has taken his lamp and gone to bed again, as so often before. Another poem on Sumner's death, "Charles Sumner," which is not a sonnet, is still less expressive, and the two finest *sonnets* of a memorial sort are those on the deaths of the elder Richard Henry Dana, "The Burial of the Poet," and of "President Garfield," neither of whom Longfellow knew intimately, though he had known the gentle Dana over a long period of time and had once had supper with Garfield at Howells's house in Cambridge. It may be hard for us to recreate Longfellow's emotion on the death of the assassinated President, but something in Garfield's nature, reinforced by the knowledge of the long agony that preceded his death, had clearly affected Longfellow deeply, and there is no denying the beauty of the use he makes in this sonnet of the great figure of Cacciaguida as Dante encounters him in Paradise. Garfield, at any rate, had been, like Dante's ancestor, a soldier in what Longfellow regarded as a kind of Crusade, and the great line from Paradiso XV is not only used in Italian as an epigraph to the sonnet but repeated in English, to moving effect, in the last line: "I came from martyrdom unto this peace!" Even more moving, if less effulgent, than this is the sonnet on Dana's burial — in the churchyard, again, at Cambridge — amid the falling snow of a winter day. The octet evokes the burial itself, with the most unstrained gravity and the quietest movement; the sestet proceeds to evoke the image of the poet's grave, the following night, in the snow and the moonlight, with one stately allusion as an accompaniment:

> And now the moon is shining on the scene,
> And the broad sheet of snow is written o'er
> With shadows cruciform of leafless trees,

> As once the winding-sheet of Saladin
> With chapters of the Koran; but, ah! more
> Mysterious and triumphant signs are these.

Not all Longfellow's sonnets, it goes without saying, are as good as these; some of them — "A Shadow," "Nature," "Moods" — are distinctly inferior poems, either because the thought is too thin even for fourteen lines, or because the idea is shopworn and boring, or because the language itself is dull. But the workmanship of a few — the choiceness of the diction, the beauty of the imagery, the refined feeling for small-scale but exacting structure — yields to the workmanship nowhere else in Longfellow, and gives us the happiest impression of the refinement and ripening of his powers in his very last years.

Not that this refinement and ripening was a sustained and continuous process: of course it was not; most, in fact, of the short poems in the later volumes are attentuated and vacuous in a manner that suggests nothing but the fatigue, the low vitality, of old age, which clearly beset Longfellow, despite his prevailing youthfulness, during many hours. In some of these poems there is a return to something very like the preachiness of the early poems and certainly like their jejune explicitness of thought: "To stay at home is best"; "We see but what we have the gift / Of seeing; what we bring we find"; "But noble souls, through dust and heat, / Rise from disaster and defeat / The stronger." Most of the guidebook pieces, written for *Poems of Places* — "Cadenabbia," "Amalfi," "To the River Yvette," and others — have lost even that freshness of sightseeing enthusiasm that lent to such early poems as "The Belfry of Bruges" and "Nuremberg" at least an ingenuous charm. Some of the memorial poems to friends — "Auf Wiedersehen" (on the death of Fields), "Charles Sumner," "Bayard Taylor" — quite fail to communicate the sense of loss with any sharpness, though in the last of these there is one image that momentarily lights up the poem. The books in Taylor's

library, where he lies dead, are said to gaze down at him from
their shelves,

> As the statues in the gloom
> Watch o'er Maximilian's tomb —

a late reminiscence on Longfellow's part of the statues, described
in *Hyperion*, in the Franciscan church of the Holy Cross at Innsbruck, which he had seen forty years earlier.

Only one of these late threnodies has anything like the poignancy of the sonnets on Dana and Garfield, and this, "The Chamber over the Gate," is in a vein of heartbroken lamentation one
does not find in them. The subject of this poem was a man whom
Longfellow may not have known at all at first hand, the son of
the Bishop of Mississippi, a young clergyman who had died "at
his post of duty and mercy," at Greenville, Mississippi, during an
epidemic of yellow fever. The young man's father, Bishop
Green, had called on Longfellow at some earlier time, and perhaps something that struck him in the older man, coming together with the memory of his anxieties over his own son, a
Union soldier during the war, moved him with a depth unac-
counted for by the external circumstances, and put him in mind
again, as "John Endicott" had done, of David's lament for Absalom in II Samuel. The Scriptural images — the chamber over
the gate, the desolate old man, the watchman on the tower, the
approaching messengers of death — could hardly be simpler, or
indeed starker, than they are, and the language has no saliency
that could possibly be specified. Yet the sense of a father's bereavement is expressed with the piercingness of an actual cry
of pain; the emotional capacities of quite ordinary language have
rarely been so movingly exemplified.

Others of these final poems have not so much the serenity
one might expect in the work of an aged writer as the buoyancy
one might look for in the work of a much younger man. This is
true of some of the ballads or balladlike poems in the later vol-

umes — of "A Dutch Picture," for example, or "The Emperor's Glove," or "The Tide Rises, the Tide Falls," or "The Leap of Roushan Beg." This last ballad, to be sure, is a very close paraphrase of a prose tale in Chodzko's volume of translations from popular Persian poetry — a paraphrase so close that, as Paul Morin once pointed out, it should probably be described as an adaptation or imitation rather than an original poem. Even so, the adaptation is one that only an accomplished narrative poet could have carried out with so much zest; the love of the Kurdish horseman for his horse, the excitement of flight, the incredible leap of the beautiful steed over an appalling chasm — these are rendered with an almost boyish speed and spirit; and the finest image in the poem is not Chodzko's but Longfellow's:

> Thus the phantom horseman passed,
> And the shadow that he cast
> Leaped the cataract underneath.

Like "Roushan Beg," the best of these later poems are mostly those that were suggested to Longfellow by his reading, as wide now as it had always been, or by circumstances that called up in his imagination some dim figure out of history or legend. This is true of "Belisarius," which, by means so simple as to defy a close look, suggests the whole tragedy of fallen greatness, the bitterness of rejection and disgrace, and the pride that, like the Duchess of Malfi's, survives even that: "I still / Am Belisarius!" It is true, too, of "Helen of Tyre"; long after finishing *The Divine Tragedy* Longfellow continued to be haunted by the figure of that half-legendary Phoenician woman, a "Jezebel" originally, as the Israelites in Tyre scornfully called her, whom the charlatan Simon Magus had deluded with the claim that she was a female emanation of the Deity, "the Intelligence Divine," and as such had already passed through a series of incarnations, as Queen Candace, Helen of Troy, and others. The deep pathos of Helen's belief, "fallen and forlorn" as she has been, in this tempting falsehood — the too-easy and touching belief of any "famished heart" — is transmitted without a touch of the meretricious, and the irony of its universal applicability is enforced, almost in an undertone, in but two lines: "O reader, stoop down and write / With thy finger in the dust." Another kind of pathos, but still the pathos of disappointment and disillusion, the bitterness of literary neglect and failure, suffuses the very brief, almost epigrammatic, "Jugurtha," based as it amusingly is on a mistaken memory, or perhaps a conscious distortion, of a passage in Plutarch's life of Caius Marius. "O Hercules! how cold your bath is!" cried Jugurtha, it appears, as he descended, wandering in his wits, into the Roman dungeon. "How cold are thy baths, Apollo!" cries Longfellow's neglected poet as he descends into the dungeons of the forgotten.

An epigrammatic conciseness is an effect of which Longfellow was more capable than has sometimes been supposed. It is the effect he achieves in two very brief late poems, one of them, "King Trisanku," suggested by a passage which he had read in a translation from a Hindu epic, the *Ramayana*. The irony of that state of suspension, "midway between earth and heaven," in which human hearts are "tossed and drifted" by their aspirations when these are held in check by their self-doubts — this irony is tersely rendered through the tale of the Hindu king who was raised to "Indra's realms" by an obliging magician and then hurled downward by the gods whom he had offended with his *húbris*. The "point" is made explicit in a third stanza but, for once, inoffensively, and the little poem has an almost Emersonian wittiness. There is a suggestion of Emerson, also, at any rate of "Hamatreya," in "Haroun Al Raschid," though its source is not of course the Vishnu Purana but the *Arabian Nights,* and the pride that is rebuked is not so much the deluded pride of ownership — ownership of the unpossessable Earth — as it is the even more radical pride of power and possessions generally. Again, the means by which this is expressed are so simple as to appear simplistic, and indeed the poem is remarkable neither in diction nor in image. But it has a kind of precision that looks easier than it is.

A passage in Iamblichus suggested another late poem, "Hermes Trismegistus," which is not epigrammatic but lyrical and meditative — or "museful." The antique and Egyptian imagery — the Nile, the desert, the pyramids, the Sphinx — is threadbare enough, and the poem, moreover, is somewhat diffuse; but in this brooding over the mythical figure of Hermes the Three Times Greatest — the Greek name for Thoth, the Egyptian god of wisdom — Longfellow manages to convey something of the range and strangeness of all the archaic speculation associated with those names; along with this, too, the intellectual humility such brooding ought to suggest to us:

> Who shall call his dreams fallacious?
>   Who has searched or sought
> All the unexplored and spacious
>   Universe of thought?
> Who, in his own skill confiding,
>   Shall with rule and line
> Mark the border-land dividing
>   Human from divine?

Longfellow has been reproached by a theological writer for the apparent agnosticism of this poem, which belongs to the last year of his life, and in fact "Hermes Trismegistus" confirms the impression Howells gives us of Longfellow's religious uncertainties at the end. There is more of Hardy in the poem, both stylistically and intellectually, though the gap is a great one, than there is, let us say, of Whittier.

The metrical pattern of "Hermes Trismegistus," though not at all a daring one, was one that Longfellow had not used before, and in his very last years he was still making small and unsensational experiments with meters that were not very familiar in English. Many years earlier, almost as early as *Evangeline,* he had tried his hand, clearly in emulation of Goethe and Schiller, at the alternating hexameters and pentameters of elegiac verse. Remembering Schiller's "Im Hexameter steigt," and perhaps also Coleridge's translation of it ("In the hexameter rises"), he had composed a distich that was rather an adaptation of Schiller than a translation, and he had even turned off a satirical literary epigram in the style of Goethe's and Schiller's *Xenien:*

> In Hexameter sings serenely a Harvard Professor;
> In Pentameter him damns censorious Poe.

Now, in his last years, having rendered two elegies of Ovid's in these distichs, he came back to the form in "Elegiac" (*Ultima Thule*) and "Elegiac Verse" (*In the Harbor*). The latter is a series of fourteen epigrams of a very slight order, though one or two of them have a mild metaphorical pleasantness; the former, "Elegiac," is a sustained poem in four four-line stanzas, and the most successful of Longfellow's experiments with the form. The famous surging and receding effect of the elegiac distich is managed here with more delicacy than is at all usual in English experiments with the measure, and the metaphors of a misty morning, the motionless sea, the sails of ships, and their departure for "Ausonian shores" — metaphors for errant thoughts and unsatisfied longings — abound in a quality that could hardly be more idiosyncratic, more deeply personal, than it is. The first stanza reads:

> Dark is the morning with mist; in the narrow mouth of the harbor
> Motionless lies the sea, under its curtain of cloud;
> Dreamily glimmer the sails of ships on the distant horizon,
> Like to the towers of a town, built on the verge of the sea.

The effect, as with all such classical measures in English, is at least a little artificial, but the artifice here has been reduced to a metrical minimum.

The very last poem Longfellow wrote, a few days before his

death, "The Bells of San Blas," was suggested to him, with his characteristic responsiveness of feeling, by an article in *Harper's*, "Typical Journeys and Country Life in Mexico," by a writer named W. H. Bishop. In a description of some of the towns on the west coast of Mexico, Bishop had said that "San Blas, larger [than Manzanillo], but still hardly more than an extensive thatched village, has, on a bluff beside it, the ruins of a once more substantial San Blas. Old bronze bells brought down from it have been mounted in rude frames a few feet high to serve the purpose of the present poor church, which is without a belfry, and this is called in irony 'the Tower of San Blas.'" A small sketch of four bells hanging in a wooden frame accompanied the passage, but there was no more than this. It was enough for Longfellow's purpose. Bells had always spoken to his imagination with a special force, and these rather pitiful church bells, once so grandly housed and now so meanly exposed, without even a belfry around them, spelled for him the whole grandeur of a proud and powerful past, both in the state and in the realm of faith — a past that one can only look back upon with reverence but that it is folly to attempt to revive. Longfellow represents the bells themselves, in a few of the stanzas, lamenting their fallen condition and praying that they may some day be restored to their old pre-eminence:

> "Then from our tower again
> We will send over land and main
>   Our voices of command,
> Like exiled kings who return
> To their thrones, and the people learn
>   That the Priest is lord of the land!"

The poem, in its first state, had ended with this stanza, but a few days later Longfellow added one other:

> O Bells of San Blas, in vain
> Ye call back the Past again!
>   The Past is deaf to your prayer;

> Out of the shadows of night
> The world rolls into light;
> It is daybreak everywhere.

He had had, no doubt, a premonition that his death was very near at hand, and he did not wish to leave as his last word an expression of backward-turning regret for the past, however noble and however devout. The day of pristine hopefulness, in the country he belonged to, had, it is true, gone by irrevocably; it was no longer the age of Emerson and Whitman; it was the age of Mark Twain and Henry Adams. But a despairing last utterance would have been wholly out of keeping for Longfellow, and there was nothing fortuitous in his ending in so sanguine a strain.

Epilogue

For a generation after his death, Longfellow's stupendous currency among readers everywhere continued unabated; from being the most popular and widely loved of American poets, he became — he was becoming, even in his lifetime — a Standard Poet; but this did not, for many years, diminish the apparent universality of his acceptance and appeal. On the crudest factual level, the story of his publishing record would be a minor chapter in the history of taste: he continued to appear, we at least know, year after year, in immense editions, editions of all sorts, on all grades of paper, with all kinds of typography, in bindings of every order of cheapness or elegance, with and without illustrations. The most familiar of his poems — it will by no means do to say always his best — had entered, as it might seem ineradicably, into the popular consciousness, fixed there in part, but only in part, by their status as educational nutriment in school readers and textbooks. He had long since become, as Van Wyck Brooks was to say, one of "Our Poets," usually six in number, who appeared everywhere in picture frames in domestic interiors — "kindly, gray-bearded, or otherwise grizzled old men." And none of the other five, or four, or six, could vie with him for a moment in bardic pre-eminence.

Such excessive literary inflation could not possibly have any stability, and nothing could have been more foreseeable, to even an undergraduate knowledge of literary history, than that Long-fellow's overblown reputation was due for a peculiarly complete collapse. This would have been true even if it were not for the existence of a general principle — it is almost a law — according to which every great literary reputation, after a longer or shorter lapse, passes through what a French writer once called its Purgatory: it is a principle that will eventually apply to the great literary reputations of our own time, both the valid and the spurious ones. Longfellow's reputation was more vulnerable than most; it was more exaggerated and it was more largely composed of "water" — of subliterary or at least dubiously literary elements. As we have seen, there had never been a time when, with critical readers and with other writers, his acceptance had really been universal, and among the younger literary generation, late in his life and after his death, the prevalent attitude was well this side of idolatry. He was mostly spoken of with respect and a kind of deference, but in what Edmund Clarence Stedman or Barrett Wendell or George Edward Woodberry has to say about Longfellow, there is a moderation of tone that amounts to coolness. "He often taught, by choice, the primary class, and the upper form is slow to forget it," said Stedman in the middle eighties; and this is pretty much the manner in which Wendell and Woodberry spoke. Perhaps, in their generation, Howells and Lafcadio Hearn were rather isolated in the warmth of their appreciation of Longfellow.

In any case, the deflation was bound to occur, and it did occur, probably not suddenly or sensationally, but with a thoroughness that was ultimately to seem final, during the few years just before the First World War. By that time, as everyone knows, the long stagnation of American, and indeed of English, poetry was at last beginning to be stirred and shaken by a new school of young poets, deeply dissatisfied with the debased language and the stale forms of the poetry that had preceded them, and in their repudiation of the bloated reputations of the earlier period,

Longfellow was bound to be a casualty, along with some greater figures. Even in his own day he had done nothing to extend the boundaries of poetic speech or to revivfy the diction of American poetry: he had been content, like the typical secondary poet, with the language he had inherited, and by the time a Revolution of the Word was ready to break out, he could not possibly play the role of a precursor or a stimulant. When Ezra Pound and H.D. appealed for "Direct treatment of the 'thing' whether subjective or objective," and when Pound advised other poets to "Use no superfluous word, no adjective, which does not reveal something," he was by implication ruling out not only Longfellow but almost all Our Poets — and, in one sense, quite properly. For the moment, they could furnish Pound and his compeers with no armament. There is lasting truth in Coleridge's remark that, among literary minds, one can distinguish between the Springs and the Tanks; Longfellow is an archetypal Tank — though when the image is applied to him it has a somewhat incongruous air.

At about the same time, there was another strain in the new literary movement that was bound to tell heavily against Longfellow. To younger writers who were deeply troubled about the aridity, the sterility, the spiritual uncreativeness of American life generally, and who were turning to the American past in the hope of discovering moral and intellectual ancestors there — to the writers for whom Van Wyck Brooks was the most serious and the most eloquent spokesman — Longfellow inevitably seemed to hold out an empty hand. Where in his work could one find the moral intensities one might find in Hawthorne's or Melville's, or the tonic individualism one might find in Emerson's, or the program of a permanent cultural revolution that might be derived from Whitman's? Clearly, nowhere; and Longfellow had to be rejected as an ancestor. "Longfellow is to poetry what the barrel-organ is to music," said Brooks in 1915 — with a finality he would later have repudiated.* "One might remove Long-fellow," said Lewis Mumford a decade later, "without changing a single possibility of American life; had Whitman died in the cradle, however, the possibilities of American life would have been definitely impoverished." He was right, in the spirit in which he made the remark. And the literary-historical sense enables us also to appreciate the spirit behind Ludwig Lewisohn's question, in the early thirties, "Who, except wretched school-children, now reads Longfellow?" "The thing to establish in America," he went on to say, "is not that Longfellow was a very small poet, but that he did not partake of the poetic character at all."

This was perhaps the most extreme judgment that found its way into print, though similar rejections were often heard in conversation. Less extreme than these were the judgments pronounced by writers of strongly left-wing or progressive convictions, though these too ended by finding Longfellow disappointing and unusable. "He was not made for battle," said V. F. Parrington, "and causes commanded an unwilling allegiance," as if this were somehow relevant to a critical judgment; there was more relevance in Parrington's remark that "One could scarcely have lived more detached from contemporary America, more effectively insulated against the electric currents of the times": the point is very much overstated, but certainly Longfellow's sensitiveness to the intellectual and moral currents of his time was not great. And, given the nadir to which his reputation had

* In the same essay, "Our Poets," Brooks made some remarks about Long-fellow that were both witty and, at least on one level, just: "To Longfellow," he said, "the world was a German picture-book, never detaching itself from the softly colored pages. He was a man of one continuous mood; it was that of a flaxen-haired German student on his *wanderjahr* along the Rhine, under the autumn sun — a sort of expurgated German student — ambling among ruined castles and reddening vines, and summoning up a thousand bright remnants of an always musical past." This is hardly a "rounded judgment" of Longfellow's whole work, but it was not really intended to be.

now sunk, one can understand the disdain for him and his work of the Marxist critics of the thirties, who had close affiliations with Parrington's populism. "His Americanisms," said V. F. Calverton, not very lucidly, "were of that sentimental school which derived its impetus from the philosophy of sweetness and light." "In the later decades of his life," said Granville Hicks, more cogently, Longfellow "became important chiefly as transmitter and interpreter of other literatures, steadily increasing the distance between him and the realities of contemporary life, meeting his fellow citizens only upon the level of domestic sentimentality." Certainly the thirties were not a period in which one could expect that even-handed justice would be done to a poet so largely nonpolitical as Longfellow.

A difficulty of a wholly different and deeper sort had been expressed many years earlier by the youthful Yeats, in his essay on "What Is 'Popular Poetry'?" How much of Longfellow's work Yeats was acquainted with may be a question, as with some of the writers just cited, but given his conviction that a degenerate "literary" poetry could be refreshed, renewed, and ennobled only by some return to the profound sources of a preliterate art among the folk, one can appreciate his impatience, to put it mildly, with what seemed to him the falsely "popular" verse of Longfellow and all his kind. Yeats had excepted Burns from his severest strictures — for did not his "expressive speech" lift him above all other popular poets? — but even Burns "has the triviality of emotion, the poverty of ideas, the imperfect sense of beauty of a poetry whose most typical expression is Longfellow." To what was Longfellow's popularity due if not to his telling of his story or his idea "so that one needs nothing but his verses to understand it"? "No words of his," Yeats continued, his voice taking on that incantatory tone he commanded so perfectly in his early prose — "No words of his borrow their beauty from those that used them before, and one can get all that there is in story and idea without seeing them, as if moving before a half-faded curtain embroidered with kings and queens, their loves and battles and their days out hunting, or else with holy letters and images of so great antiquity that nobody can tell the god or goddess they would commend to an unfading memory." One rather forgets Longfellow and his work by the end of this lovely hypnotic sentence, but the whole passage confronts us, nevertheless, with a genuine critical question.

So, too, does the revolution in taste, associated with the names of Eliot and, later, Richards, Tate, Ransom, and others, which resulted in a rejection, sometimes sweeping, sometimes more discriminating, of romantic nineteenth-century poetry generally and a revival of interest in the more tightly woven, more intellectually intense, more paradoxical poetry of the seventeenth century, before the "dissociation of sensibility" had taken place. The valuation, in poetry, of such qualities as ambiguity, tension, and irony was bound to result in a repudiation of much of romantic poetry, with its personal spontaneities, its rhetoric of eloquence, and its confessional directness, and this repudiation was fortified by the Symbolist cultivation of indirectness, indefiniteness, obliqueness — of the "nuance," the "indécis," the "absence de signification." Inevitably a poet like Longfellow suffered heavily, along with more important writers, from this shift in taste, and when we add that all this was accompanied by the emergence of a school of formalist and explicative criticism, of close reading and textual analysis, we shall hardly find it surprising that any esteem for a poet so unresponsive to these methods faded away almost to the vanishing point. The only poem of Longfellow's included in the immensely influential textbook *Understanding Poetry*, by Cleanth Brooks and Robert Penn Warren, is "A Psalm of Life," a liking for which is cited as a case of the fallacy of "message-hunting," as indeed it is. Yet the effect is hardly to lure young readers on to a perusal of Longfellow generally.

The question now is whether either they or older readers

should be so lured. Certainly Longfellow will never again "enjoy" the excessive popularity he enjoyed in his own time and for some years afterward, and this is as it should be. The general memory cannot and ought not to be burdened with the works of all writers who have ever been, or even who were a century ago, "in every home," and Longfellow spoke too directly to the general taste of his own age ever to have a great claim on the general taste of a later age. Is his work, however, or some part of it, now worth preserving in what, for convenience, can only be called the literary memory? A much broader question than this, as a matter of fact, is involved — a question that is raised by much more than a reading of Longfellow. How much, in general, of the writing of the past is worth preserving? There have been two kinds of answers to this question, implied (as a rule) rather than made explicit, in the history of criticism and taste — the answer of elimination and the answer of inclusion. Minds of a certain order have a strong bias toward elimination, and whole periods of taste — the neoclassical period, for example — have been dominated by them. Our own age is one of these, and some great critical reputations have been based _partly_ on the success with which the critics in question have shown reasons for holding on to as few writers in the past as possible. The passion for proscription, in literature as in other realms, is one of the prevailing passions of our time, and better writers, as well as worse writers, than Longfellow have found themselves on the lists of the proscribed.

A genuine concern for discrimination, in a culture that seems to have thrown overboard the very notion of discrimination, often lies behind these ostracisms. But there is a danger in the habit of leaving out, just as in the habit of taking in, and we may well be moving into a period when, by the familiar dialectical process, the case for inclusion may be heard more frequently than it has been for a long time. Literary taste can be hospitable and comprehensive without necessarily losing sight of real distinctions, and there is such a thing as a wholesome fear of losing something precious as well as of being deceived by something second-rate. A vigorous taste is not inevitably a coarse one; an eclectic taste is not inevitably promiscuous, and there is now a certain urgency in the necessity for restoring some damaged reputations as well as for disposing of others. The canon of acceptable writers has grown alarmingly small.

Americans are notoriously obsessed with the question of status, and to say that a writer is a minor writer, to many American readers, is as if one were to say that he is negligible. This is not true, or it is much less true, in Europe, where steadily, through the most seismic upheavals of taste, writers of the second or even the third order continue to be edited, to be published, and to be read. They are often, too, the objects of thoughtful critical discussion, and the general consciousness is appreciably enriched as a result. By an understandable paradox, we are much more "democratic" in our receptiveness, and much less catholic. Our memories, too, are shorter, and once a writer has receded from the foreground of our attention, he runs the risk of being forgotten irretrievably, especially if he can be disposed of as a minor writer.

All this is only preparatory to suggesting that Longfellow is better worth preserving in the literary memory than he has long been regarded as being. Let us agree, once for all, that he is a minor writer — and then go on to observe that the distinction between major writers and minor writers, like the distinction between the major and the minor prophets, is at best a rough-and-ready one. It has to be made, no doubt, but only then does the real work of discrimination begin. When one's mind is filled with Vergil or Dante or Shakespeare, most writers in world literature appear to be, and indeed are, minor writers — but the observation is not a very useful one. There are infinite degrees of power, of reach, of profundity among "major" writers, and almost as many degrees of fineness, of purity, of versatility, of experimental adventurousness among "minor" ones. Some of these latter are to be described as, however remarkable in their special ways, essentially *small* writers — limited in their interests, restricted in their modes of expression, and sometimes simply thin in the mere bulk of their work. Side by side with such writers — with Robert Blair or Thomas Moore or George Darley, with Joseph Rodman Drake or Jones Very or Henry Timrod — Longfellow may continue to seem minor, but one rebels against describing him as small. There is a certain largeness not only in his conception of his role but in his actual performance, which is inconsistent with the label of littleness, even of perfection in littleness; his mind was simply, with all its limitations, too venturesome to allow him to remain content with the mastery of one or two forms or modes, and if this meant that he sometimes essayed to do a larger kind of thing than his gifts warranted, the result often has the value of interesting failure, and sometimes a greater value than that. The author of *Hiawatha*, of *Tales of a Wayside Inn*, of *Michael Angelo* was a lesser but not a little writer, a minor poet but not a poetaster.

If he is to be restored to a modest rank in the literary memory, this will depend largely on the rehabilitation, in the scale of critical values, of the poetic virtues of directness, of simplicity in statement, of the incomplex, of "easiness" on a certain level — of what Marcel Raymond has called "a certain ingenuousness." These have never been the virtues of poetry of a very high order, and they are certainly not virtues that our own age can be expected spontaneously to esteem very highly. There are a dozen good reasons why the only poetry that has had much authenticity for our difficult and self-divided time has been poetry of a certain difficulty — emotionally perplexed, intellectually hard-earned, stylistically dense. And after the experiments of the Symbolists and their successors it has not been easy to do justice to poets who "signified" no more, or not much more, than they plainly stated; to poets whose penumbra of implication extended less far than the clearly lighted surface of statement. Yet the long history of poetry abounds in poets of essentially this sort — granted always that the plainest poetic statement is never without a resonance beyond language. Unless we are to throw into the discard all writers who do not satisfy our post-metaphysical and post-symbolist needs, we shall wish to preserve many of these poets in our memory, and keep them available for states of feeling that respond to their styles. A good deal of Longfellow belongs to this valid order of poetry, and perhaps it has already been indicated fairly fully that the rejection of everything he wrote would entail a genuine loss. This would be somewhat truer of American readers than of others.

There remains the question which Yeats's essay broaches — the question whether Burns and Longfellow and all such poets must be cast aside as representing nothing better than "popular" poetry in the base and degraded sense. There *is* no question, of course, if only true folk poetry and the literate poetry that derives authentically from it are to be taken as acceptable. But this is much too arbitrary and doctrinaire a position to be any longer critically maintained, and Yeats's later work is very far from supporting any such view. To go back to Longfellow, it may be useful to suggest a distinction not between two kinds but among three kinds of popular poetry: these would be folk poetry, demotic poetry, and masscult "poetry." Folk poetry is of course the poetry of preliterate peoples or of illiterate peoples living aloof from a reading and writing culture. One might describe as demotic poetry the kind of writing that, in a literate culture, has a very wide body of more or less educated but not sophisticated or exacting readers; poetry of this kind hardly appeared before the invention of printing, and it did not really flourish until, in the eighteenth and nineteenth centuries, literacy had spread downward and outward among the middle classes, and had produced a "reading public" of large but still limited dimensions. The great age of demotic poetry was the nineteenth century, when such poets as Scott, Byron, and Tennyson (in much of their work) could flourish; it seems unlikely that this literary phenomenon will ever be repeated. Even in the nineteenth century there began to appear a kind of cheaply manufactured, as it were machine-produced "poetry" — newspaper verse, domestic doggerel, rhymes about miners and prospectors, and the like — which may conveniently be called masscult poetry. It still exists, but its most successful practitioners seem to have died out, and perhaps it too has a melancholy future.

There are elements of all these kinds of popular poetry in Longfellow. There was even, as we have seen, a touch of the true folk poet in him, as there was in some of the German poets — as there was also in Scott — but it was overlain by too many layers of literacy and even of learning to hold its own successfully, and of course Longfellow is in no strict sense, as Yeats was right in pointing out, a folk poet. At times, with the clearest conscience in the world, he could sink to the level of masscult poetry; this was mostly in his earlier years, though even in his middle decades, with poems like "The Children's Hour" and "Christmas Bells," he could return to that vein; there is little or none of it from *Aftermath* on. In the great bulk of his work, however, he is a demotic poet pure and simple, like Bryant, Whittier, and Holmes — only richer in resources, more various, more *genialisch* than any of them. And there are poems, early and late, which do not belong to the sphere of popular poetry at all; poems that are simply expressions of an authentic poetic gift, of course of a secondary order. These are the poems most worth holding on to, but much of the rest of his work deserves to be retained in the literary memory in much the same spirit in which Byron's narrative poems, or Tennyson's ballads, or the best of Whittier's demotic pieces deserve to be retained. It is still pleasure-giving to a catholic taste; it still speaks appealingly, for an American mind, to the sense of the American past; and now and then it disengages itself from historic circumstances and takes on the aspect, modestly and even obscurely, of timelessness. Our literature is not so rich in writing of this kind that we can afford to discard any of it.

Index